Richard III

Dominic Oliver, Volume Editor
Beth Wood, Activity Writer
Margaret Graham, Consultant

John O'Connor, Editor
Dr Stewart Eames, Textual Consultant

PEARSON
Longman

Pearson Education Limited
Edinburgh Gate
Harlow
Essex
CM20 2JE
England
and Associated Companies throughout the World

ISBN 0582 848725

Printed in China
SWTC/01

First published 2004

The Publisher's policy is to use paper manufactured from sustainable forests.

We are grateful to the following for permission to reproduce copyright photographs:

Clive Barda/ArenaPAL page 14 bottom; Donald Cooper pages 3, 5, 10 top, 11 bottom, 12, 13, 15 top, 46, 47 bottom, 180, 181, 200, 201 bottom, 274 bottom, 275, 283; Ronald Grant Archive pages 10 bottom, 14 top, 201 top, 292; The Image Bank/Andrea Pistolesi page 289; Robbie Jack pages 47 top, 285, 291; Mayfair/Bayly/Pare/The Kobal Collection/Bailey, Alex page 4; Ivan Kyncl/ArenaPAL page 11 top; Royal Shakespeare Company/Reg Wilson page 282; Shakespeare's Globe/Donald Cooper pages 15 bottom, 274 top.

Cover photograph: Donald Cooper

Picture researcher: Louise Edgeworth

ACT 1: SCENE BY SCENE

1 Richard enters and tells us of the victory of his family in the recent wars. While others relax, he is an unhappy misfit and plans to cause serious trouble. His brother, Clarence, is being taken to prison because of Richard's plotting, but Clarence thinks that Richard is his closest friend.

2 Lady Anne leads a funeral procession for King Henry the Sixth, who had been her father-in-law. Although Richard was the killer of both King Henry and Anne's husband, Prince Edward, amazingly he persuades her to consider marrying him.

3 King Edward the Fourth's family are very worried about his health. Family rivalries lead to a fierce argument. Old Queen Margaret, widow of King Henry the Sixth, places curses on many of those present. After Margaret exits, everyone, except Richard, goes to see the King. Richard sends two murderers to kill Clarence.

4 Clarence is violently murdered in the Tower of London.

ACT 2: SCENE BY SCENE

1 King Edward knows that the court is split into two groups: those for and against Queen Elizabeth. He tries to make peace amongst his quarrelling family. The news of Clarence's death shocks everyone except Richard.

2 Queen Elizabeth brings news that King Edward is dead. It is agreed that the young Prince Edward should be crowned King as soon as possible, but Richard and Buckingham secretly plot to take control of this.

3 Citizens talk about the dangerous state the country is in.

4 Queen Elizabeth waits for her son, Prince Edward. News reaches her that Richard has imprisoned some of her friends and family, so she takes her younger son, the Duke of York, to a safe place.

ACT 3: SCENE BY SCENE

1 Richard gets control of the young Prince Edward and his brother, the Duke of York. They follow his advice, but are not happy to be sent to stay in the Tower of London.

2 Hastings sets off confidently for a meeting at the Tower of London, despite warnings from Lord Derby that their lives are in danger.

3 Queen Elizabeth's relatives, Rivers, Grey and Vaughan, are taken to execution on Richard's orders.

4 At a meeting at the Tower of London, Richard falsely accuses Hastings of being a traitor and Hastings is hurried off to execution.

5 Richard and Buckingham try to convince the Lord Mayor of London that Hastings deserved to die. Buckingham agrees to spread lies about King Edward the Fourth and his children.

6 A legal clerk talks about the injustice of killing Hastings.

7 Buckingham has failed to get support for Richard from the citizens of London. Richard first pretends to the Lord Mayor that he does not want to be King and then that he has been persuaded that it is a good idea. His coronation is arranged for the next day.

ACT 4: SCENE BY SCENE

1 Queen Elizabeth, accompanied by other members of the Royal family and Lady Anne, is prevented from visiting her sons in the Tower of London. She and her companions are shocked to learn that Richard is to become King.

2 Now King, Richard wants the Princes to be killed. Buckingham is reluctant to help and decides to escape, frightened that he will be Richard's next victim.

3 Tyrrel, the man who organised the Princes' murders, describes their pitiful deaths. Lady Anne is dead (probably at Richard's hands) and Richard plans to marry Queen Elizabeth's daughter. News that Buckingham and Richmond plan to attack is brought to Richard.

4 Queen Elizabeth, the Duchess of York and Margaret all mourn together. Despite throwing terrible insults and curses at Richard, Queen Elizabeth seems to agree to allow her daughter to marry him. Richmond's army has landed but Buckingham is captured.

5 Derby secretly promises to support Richmond, even though Richard has his son as a hostage.

ACT 5: SCENE BY SCENE

1 Buckingham is refused permission to speak to Richard and is taken away to be executed.

2 Richmond gives an inspiring speech in which he promises to defeat Richard and to bring peace to the country.

3 On the night before the battle, the ghosts of Richard's victims haunt him and fill him with fear. They also visit Richmond, giving him praise and hope for victory. Both men give speeches to their men before the battle starts.

4 The battle begins and Richard fights fiercely, refusing to escape.

5 Richmond kills Richard in the battle. He accepts the crown and proclaims a new era of peace for the country. He announces that he will marry Princess Elizabeth and so bring together the Houses of Lancaster and York.

THE ROYAL FAMILY AND COURTIERS

DUCHESS OF YORK
Mother of King Edward IV, the Duke of Clarence and Richard, Duke of Gloucester
She mourns the deaths of her sons, Clarence and Edward IV, but curses her other son, Richard.

KING EDWARD IV
Married to Queen Elizabeth
He tries to make peace between Richard's supporters and his wife's family, but dies soon after Clarence's death.

GEORGE, DUKE OF CLARENCE
Brother of Richard, Duke of Gloucester and King Edward IV
He is killed in the Tower of London on Richard's orders.

RICHARD, DUKE OF GLOUCESTER
Brother of King Edward IV and the Duke of Clarence
He later becomes King Richard III.

QUEEN ELIZABETH
Mother of the young Prince Edward, of Richard, Duke of York, and Princess Elizabeth
She fails to protect her sons against Richard, but later agrees to her daughter's marriage to Richmond.

LADY ANNE
Widow of Prince Edward of Lancaster, son of King Henry VI
She later marries Richard, Duke of Gloucester.

EDWARD, PRINCE OF WALES
Son of King Edward IV and Queen Elizabeth
He becomes King Edward V, but is never crowned because he is murdered in the Tower of London on Richard's orders.

RICHARD, DUKE OF YORK
Son of King Edward IV and Queen Elizabeth
He is murdered in the Tower of London with his brother, Edward.

MARGARET
Widow of King Henry VI
She hates King Edward IV's family, cursing them and taking great pleasure in their sufferings.

EARL RIVERS
Brother of Queen Elizabeth
An uncle and supporter of Prince Edward, he is killed on Richard's orders.

MARQUIS OF DORSET and **LORD GREY**
Sons of Queen Elizabeth by her first marriage
Supporters of Prince Edward; Grey is killed on Richard's orders while Dorset escapes.

SIR THOMAS VAUGHAN
A supporter of Prince Edward's claim to the throne
He is executed by Richard, along with Rivers and Grey.

RICHARD'S ALLIES

DUKE OF BUCKINGHAM
Richard's closest friend and supporter
He eventually falls out with Richard and rebels against him.

LORD HASTINGS
One of Richard's supporters
He later refuses to help Richard seize the throne and is executed.

DUKE OF NORFOLK
He dies fighting for Richard at the battle of Bosworth.

EARL OF SURREY
Son of the Duke of Norfolk
He is given command of the front-line troops at Bosworth.

LORD LOVELL, SIR WILLIAM CATESBY and **SIR RICHARD RATCLIFFE**
Servants and supporters of Richard

SIR ROBERT BRAKENBURY
The official in charge of the Tower of London

SIR JAMES TYRREL
He organises the murders of Edward, Prince of Wales and Richard, Duke of York in the Tower of London.

RICHMOND AND HIS ALLIES

HENRY, EARL OF RICHMOND
Related to the Lancastrian family line
He raises an army, invades England and fights against Richard at Bosworth. After defeating Richard he becomes King Henry VII, the first of the Tudors.

EARL OF DERBY
Lord Stanley
Although pressured into declaring support for Richard he secretly supports Richmond.

EARL OF OXFORD, SIR JAMES BLUNT, SIR WALTER HERBERT and SIR WILLIAM BRANDON
They fight for Richmond at Bosworth.

CHURCHMEN

CARDINAL BOURCHIER
Archbishop of Canterbury
He persuades Queen Elizabeth to release her son into Richard's hands.

ARCHBISHOP OF YORK
He advises Queen Elizabeth to take sanctuary because her relatives have been imprisoned by Richard.

JOHN MORTON
Bishop of Ely
He deserts Richard to join Richmond.

CHRISTOPHER URSWICK
A priest

SERVANTS, OFFICIALS, AND INTERESTED CITIZENS

LORD MAYOR OF LONDON
Although unwilling at first, he is persuaded to support Richard.

SCRIVENER
A legal clerk

CITIZENS
They discuss King Edward IV's death and wonder what the future holds.

TRESSEL and BERKELEY
Attendants to Lady Anne

KEEPER
Clarence's jailer

MURDERERS
They kill Clarence in the Tower of London.

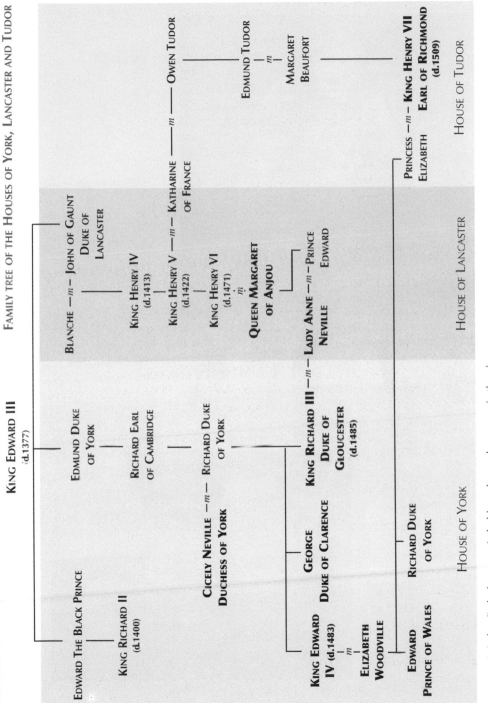

FAMILY TREE OF THE HOUSES OF YORK, LANCASTER AND TUDOR

KING EDWARD III (d.1377)

EDWARD THE BLACK PRINCE

KING RICHARD II (d.1400)

EDMUND DUKE OF YORK

RICHARD EARL OF CAMBRIDGE

CICELY NEVILLE —m— RICHARD DUKE OF YORK

GEORGE DUKE OF CLARENCE

KING EDWARD IV (d.1483) —m— ELIZABETH WOODVILLE

KING RICHARD III DUKE OF GLOUCESTER (d.1485) —m— LADY ANNE NEVILLE

EDWARD PRINCE OF WALES

RICHARD DUKE OF YORK

HOUSE OF YORK

BLANCHE —m— JOHN OF GAUNT DUKE OF LANCASTER

KING HENRY IV (d.1413)

KING HENRY V (d.1422) —m— KATHARINE OF FRANCE —m— OWEN TUDOR

KING HENRY VI (d.1471)

QUEEN MARGARET OF ANJOU —m— PRINCE EDWARD

LADY ANNE NEVILLE

HOUSE OF LANCASTER

EDMUND TUDOR —m— MARGARET BEAUFORT

PRINCESS ELIZABETH —m— KING HENRY VII EARL OF RICHMOND (d.1509)

HOUSE OF TUDOR

m = married, d = died; characters in bold are those who appear in the play.

9

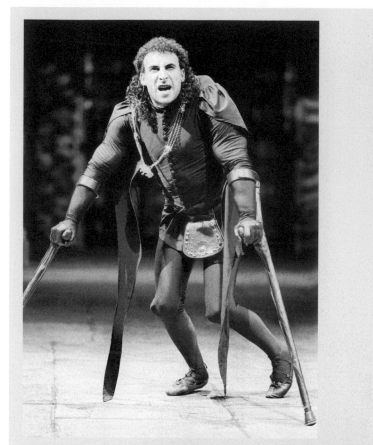

RSC, 1984

Richard III, 1995 (directed by R. Loncraine)

Crucible Theatre, 2002

RSC, 1992

RSC, 1988

Shakespeare's Globe, 2003

English Shakespeare Company, 1989

RSC, 1984

Richard III, 1995 (directed by R. Loncraine)

RSC, 1995

RSC, 1992

Shakespeare's Globe, 2003

The Royal family

KING EDWARD *the Fourth*

QUEEN ELIZABETH *his wife*

DUKE OF CLARENCE

RICHARD, DUKE OF GLOUCESTER *(later King Richard the Third)* } *brothers of King Edward*

Old DUCHESS OF YORK *mother of King Edward, Clarence and Richard*

PRINCE OF WALES

DUKE OF YORK } *young sons of King Edward (the Princes in the Tower)*

Young SON *and* DAUGHTER *of Clarence*

EARL RIVERS *brother of Queen Elizabeth*

MARQUIS OF DORSET

LORD GREY } *sons of Queen Elizabeth's earlier marriage*

Past and future royalty

Old QUEEN MARGARET *widow of King Henry the Sixth*

LADY ANNE *widow of King Henry's son, Prince Edward*

EARL OF RICHMOND *(later King Henry the Seventh)*

Lords, Knights and Churchmen

LORD HASTINGS	DUKE OF BUCKINGHAM
EARL OF DERBY *(Lord Stanley)*	DUKE OF NORFOLK
LORD LOVELL	EARL OF OXFORD
EARL OF SURREY	SIR WILLIAM CATESBY
SIR RICHARD RATCLIFFE	SIR THOMAS VAUGHAN
SIR JAMES TYRREL	SIR WALTER HERBERT
SIR JAMES BLUNT	SIR WILLIAM BRANDON

SIR ROBERT BRAKENBURY *Lieutenant of the Tower*

ARCHBISHOP OF YORK

CARDINAL BOURCHIER *Archbishop of Canterbury*

BISHOP OF ELY

Two other BISHOPS

CHRISTOPHER URSWICK *a priest*

Another PRIEST

Other LORDS *and* GENTLEMEN

Officers, servants and the people

TRESSEL *and* BERKELEY *gentlemen attending Lady Anne*

MURDERERS

A PURSUIVANT

KEEPER *in the Tower*

A SCRIVENER

CITIZENS *of London*

PAGE *to King Richard*

LORD MAYOR *of London*

SHERIFF OF WILTSHIRE

MESSENGERS, GUARDS, ATTENDANTS *and* SOLDIERS

Ghosts of Richard's victims

PRINCE EDWARD *son of King Henry the Sixth*

KING HENRY *the Sixth*

CLARENCE

RIVERS, GREY *and* VAUGHAN

HASTINGS

THE YOUNG PRINCES *murdered in the Tower*

LADY ANNE

BUCKINGHAM

The action takes place in England.

In this scene ...

- Richard enters and sets the scene.
- He comforts his brother Clarence who is being sent to the Tower by King Edward, even though Richard himself is really behind his imprisonment.
- Lord Hastings informs Richard that the King is seriously ill.
- Alone, Richard speaks of his plans to murder Clarence, and to marry Lady Anne despite the fact that it was he who killed her father and husband.

Richard speaks his thoughts about the end of the civil wars and the victory of his family. As he feels unable to share in the pleasures of the peace, he is determined to behave wickedly.

Think about

- Richard's family has won, but what is Richard's attitude to the end of the war?

- Do you think Richard is born evil, circumstances have forced him to be evil, or that it is his choice?

2 **son of York**: a pun. As well as the weather and season image, Richard is referring to his brother King Edward IV, son of Richard of York.

3 **loured**: frowned

6 **arms**: weapons

7 **alarums**: calls to battle

8 **dreadful**: frightening
measures: dances

9 **Grim-visaged**: Stern-faced
front: forehead

10 **barbèd steeds**: armoured horses

11 **adversaries**: enemies

12 **capers**: dances

13 **lascivious**: lustful
lute: stringed, guitar-like instrument

14 **sportive tricks**: sexual games

15 **amorous looking-glass**: lover's mirror

16 **rudely stamped**: made with rough or ugly appearance

17 **wanton ambling nymph**: a girl who moves flirtatiously

18 **curtailed ... proportion**: not attractively formed

19 **feature**: well-shaped body
dissembling: deceiving

20 **sent before my time**: born prematurely

23 **halt**: limp

24 **piping time of peace**: time of peaceful music

27 **descant**: commentate

A street near the Tower of London.

Enter RICHARD, *Duke of Gloucester, alone.*

RICHARD   Now is the winter of our discontent
Made glorious summer by this son of York –
And all the clouds that loured upon our house
In the deep bosom of the ocean buried.
Now are our brows bound with victorious wreaths;   5
Our bruisèd arms hung up for monuments;
Our stern alarums changed to merry meetings,
Our dreadful marches to delightful measures.
Grim-visaged war hath smoothed his wrinkled front,
And now, instead of mounting barbèd steeds   10
To fright the souls of fearful adversaries,
He capers nimbly in a lady's chamber
To the lascivious pleasing of a lute.
But I – that am not shaped for sportive tricks,
Nor made to court an amorous looking-glass –   15
I – that am rudely stamped, and want love's majesty
To strut before a wanton ambling nymph –
I – that am curtailed of this fair proportion,
Cheated of feature by dissembling nature,
Deformed, unfinished, sent before my time   20
Into this breathing world scarce half made up –
And that so lamely and unfashionable
That dogs bark at me as I halt by them –
Why, I, in this weak piping time of peace,
Have no delight to pass away the time –   25
Unless to spy my shadow in the sun
And descant on mine own deformity.
And therefore, since I cannot prove a lover
To entertain these fair well-spoken days,
I am determinèd to prove a villain   30
And hate the idle pleasures of these days.

Richard reveals how he has plotted the downfall of his brother, Clarence. He pretends to be shocked when he meets Clarence, who is being taken to the Tower of London under armed guard.

32 **inductions**: preparations
33 **libels**: lies about a person

37 **subtle**: clever / deceitful
38 **mewed up**: caged (like a hawk)
39 **'G'**: The Duke of Clarence is called George.

43 **waits upon**: attends
   your Grace: title given to senior lords or ladies
44 **Tend'ring**: being concerned about
45 **conduct**: guard
   convey: take
   Tower: Tower of London

47 **Alack**: Alas
48 **commit**: imprison
49 **belike**: perhaps
50 **new-christened**: named again

54 **hearkens after**: listens to
55 **cross-row**: alphabet

57 **issue**: children
   disinherited: stopped from becoming kings
60 **toys**: foolish ideas

Think about

- If you were the actor, how would you show Richard's transformation from a gleeful villain to an apparently caring brother? Think about gestures and facial expressions, for example.

- The prophecy mentions the letter 'G'. Richard's title is Duke of Gloucester, so why isn't he also under suspicion?

Plots have I laid, inductions dangerous,
By drunken prophecies, libels, and dreams,
To set my brother Clarence and the King
In deadly hate the one against the other.   35
And if King Edward be as true and just
As I am subtle, false, and treacherous,
This day should Clarence closely be mewed up –
About a prophecy which says that 'G'
Of Edward's heirs the murderer shall be.   40
Dive, thoughts, down to my soul! Here Clarence comes.

Enter George, Duke of CLARENCE, *with guards, and* BRAKENBURY
(Lieutenant of the Tower).

Brother, good day. What means this armèd guard
That waits upon your Grace?

CLARENCE   His Majesty,
Tend'ring my person's safety, hath appointed
This conduct to convey me to the Tower.   45

RICHARD   Upon what cause?

CLARENCE   Because my name is George.

RICHARD   Alack, my lord, that fault in none of yours:
He should, for that, commit your godfathers!
O, belike his Majesty hath some intent
That you should be new-christened in the Tower.   50
But what's the matter, Clarence? May I know?

CLARENCE   Yea, Richard, when I know – for I protest
As yet I do not. But, as I can learn,
He hearkens after prophecies and dreams,
And from the cross-row plucks the letter G,   55
And says a wizard told him that by 'G'
His issue disinherited should be.
And, for my name of George begins with G,
It follows in his thought that I am he.
These, as I learn, and such like toys as these,   60
Hath moved his Highness to commit me now.

Richard pretends that it is the Queen who is to blame for Clarence's arrest and tells him that she and Jane Shore are important influences on the King. Brakenbury says that it is against his orders for anyone to talk to Clarence, but he is teased by Richard.

64 **Lady Grey**: Queen Elizabeth's name by her first marriage

65 **tempers ... extremity**: persuades him into extreme behaviour

66 **worship**: honour

67 **Antony Woodville**: Earl Rivers, the Queen's brother

69 **delivered**: released

72 **kindred**: family
night-walking heralds: secret messengers

73 **betwixt**: between
Mistress Shore: Jane Shore, the King's lover

74 **suppliant**: someone who asks a favour

75 **delivery**: release

76 **her deity**: i.e. Jane Shore

77 **Lord Chamberlain**: i.e. Hastings

80 **wear her livery**: i.e. be her servants

81 **o'er-worn**: worn out
widow: i.e. Queen Elizabeth

82 **dubbed them gentlewomen**: gave them status

83 **gossips**: busy-bodies

84 **beseech**: beg

85 **straitly ... charge**: strictly ordered

86 **have private conference**: talk privately

87 **of ... soever**: of whatever rank

88 **An't**: If it

89 **partake of**: listen to

92 **well struck in years**: no longer youthful

94 **bonny**: pretty
passing: exceptionally

Think about

- Brakenbury is acting on the King's orders. How do you think he feels as he listens to this conversation between the King's brothers, Richard and Clarence?

RICHARD Why, this it is when men are ruled by women!
'Tis not the King that sends you to the Tower.
My Lady Grey his wife, Clarence – 'tis she
That tempers him to this extremity.   65
Was it not she and that good man of worship,
Antony Woodville, her brother there,
That made him send Lord Hastings to the Tower,
From whence this present day he is delivered?
We are not safe, Clarence, we are not safe!   70

CLARENCE By heaven, I think there's no man is secure
But the Queen's kindred, and night-walking heralds
That trudge betwixt the King and Mistress Shore.
Heard you not what an humble suppliant
Lord Hastings was, for her delivery?   75

RICHARD Humbly complaining to her deity
Got my Lord Chamberlain his liberty.
I'll tell you what – I think it is our way,
If we will keep in favour with the King,
To be her men and wear her livery!   80
The jealous o'er-worn widow and herself,
Since that our brother dubbed them gentlewomen,
Are mighty gossips in our monarchy.

BRAKENBURY I beseech your Graces both to pardon me.
His Majesty hath straitly given in charge   85
That no man shall have private conference,
Of what degree soever, with your brother.

RICHARD Even so. An't please your worship, Brakenbury,
You may partake of any thing we say.
We speak no treason, man! We say the King   90
Is wise and virtuous, and his noble queen
Well struck in years, fair, and not jealous.
We say that Shore's wife hath a pretty foot,
A cherry lip, a bonny eye, a passing pleasing tongue;
And that the Queen's kindred are made gentlefolks.   95
How say you, sir? Can you deny all this?

BRAKENBURY With this, my lord, myself have nought to do.

Richard promises to do everything he can to get Clarence released. Left alone on the stage, Richard gleefully reveals his plot to have Clarence killed. Lord Hastings, recently released from the Tower of London, enters.

98 **Naught**: Nothing
99 **naught**: i.e. something sexual

102 **knave**: dishonest person

103 **withal**: i.e. also
104 **Forbear … conference**: stop talking

105 **charge**: orders

106 **abjects**: oppressed and humble servants

109 **King Edward's widow**: i.e. Queen Elizabeth
110 **enfranchise**: free
112 **Touches**: hurts

115 **lie for you**: 1 take your place; 2 tell lies

116 **must perforce**: have no choice

Think about

- Richard's speeches are full of double meanings. What differences are there between what the other characters hear and what he really means? For example, think about what possible meanings there are to Richard's declaration that Clarence's 'imprisonment shall not be long' (line 114).

- What is your first impression of Hastings?

125 **brooked**: endured

127 **to … thanks**: pay them back

RICHARD	Naught to do with Mistress Shore! I tell thee, fellow,
	He that doth naught with her – excepting one –
	Were best to do it secretly alone. 100
BRAKENBURY	What one, my lord?
RICHARD	Her husband, knave! Wouldst thou betray me?
BRAKENBURY	I do beseech your Grace to pardon me, and withal
	Forbear your conference with the noble Duke.
CLARENCE	We know thy charge, Brakenbury, and will obey. 105
RICHARD	We are the Queen's abjects and must obey.
	Brother, farewell. I will unto the King.
	And whatsoe'er you will employ me in –
	Were it to call King Edward's widow 'sister' –
	I will perform it to enfranchise you. 110
	Meantime, this deep disgrace in brotherhood
	Touches me deeper than you can imagine.
CLARENCE	I know it pleaseth neither of us well.
RICHARD	Well, your imprisonment shall not be long.
	I will deliver you, or else lie for you. 115
	Meantime, have patience.
CLARENCE	I must perforce. Farewell.

Exit CLARENCE, *escorted by* BRAKENBURY *and guards.*

RICHARD	Go tread the path that thou shalt ne'er return.
	Simple, plain Clarence, I do love thee so
	That I will shortly send thy soul to heaven –
	If heaven will take the present at our hands. 120
	But who comes here? The new-delivered Hastings?

Enter Lord HASTINGS.

HASTINGS	Good time of day unto my gracious lord!
RICHARD	As much unto my good Lord Chamberlain!
	Well are you welcome to the open air.
	How hath your lordship brooked imprisonment? 125
HASTINGS	With patience, noble lord, as prisoners must.
	But I shall live, my lord, to give them thanks
	That were the cause of my imprisonment.

Hastings tells Richard that the King is dangerously ill. Alone once again, Richard hopes that the King will not die before Clarence is killed. He reveals his plan to marry Lady Anne, the widow of Prince Edward, the son of King Henry the Sixth, both of whom had been killed by Richard.

131   prevailed: worked successfully

132–3   More pity ... at liberty: The mewed (caged) eagles are Clarence and Hastings; the kites and buzzards (inferior, scavenging birds) who are free to hunt are the Queen's followers at court.

134   abroad: is around

136   melancholy: depressed

137   fear him mightily: are very afraid he is going to die

138   by: in the name of (Richard is swearing an oath.)

139   evil diet: unhealthy way of life

140   overmuch ... person: overindulged himself

146   packed with posthorse: i.e. sent as quickly as possible

147   urge ... Clarence: persuade him to hate Clarence more

148   steeled: strengthened

149   deep intent: hidden purpose

153   Warwick's youngest daughter: i.e. Lady Anne

154   her husband and her father: i.e. Edward Prince of Wales and King Henry VI

155   readiest ... amends: easiest way to make it up to the girl

158   secret close intent: concealed purpose

160   run ... market: am getting ahead of myself

Think about

- What do you find in Richard's speeches so far that is a) frightening, and b) funny?

- What impression do you have of Richard at the end of this scene? Think about how an actor could play the character.

RICHARD	No doubt, no doubt: and so shall Clarence too –
	For they that were your enemies are his, 130
	And have prevailed as much on him as you.
HASTINGS	More pity that the eagles should be mewed
	Whiles kites and buzzards prey at liberty.
RICHARD	What news abroad?
HASTINGS	No news so bad abroad as this at home: 135
	The King is sickly, weak, and melancholy,
	And his physicians fear him mightily.
RICHARD	Now, by Saint John, that news is bad indeed!
	O, he hath kept an evil diet long
	And overmuch consumed his royal person! 140
	'Tis very grievous to be thought upon.
	Where is he? In his bed?
HASTINGS	He is.
RICHARD	Go you before, and I will follow you.

Exit HASTINGS.

He cannot live, I hope – and must not die   145
Till George be packed with posthorse up to heaven.
I'll in to urge his hatred more to Clarence
With lies well steeled with weighty arguments.
And, if I fail not in my deep intent,
Clarence hath not another day to live: 150
Which done, God take King Edward to his mercy,
And leave the world for me to bustle in!
For then I'll marry Warwick's youngest daughter.
What though I killed her husband and her father?
The readiest way to make the wench amends   155
Is to become her husband and her father:
The which will I – not all so much for love
As for another secret close intent
By marrying her which I must reach unto.
But yet I run before my horse to market.   160
Clarence still breathes; Edward still lives and reigns.
When they are gone, then must I count my gains.

Exit.

In this scene ...

- Anne enters with the body of her father-in-law, King Henry the Sixth, who was killed by Richard before the play started.
- Richard interrupts Anne's mourning. Anne curses him and calls for Richard's death for killing her husband and father-in-law.
- Richard offers Anne his sword so that she can kill him but she cannot do it. Amazingly, and after much resistance from Anne, Richard persuades her to consider marrying him.

Anne is mourning for her dead father-in-law, King Henry the Sixth. She curses Richard, who killed both Henry and her husband Edward, Henry's son.

Think about

- Some productions stage Anne's entrance as a grand procession. Others make the scene more small-scale and intimate. How would you stage it, and why?

2 **shrouded**: covered
   hearse: coffin
3 **obsequiously**: respectfully as a mourner
5 **key-cold**: deathly cold (like a metal key)
7 **remnant**: last representative
   blood: i.e. family
8 **invocate**: call upon

12 **windows**: i.e. wounds
13 **helpless balm**: i.e. useless tears
14 **the hand**: i.e. Richard's hand

17 **More ... betide**: May a more terrible fortune fall upon

20 **venomed**: poisonous
21 **abortive**: monstrous
22 **Prodigious ... light**: abnormal and prematurely born
23 **aspect**: appearance
25 **unhappiness**: evil

28 **thee**: i.e. King Henry VI
29 **Chertsey**: Chertsey monastery

Another street in London.

Enter bearers carrying a coffin with the corpse of King Henry

the Sixth, escorted by guards. Lady ANNE *(widow of the dead*

*King's son) follows as a mourner, with Gentlemen (*TRESSEL,

BERKELEY, *and others).*

ANNE   Set down, set down your honourable load –
                        If honour may be shrouded in a hearse –
                        While I awhile obsequiously lament
                        Th' untimely fall of virtuous Lancaster.
                        Poor key-cold figure of a holy King!   5
                        Pale ashes of the house of Lancaster!
                        Thou bloodless remnant of that royal blood!
                        Be it lawful that I invocate thy ghost
                        To hear the lamentations of poor Anne,
                        Wife to thy Edward, to thy slaughtered son,   10
                        Stabbed by the self-same hand that made these wounds.
                        Lo, in these windows that let forth thy life
                        I pour the helpless balm of my poor eyes.
                        Cursed be the hand that made these fatal holes!
                        Cursed the heart that had the heart to do it!   15
                        Cursed the blood that let this blood from hence!
                        More direful hap betide that hated wretch
                        That makes us wretched by the death of thee
                        Than I can wish to adders, spiders, toads,
                        Or any creeping venomed thing that lives!   20
                        If ever he have child, abortive be it,
                        Prodigious, and untimely brought to light,
                        Whose ugly and unnatural aspect
                        May fright the hopeful mother at the view,
                        And that be heir to his unhappiness!   25
                        If ever he have wife, let her be made
                        More miserable by the death of him
                        Than I am made by my young lord and thee!
                        Come, now towards Chertsey with your holy load,

Richard interrupts the funeral procession. Anne curses him and calls attention to the body's wounds, which suddenly bleed again.

30 Paul's: St. Paul's Cathedral
   interrèd: buried
31 still as: whenever

40 Advance thy halberd: Raise your spear

42 spurn upon: stamp on

46 Avaunt: Get away
   minister: agent
47 but: only

49 charity: pity's sake
   curst: sharp-tongued
50 hence: go away

52 exclaims: shouts of complaint
53 heinous: terrible
54 pattern: great example

56 congealed: dried up

58 exhales this blood: causes this bleeding

Think about

• When Richard enters, only Anne does not seem afraid. Do you think she is acting, or is she genuinely fearless at this point?

• If you were the director, how would you present the corpse in this scene?

Taken from Paul's to be interrèd there –   30
And still as you are weary of this weight
Rest you, whiles I lament King Henry's corpse.

The bearers take up the coffin.

Enter RICHARD.

RICHARD   Stay, you that bear the corpse, and set it down.

ANNE   ⚘ What black magician conjures up this fiend
To stop devoted charitable deeds?   35

RICHARD   Villains, set down the corpse; or, by Saint Paul,
I'll make a corpse of him that disobeys!

GENTLEMAN 1   My lord, stand back, and let the coffin pass.

RICHARD   Unmannered dog! Stand thou, when I command.
Advance thy halberd higher than my breast –   40
Or, by Saint Paul, I'll strike thee to my foot
And spurn upon thee, beggar, for thy boldness.

The bearers set down the coffin.

ANNE   What, do you tremble? Are you all afraid?
Alas, I blame you not, for you are mortal,
And mortal eyes cannot endure the devil.   45
✴ Avaunt, thou dreadful minister of hell!
Thou hadst but power over his mortal body:
His soul thou canst not have. Therefore be gone!

RICHARD   Sweet saint, for charity, be not so curst.

ANNE   Foul devil, for God's sake, hence and trouble us not –   50
For thou hast made the happy earth thy hell,
Filled it with cursing cries and deep exclaims!
If thou delight to view thy heinous deeds,
Behold this pattern of thy butcheries.
O, gentlemen, see, see! Dead Henry's wounds   55
Open their congealed mouths and bleed afresh!
Blush, blush, thou lump of foul deformity,
For 'tis thy presence that exhales this blood
From cold and empty veins where no blood dwells.
Thy deeds inhuman and unnatural   60

Anne continues to furiously rage at Richard. He tries to reason with her and divert her anger. He denies killing her husband Edward.

61 **deluge**: flood

65 **quick**: alive

68 **charity**: kindness
69 **renders**: gives back

71 **No beast … but**: Even the fiercest animal

75 **Vouchsafe**: Allow me
76 **leave**: permission
77 **circumstance … myself**: explaining the details to clear myself
78 **diffused infection**: widespread sickness

82 **patient leisure**: i.e. time

84 **excuse current**: genuine excuse

85 **despair**: complete lack of hope (a sin)

89 **Say**: Suppose
    slew: killed

90 **by thee**: killed by you

Think about

- Look at the language Richard uses to calm Anne and to excuse himself. What does this show about the attitude he has towards Anne and to his past crimes against her family? Do you think he is being sincere?

- How do you think Anne's responses to Richard should be delivered?

	Provokes this deluge most unnatural.
	O God, which this blood mad'st, revenge his death!
	O earth, which this blood drink'st, revenge his death!
	Either heaven with lightning strike the murderer dead;
	Or earth gape open wide and eat him quick –
	As thou dost swallow up this good King's blood,
	Which his hell-governed arm hath butcherèd.

RICHARD Lady, you know no rules of charity,
Which renders good for bad, blessing for curses.

ANNE Villain, thou knowest nor law of God nor man! 70
No beast so fierce but knows some touch of pity.

RICHARD But I know none, and therefore am no beast.

ANNE O wonderful, when devils tell the truth!

RICHARD More wonderful when angels are so angry.
Vouchsafe, divine perfection of a woman, 75
Of these supposèd crimes to give me leave
By circumstance but to acquit myself.

ANNE Vouchsafe, diffused infection of a man,
For these known evils but to give me leave
By circumstance to curse thy cursèd self. 80

RICHARD Fairer than tongue can name thee, let me have
Some patient leisure to excuse myself.

ANNE Fouler than heart can think thee, thou canst make
No excuse current but to hang thyself.

RICHARD By such despair I should accuse myself. 85

ANNE And by despairing shalt thou stand excused
For doing worthy vengeance on thyself
That didst unworthy slaughter upon others.

RICHARD Say that I slew them not?

ANNE Then say they were not slain.
But dead they are, and, devilish slave, by thee! 90

RICHARD I did not kill your husband.

ANNE Why, then he is alive

Richard admits to killing King Henry and to trying to kill Queen Margaret. He dares to suggest himself to Anne as someone who could replace her husband.

92 **Edward**: i.e. the King

94 **falchion**: a kind of sword
smoking: steaming (i.e. still hot from the killing)
95 **bend**: i.e. aim

100 **on aught but**: about anything except

101 **grant ye**: agree that I did

102 **hedgehog**: a scornful reference to Richard's emblem, the hog or boar

107 **holp**: helped
108 **fitter**: better suited

110 **place else**: other place

112 **Ill rest betide**: Bad sleep come to

116 **keen**: sharp

118 **timeless**: ill-timed

---Think about

• How do you react to Richard's suggestion that he go to bed with Anne? Do you think he is serious, or is he just seeing how far he can go?

34

RICHARD	Nay, he is dead, and slain by Edward's hands.
ANNE	In thy foul throat thou liest! Queen Margaret saw Thy murderous falchion smoking in his blood – The which thou once didst bend against her breast, 95 But that thy brothers beat aside the point.
RICHARD	I was provokèd by her slanderous tongue That laid their guilt upon my guiltless shoulders.
ANNE	Thou wast provokèd by thy bloody mind, That never dream'st on aught but butcheries. 100 Didst thou not kill this King?
RICHARD	I grant ye.
ANNE	Dost grant me, hedgehog? Then, God grant me too Thou mayst be damnèd for that wicked deed! O, he was gentle, mild, and virtuous!
RICHARD	The better for the King of Heaven, that hath him. 105
ANNE	He is in heaven, where thou shalt never come.
RICHARD	Let him thank me that holp to send him thither – For he was fitter for that place than earth.
ANNE	And thou unfit for any place but hell!
RICHARD	Yes, one place else, if you will hear me name it. 110
ANNE	Some dungeon.
RICHARD	Your bed-chamber.
ANNE	Ill rest betide the chamber where thou liest!
RICHARD	So will it, madam, till I lie with you.
ANNE	I hope so.
RICHARD	I know so. But, gentle Lady Anne, 115 To leave this keen encounter of our wits, And fall something into a slower method – Is not the causer of the timeless deaths Of these Plantagenets, Henry and Edward, As blameful as the executioner? 120
ANNE	Thou wast the cause and most accursed effect.

Richard tries to claim that Anne's beauty was the cause of his murderous actions. Outraged, Anne hopes for revenge on Richard. Richard again suggests he could replace her husband and she spits at him.

126   **homicide**: murderer
127   **rend**: tear

134   **would**: wish

139   **bereft thee**: took from you by force

142   **He lives**: There is a man

143   **Plantagenet**: Richard, King Henry VI, and his son Prince Edward shared that name since they were all descended from King Edward III.
144   **self-same**: same

146   **mortal**: deadly

---Think about---

• Having said that Anne's beauty was the cause of his crimes, Richard quite calmly accepts her spitting at him. How would you direct this moment to make it convincing?

RICHARD		Your beauty was the cause of that effect –
		Your beauty that did haunt me in my sleep
		To undertake the death of all the world
		So I might live one hour in your sweet bosom.	125

ANNE   If I thought that, I tell thee, homicide,
            These nails should rend that beauty from my cheeks.

RICHARD   These eyes could not endure that beauty's wreck:
            You should not blemish it if I stood by.
            As all the world is cheerèd by the sun,   130
            So I by that. It is my day, my life.

ANNE   Black night o'ershade thy day, and death thy life!

RICHARD   Curse not thyself, fair creature: thou art both.

ANNE   I would I were, to be revenged on thee.

RICHARD   It is a quarrel most unnatural,   135
            To be revenged on him that loveth thee.

ANNE   It is a quarrel just and reasonable,
            To be revenged on him that killed my husband.

RICHARD   He that bereft thee, lady, of thy husband
            Did it to help thee to a better husband.   140

ANNE   His better doth not breathe upon the earth.

RICHARD   He lives that loves thee better than he could.

ANNE   Name him.

RICHARD   Plantagenet.

ANNE   Why, that was he.

RICHARD   The self-same name, but one of better nature.

ANNE   Where is he?

RICHARD   Here. (*She spits at him.*) Why dost thou
            spit at me?   145

ANNE   Would it were mortal poison, for thy sake!

RICHARD   Never came poison from so sweet a place.

Richard says that nothing except Anne's beauty can make him cry, despite all the suffering he has seen and felt. He offers her his sword so that she can kill him.

151 **basilisks**: mythical creatures who could kill with a look

155 **aspects**: appearances

158 **Rutland**: Richard's younger brother, whose murder was plotted by Margaret
159 **black-faced**: darkly angry, frightening
Clifford: Rutland's murderer
160 **thy warlike father**: the Earl of Warwick, also dead in the wars
164 **bedashed**: spattered

166 **exhale**: draw out

168 **sued to**: asked favours of
169 **smoothing**: flattering
170 **proposed**: i.e. offered as
fee: reward
171 **sues**: begs

Think about

- Who do you think is in control at this point?

- Whose side are you on?

ANNE	⏁ Never hung poison on a <u>fouler toad</u>.	
	Out of my sight! Thou dost infect mine eyes.	
RICHARD	Thine eyes, sweet lady, have infected mine.	150
ANNE	Would they were basilisks to strike thee dead!	

RICHARD	I would they were, that I might die at once –	
	For now they kill me with a living death.	
	Those eyes of thine from mine have drawn salt tears,	
	Shamed their aspects with store of childish drops –	155
	These eyes, which never shed remorseful tear,	
	No, when my father York and Edward wept	
	To hear the piteous moan that Rutland made	
	When black-faced Clifford shook his sword at him –	
	Nor when thy warlike father, like a child,	160
	Told the sad story of my father's death,	
	And twenty times made pause to sob and weep	
	That all the standers-by had wet their cheeks	
	Like trees bedashed with rain. In that sad time	
	My manly eyes did scorn an humble tear;	165
	And what these sorrows could not thence exhale	
	Thy beauty hath, and made them blind with weeping.	
	I never sued to friend nor enemy;	
	My tongue could never learn sweet smoothing word.	
	But, now thy beauty is proposed my fee,	170
	My proud heart sues, and prompts my tongue to speak.	

She looks scornfully at him.

	Teach not thy lip such scorn – for it was made	
	For kissing, lady, not for such contempt.	
	If thy revengeful heart cannot forgive,	
	Lo here I lend thee this sharp-pointed sword –	175
	Which if thou please to hide in this true breast	
	And let the soul forth that adoreth thee,	
	I lay it naked to the deadly stroke,	
	And humbly beg the death upon my knee.	

He kneels, pulling open his shirt. She grips the sword and moves as if to stab him.

Anne cannot kill him. Richard offers to kill himself if she will tell him to, but she will not. She accepts his ring and puts it on her finger.

182 dispatch: 1 hurry up; 2 kill me
183 set me on: made me do it

185 dissembler: pretender

190–1 This hand ... love: Richard claims to have killed Anne's husband because he himself loved her, and he now offers again to kill himself.

192 shalt ... accessary: you will share the blame

194 figured: shown

197 put up: put away

Think about

- Why does Anne not stab Richard? How close do you think she is to doing so?

- Look closely at lines 193 to 203. What is the effect of each character speaking such short lines?

202 Vouchsafe: Please agree

Nay, do not pause: for I did kill King Henry –   **180**
But 'twas thy beauty that provokèd me.
Nay, now dispatch: 'twas I that stabbed young Edward –
But 'twas thy heavenly face that set me on.

She lets the sword fall.

Take up the sword again, or take up me.

ANNE   Arise, dissembler. Though I wish thy death,   **185**
I will not be thy executioner.

RICHARD   Then bid me kill myself, and I will do it.

ANNE   I have already.

RICHARD   That was in thy rage.
Speak it again – and even with the word
This hand, which for thy love did kill thy love,   **190**
Shall for thy love kill a far truer love.
To both their deaths shalt thou be accessary.

ANNE   I would I knew thy heart.

RICHARD   'Tis figured in my tongue.

ANNE   I fear me both are false.   **195**

RICHARD   Then never was man true.

ANNE   Well, well, put up your sword.

RICHARD   Say, then, my peace is made.

ANNE   That shalt thou know hereafter.

RICHARD   But shall I live in hope?   **200**

ANNE   All men, I hope, live so.

RICHARD   Vouchsafe to wear this ring.

ANNE   To take is not to give.

She puts on the ring.

Richard persuades Anne to let him take over the arrangements for King Henry's funeral. After Anne leaves he is triumphant over his success in wooing her, but says that he will soon be rid of her.

204   Look how: i.e. Just as
encompasseth: goes round

211   sad designs: plans (i.e. the funeral arrangements for King Henry VI)
213   presently repair to: immediately go to
Crosby House: one of Richard's houses
214   interred: buried

217   expedient: swift
218   divers unknown: various secret
219   boon: favour

220   joys: delights
221   penitent: regretful of your crime

227   White Friars: a priory
attend my coming: wait for me

228   humour: mood

Think about

• How should Anne be reacting to Richard as the scene comes to an end? What do you think she is thinking?

RICHARD	Look how my ring encompasseth thy finger:
	Even so thy breast encloseth my poor heart.
	Wear both of them, for both of them are thine.
	And if thy poor devoted servant may
	But beg one favour at thy gracious hand,
	Thou dost confirm his happiness for ever.
ANNE	What is it?
RICHARD	That it may please you leave these sad designs
	To him that hath most cause to be a mourner,
	And presently repair to Crosby House;
	Where – after I have solemnly interred
	At Chertsey monast'ry this noble King,
	And wet his grave with my repentant tears –
	I will with all expedient duty see you.
	For divers unknown reasons, I beseech you,
	Grant me this boon.
ANNE	With all my heart – and much it joys me too
	To see you are become so penitent.
	Tressel and Berkeley, go along with me.
RICHARD	Bid me farewell.
ANNE	'Tis more than you deserve.
	But since you teach me how to flatter you,
	Imagine I have said farewell already.

205

210

215

220

225

Exit Lady **ANNE**, *with Gentlemen (*TRESSEL *and* BERKELEY*).*

RICHARD	Sirs, take up the corpse.
GENTLEMAN	Towards Chertsey, noble lord?
RICHARD	No, to White Friars. There attend my coming.

Bearers carry the coffin away, escorted by guards and
Gentlemen. **RICHARD** *remains, alone.*

Was ever woman in this humour wooed?
Was ever woman in this humour won?
I'll have her – but I will not keep her long.
What! I that killed her husband and his father –
To take her in her heart's extremest hate,
With curses in her mouth, tears in her eyes,

230

43

Alone, Richard talks triumphantly about his evil actions and ugly appearance, pleased and surprised that despite these difficulties he has been so persuasive and successful.

234   **witness … hatred by**: i.e. body of King Henry VI nearby
235   **bars**: obstacles
236   **suit**: wooing
237   **dissembling looks**: the ability to pretend / deceive
238   **all … nothing**: with everything against me and nothing for me

244   **Framed … nature**: outstandingly gifted

246   **afford**: supply (i.e. another like him)
247   **abase**: lower
248   **cropped**: cut off
        golden prime: i.e. his best years
250   **Edward's moiety**: half Edward's value
251   **halts**: limps
252   **denier**: a small French coin of very little value

255   **proper**: handsome
256   **be at charges for**: i.e. buy
        looking-glass: mirror
257   **entertain**: employ
        score: twenty
259   **Since I … myself**: i.e. Now that I am pleased to know how handsome I am
261   **turn**: tip
        yon fellow: the body of King Henry VI

Think about

• What is Richard's attitude to Anne?

• Richard's wooing of Anne is one of his great triumphs. Were you convinced by it? How do you feel about him at the end of this scene?

The bleeding witness of my hatred by –
Having God, her conscience, and these bars against me –   **235**
And I no friends to back my suit at all
But the plain devil and dissembling looks?
And yet to win her, all the world to nothing!
Ha!
Hath she forgot already that brave prince,   **240**
Edward, her lord – whom I, some three months since,
Stabbed in my angry mood at Tewkesbury?
A sweeter and a lovelier gentleman –
Framed in the prodigality of nature,
Young, valiant, wise, and no doubt right royal –   **245**
The spacious world cannot again afford.
And will she yet abase her eyes on me,
That cropped the golden prime of this sweet prince
And made her widow to a woeful bed?
On me, whose all not equals Edward's moiety?   **250**
On me, that halts and am misshapen thus?
My dukedom to a beggarly denier,
I do mistake my person all this while!
Upon my life, she finds, although I cannot,
Myself to be a marvellous proper man!   **255**
I'll be at charges for a looking-glass,
And entertain a score or two of tailors
To study fashions to adorn my body.
Since I am crept in favour with myself,
I will maintain it with some little cost.   **260**
But first I'll turn yon fellow in his grave,
And then return lamenting to my love.
Shine out, fair sun, till I have bought a glass,
That I may see my shadow as I pass.

Exit.

45

RSC, 1984

RSC, 2001

Shakespeare's Globe, 2003

RSC, 1995

In this scene ...

- Queen Elizabeth is worried that her husband, King Edward the Fourth, is going to die and that her son, the young Prince Edward, is too young to rule.
- Queen Elizabeth is concerned that Richard has been appointed as Protector to Prince Edward and his brother, the Duke of York, and she and Richard insult one another bitterly.
- Queen Margaret, widow of King Henry the Sixth, spits out curses, focusing particularly on Richard. She warns Buckingham not to trust Richard, but he ignores her.
- Richard sends two murderers to kill Clarence.

Elizabeth and her relatives discuss King Edward's illness. She claims that Richard, who will rule as Protector if the King dies, hates her and her family.

3 **brook it ill**: take it badly
4 **entertain good comfort**: cheer up

6 **betide on**: happen to

9 **goodly son**: i.e. Prince Edward

11–12 **Ah ... Gloucester**: Richard has been chosen as the official guardian (Protector) of the Prince as he is too young to rule.
14 **concluded**: legally decided
15 **determined**: agreed
16 **miscarry**: dies

Think about

- The change of scene here marks a shift from Richard's excited plotting to the anxious members of the royal family. How could you stage this moment to emphasise the change in mood?

- What is it that is most worrying to Elizabeth and her relatives?

20 **Countess Richmond**: Richmond's mother, widow of Edmund Tudor, now married to the Earl of Derby
22 **notwithstanding**: although

London: the palace of KING EDWARD the Fourth.

Enter Queen ELIZABETH, with her brother Lord RIVERS, and her

sons, Lord GREY and the Marquis of DORSET (her earlier

'Woodville' family).

RIVERS	Have patience, madam. There's no doubt his Majesty
	Will soon recover his accustomed health.
GREY	In that you brook it ill, it makes him worse.
	Therefore, for God's sake, entertain good comfort,
	And cheer his Grace with quick and merry eyes.

5

ELIZABETH	If he were dead, what would betide on me?
GREY	No other harm but loss of such a lord.
ELIZABETH	The loss of such a lord includes all harms.
GREY	The heavens have blessed you with a goodly son
	To be your comforter when he is gone.

10

ELIZABETH	⎧Ah, he is young; and his minority
	⎨ Is put unto the trust of Richard Gloucester,
	⎩ A man that loves not me, nor none of you.
RIVERS	Is it concluded he shall be Protector?
ELIZABETH	It is determined, not concluded yet.
	But so it must be, if the King miscarry.

15

Enter the Duke of BUCKINGHAM and Lord Stanley, Earl of DERBY.

GREY	Here comes the Lords of Buckingham and Derby.
BUCKINGHAM	Good time of day unto your royal Grace!
DERBY	God make your Majesty joyful as you have been.
ELIZABETH	The Countess Richmond, good my Lord of Derby,
	To your good prayer will scarcely say amen.
	Yet, Derby, notwithstanding she's your wife
	And loves not me, be you, good lord, assured
	I hate not you for her proud arrogance.

20

Buckingham and Derby have visited the King, and say that he wants to make peace between the competing groups at court. Richard enters and attacks Elizabeth and her relatives for being deceitful and complaining about him to the King.

Think about

- Richard claims that he cannot 'flatter' and 'deceive' (lines 47 and 48), but we have just watched him do that with Anne. Why is he protesting that he is a straightforward man? Do you think anyone in the play believes him?

26 **envious slanders**: malicious untruths

29 **wayward**: obstinate / misguided
   grounded malice: firm hatred

33 **amendment**: recovery

36 **atonement**: reconciliation

39 **warn**: summon

41 **I fear … height**: I'm afraid things will only get worse from now on

44 **forsooth**: indeed
45 **lightly**: superficially
46 **dissentious**: trouble-making

48 **smooth … cog**: flatter, deceive and sweet-talk
49 **Duck with … courtesy**: bow in a foolish (foreign) and insincere way
50 **rancorous**: spiteful
53 **silken**: smooth
   insinuating Jacks: i.e. low-born people who 1 spread stories by hints; 2 use subtle ways to gain a position
54 **presence**: company
57 **faction**: followers / group

DERBY	I do beseech you: either not believe	**25**
	The envious slanders of her false accusers –	
	Or, if she be accused on true report,	
	Bear with her weakness, which I think proceeds	
	From wayward sickness and no grounded malice.	
ELIZABETH	Saw you the King today, my Lord of Derby?	**30**
DERBY	But now the Duke of Buckingham and I	
	Are come from visiting his Majesty.	
ELIZABETH	What likelihood of his amendment, lords?	
BUCKINGHAM	Madam, good hope. His Grace speaks cheerfully.	
ELIZABETH	God grant him health! Did you confer with him?	**35**
BUCKINGHAM	Ay, madam. He desires to make atonement	
	Between the Duke of Gloucester and your brothers,	
	And between them and my Lord Chamberlain;	
	And sent to warn them to his royal presence.	
ELIZABETH	Would all were well! But that will never be.	**40**
	I fear our happiness is at the height.	

Enter RICHARD, with HASTINGS (Lord Chamberlain).

RICHARD	They do me wrong, and I will not endure it!	
	Who is it that complains unto the King	
	That I, forsooth, am stern and love them not?	
	By holy Paul, they love his Grace but lightly	**45**
	That fill his ears with such dissentious rumours.	
	Because I cannot flatter and look fair,	
	Smile in men's faces, smooth, deceive, and cog,	
	Duck with French nods and apish courtesy,	
	I must be held a rancorous enemy.	**50**
	Cannot a plain man live and think no harm	
	But thus his simple truth must be abused	
	With silken, sly, insinuating Jacks?	
GREY	To who in all this presence speaks your Grace?	
RICHARD	To thee, that hast nor honesty nor grace.	**55**
	When have I injured thee? When done thee wrong?	
	Or thee, or thee, or any of your faction?	
	A plague upon you all! His royal Grace –	

Elizabeth says that it is not her family who have been complaining, but that the King himself wants to find out the truth about the quarrels. Richard blames her for Clarence's imprisonment, which she denies.

60 **scarce … while**: even for a short time
61 **lewd**: mischievous

63–8 **on his … the ground**: acting on his own initiative, has probably guessed from your actions that you secretly hate me and my family, and has sent to find out why you feel like this

71–2 **Jack**: a common man (Richard is teasing the Queen about having married above herself.)

74 **advancement**: promotion

77 **means**: influence (over the King)

80 **ennoble**: make into an aristocrat
81 **noble**: a coin worth less than half a pound (a pun)
82 **Him**: God
    careful height: troublesome high position
83 **hap**: fortune
84 **incense**: anger
87 **injury**: i.e. injustice
88 **suspects**: suspicions
89–90 **mean Of**: reason behind

Think about

• This scene is full of accusations and jealousy. From what you have seen so far, do you think Edward has been an effective King? Could anyone be effective against Richard's plots?

• Is Richard justified in making his accusations about Elizabeth and her family, from what you know so far?

	Whom God preserve better than you would wish! –	
	Cannot be quiet scarce a breathing while	60
	But you must trouble him with lewd complaints.	
ELIZABETH	Brother of Gloucester, you mistake the matter.	
	The King, on his own royal disposition	
	And not provoked by any suitor else –	
	Aiming, belike, at your interior hatred	65
	That in your outward action shows itself	
	Against my children, brothers, and myself –	
	Makes him to send that he may learn the ground.	
RICHARD	I cannot tell. The world is grown so bad	
	That wrens make prey where eagles dare not perch.	70
	Since every Jack became a gentleman,	
	There's many a gentle person made a Jack.	
ELIZABETH	Come, come, we know your meaning, brother	
	Gloucester:	
	You envy my advancement and my friends'.	
	God grant we never may have need of you!	75
RICHARD	Meantime, God grants that I have need of you.	
	Our brother is imprisoned by your means,	
	Myself disgraced, and the nobility	
	Held in contempt – while great promotions	
	Are daily given to ennoble those	80
	That scarce some two days since were worth a noble.	
ELIZABETH	By Him that raised me to this careful height	
	From that contented hap which I enjoyed,	
	I never did incense his Majesty	
	Against the Duke of Clarence – but have been	85
	An earnest advocate to plead for him.	
	My lord, you do me shameful injury	
	Falsely to draw me in these vile suspects!	
RICHARD	You may deny that you were not the mean	
	Of my Lord Hastings' late imprisonment.	90
RIVERS	She may, my lord. For –	

Richard continues to insult Elizabeth, and she threatens to tell the King about his behaviour. Queen Margaret enters listening to the argument. She verbally attacks both Elizabeth and Richard.

94   **preferments**: promotions

96   **lay ... desert**: say you were promoted through your own great merit
97   **marry**: indeed (i.e. By the Virgin Mary, an oath)
99   **Marry**: 1 Indeed; 2 To get married
100   **stripling**: youth
101   **Iwis**: Certainly
       grandam: grandmother

103   **upbraidings**: insults
       scoffs: name-calling / taunts
104   **acquaint**: tell

107   **with this condition**: in this situation
108   **baited**: tormented

111   **state**: rank
       seat: throne
       is due: should belong
113   **Look ... said**: Whatever I have said
114   **avouch't**: confirm it
115   **adventure**: risk
116   **pains**: efforts / troubles

Think about

- Historically, Queen Margaret was dead before King Edward the Fourth's final illness. Why do you think Shakespeare introduces her at this point in the play?

119   **Tewkesbury**: the Battle of Tewkesbury in 1471
120   **Ere**: Before
121   **pack-horse**: ordinary labourer

123   **liberal**: generous

RICHARD	She may, Lord Rivers? Why, who knows not so?
	She may do more, sir, than denying that.
	She may help you to many fair preferments
	And then deny her aiding hand therein, 95
	And lay those honours on your high desert.
	What may she not? She may – ay, marry, may she –
RIVERS	What, marry, may she?
RICHARD	What, marry, may she? Marry with a king –
	A bachelor, and a handsome stripling too. 100
	Iwis your grandam had a worser match!
ELIZABETH	My Lord of Gloucester, I have too long borne
	Your blunt upbraidings and your bitter scoffs.
	By heaven, I will acquaint his Majesty
	Of those gross taunts that oft I have endured! 105

Enter old Queen MARGARET *(widow of King Henry the Sixth),*
listening behind them.

	I had rather be a country servant-maid
	Than a great queen with this condition –
	To be so baited, scorned, and stormed at.
	Small joy have I in being England's Queen.
MARGARET	*(Aside)* And lessened be that small, God, I beseech Him! 110
	Thy honour, state, and seat, is due to me.
RICHARD	What! Threat you me with telling of the King?
	Tell him and spare not! Look what I have said
	I will avouch't in presence of the King.
	I dare adventure to be sent to th' Tower. 115
	'Tis time to speak – my pains are quite forgot!
MARGARET	*(Aside)* Out, devil! I do remember them too well.
	Thou kill'dst my husband Henry in the Tower,
	And Edward, my poor son, at Tewkesbury!
RICHARD	Ere you were queen, ay, or your husband king, 120
	I was a pack-horse in his great affairs,
	A weeder-out of his proud adversaries,
	A liberal rewarder of his friends.
	To royalize his blood I spent mine own.
MARGARET	*(Aside)* Ay, and much better blood than his or thine. 125

Richard claims to pity his brother Clarence, and to be inexperienced in the ways of the world. The insults and accusations continue to fly in all directions. Rivers claims to be loyal, but is brushed aside.

127 **Were factious for**: took the side of

129 **battle**: i.e. army
130 **put in your minds**: remind you

132 **Withal**: also

134 **father**: father-in-law
135 **forswore himself**: broke an oath

138 **meed**: reward
     mewed up: imprisoned
139 **flint**: hard as stone

142 **Hie thee to hell**: Hurry to hell (i.e. go to hell)
143 **cacodemon**: evil spirit

145 **Which ... urge**: which you bring up

148 **pedlar**: travelling salesman who sells small objects

156 **hold me** : remain

Think about

- Richard emphasises his loyalty and denies that he wants to be King. Elizabeth claims that she has no pleasure in being Queen. Do you believe what either of them say?

- What is the effect of Margaret speaking in asides (words that only the audience can hear)?

RICHARD	In all which time you and your husband Grey	
	Were factious for the house of Lancaster –	
	And, Rivers, so were you. Was not your husband	
	In Margaret's battle at Saint Albans slain?	
	Let me put in your minds, if you forget,	130
	What you have been ere this, and what you are –	
	Withal, what I have been, and what I am.	

MARGARET   (*Aside*) A murderous villain, and so still thou art!

RICHARD   Poor Clarence did forsake his father, Warwick,
Ay, and forswore himself – which Jesu pardon! –   135

MARGARET   (*Aside*) Which God revenge!

RICHARD   – To fight on Edward's party for the crown.
And for his meed, poor lord, he is mewed up.
I would to God my heart were flint like Edward's,
Or Edward's soft and pitiful like mine.   140
I am too childish-foolish for this world.

MARGARET   (*Aside*) Hie thee to hell for shame and leave this world,
Thou cacodemon! There thy kingdom is!

RIVERS   My Lord of Gloucester, in those busy days
Which here you urge to prove us enemies,   145
We followed then our lord, our sovereign king.
So should we you, if you should be our king.

RICHARD   If I should be! I had rather be a pedlar.
Far be it from my heart, the thought thereof!

ELIZABETH   As little joy, my lord, as you suppose   150
You should enjoy were you this country's king,
As little joy you may suppose in me
That I enjoy, being the Queen thereof.

MARGARET   (*Aside*) A little joy enjoys the Queen thereof –
For I am she, and altogether joyless.   155
I can no longer hold me patient.

She comes forward.

Margaret claims to be superior in both authority and the right to sorrow. Richard reminds her how badly she treated his father, and that she had his young brother, Rutland, killed. Margaret argues that they have only turned on her as a diversion from attacking each other.

157 **wrangling**: angrily arguing
158 **pilled**: stolen / pillaged

160–1 **If not … rebels**: If you do not bow to me because I am Queen and you are my subjects, at least you shake because you took the throne from me and know that you are rebels
164 **repetition**: retelling
 marred: ruined

168 **yield**: give
 abode: staying here
170 **allegiance**: loyalty

172 **usurp**: take wrongfully

174 **crown … paper**: Richard's father, the Duke of York, was humiliated by being made to wear a paper crown after defeat at the Battle of Wakefield
176 **clout**: cloth
177 **Steeped**: soaked
179 **Denounced**: angrily proclaimed
180 **plagued**: i.e. punished
181 **right**: avenge
182 **that babe**: young Rutland, Richard's brother

185 **No man but**: Everyone

Think about

- Is Richard's treatment of Margaret here fair?

- Why do you think the lords make their comments, and what effect do they have on the tension in this scene?

190 **prevail**: succeed

	Hear me, you wrangling pirates, that fall out	
	In sharing that which you have pilled from me!	
	Which of you trembles not that looks on me?	
	If not, that I am Queen, you bow like subjects,	**160**
	Yet that, by you deposed, you quake like rebels?	
	Ah, gentle villain, do not turn away!	

RICHARD   Foul wrinkled witch, what mak'st thou in my sight?

MARGARET   But repetition of what thou hast marred –
That will I make before I let thee go.   **165**

RICHARD   Wert thou not banishèd on pain of death?

MARGARET   I was. But I do find more pain in banishment
Than death can yield me here by my abode.
A husband and a son thou ow'st to me –
And thou a kingdom – all of you allegiance.   **170**
This sorrow that I have by right is yours;
And all the pleasures you usurp are mine.

RICHARD   The curse my noble father laid on thee,
When thou didst crown his warlike brows with paper
And with thy scorns drew'st rivers from his eyes –   **175**
And then to dry them gav'st the Duke a clout
Steeped in the faultless blood of pretty Rutland –
His curses then from bitterness of soul
Denounced against thee are all fall'n upon thee –
And God, not we, hath plagued thy bloody deed.   **180**

ELIZABETH   So just is God to right the innocent.

HASTINGS   O, 'twas the foulest deed to slay that babe,
And the most merciless that e'er was heard of!

RIVERS   Tyrants themselves wept when it was reported.

DORSET   No man but prophesied revenge for it.   **185**

BUCKINGHAM   Northumberland, then present, wept to see it.

MARGARET   What, were you snarling all before I came,
Ready to catch each other by the throat,
And turn you all your hatred now on me?
Did York's dread curse prevail so much with heaven   **190**
That Henry's death, my lovely Edward's death,

Margaret curses everyone, predicting death and suffering in the future. Richard insults her.

193 **answer**: compensate
peevish brat: miserable child
195 **quick**: sharp (the opposite of 'dull')
196 **surfeit**: overindulgence

200 **like untimely**: similarly premature

205 **Decked**: dressed
stalled: installed

212 **natural age**: full lifetime
213 **unlooked**: unexpected

214 **charm**: i.e. spell

Think about

- Look at Margaret's curses. Pick out language that makes you think that she is a) a commentator; b) a reminder that the guilty will be punished; and c) a predictor of the future.

- How might an audience react to Margaret's curses? For example, think about whether they expect they will come true.

---

221 **be-gnaw**: chew at

227 **elvish-marked**: marked by evil fairies as one of their own
abortive: unnatural / deformed
rooting hog: a reference both to Richard's emblem, the boar, and to his hunch-backed shape
228 **sealed**: marked forever
nativity: birth
229 **slave of nature**: lowest form of life

Their kingdom's loss, my woeful banishment,
Should all but answer for that peevish brat?
Can curses pierce the clouds and enter heaven?
Why then, give way, dull clouds, to my quick curses!   **195**
Though not by war, by surfeit die your king,
As ours by murder, to make him a king!
Edward thy son, that now is Prince of Wales,
For Edward our son, that was Prince of Wales,
Die in his youth by like untimely violence!   **200**
Thyself a queen, for me that was a queen,
Outlive thy glory, like my wretched self!
Long may'st thou live to wail thy children's death,
And see another, as I see thee now,
Decked in thy rights, as thou art stall'd in mine!   **205**
Long die thy happy days before thy death –
And, after many lengthened hours of grief,
Die neither mother, wife, nor England's Queen!
Rivers and Dorset, you were standers by,
And so wast thou, Lord Hastings, when my son   **210**
Was stabbed with bloody daggers. God, I pray Him,
That none of you may live his natural age,
But by some unlooked accident cut off!

RICHARD   Have done thy charm, thou hateful withered hag!

MARGARET   And leave out thee? Stay, dog, for thou shalt hear me.   **215**
If heaven have any grievous plague in store
Exceeding those that I can wish upon thee,
O, let them keep it till thy sins be ripe,
And then hurl down their indignation
On thee, the troubler of the poor world's peace!   **220**
The worm of conscience still be-gnaw thy soul!
Thy friends suspect for traitors while thou liv'st,
And take deep traitors for thy dearest friends!
No sleep close up that deadly eye of thine,
Unless it be while some tormenting dream   **225**
Affrights thee with a hell of ugly devils!
Thou elvish-marked, abortive, rooting hog! –
Thou that wast sealed in thy nativity
The slave of nature and the son of hell,

Margaret focuses her strongest curse on Richard, but he turns her words back on her. Margaret then aims her hatred at the others.

230 **slander**: insult to
heavy: 1 pregnant; 2 sad
232 **rag**: leftover scrap

234 **cry thee mercy**: beg your pardon

237 **period**: ending

240 **painted**: imitation
vain flourish: empty show
241 **strew'st ... spider**: do you scatter sweet words on that swollen (bottle-shaped) spider (i.e. Richard)
243 **whet'st**: sharpen
245 **bunch-backed**: hunch-backed
246 **False-boding**: False-prophesying
247 **move**: try

249 **well served**: properly prompted by your conscience

Think about

• List the images of disability and beastliness thrown at Richard here and on the previous page. Now look back at Richard's speech at the beginning of Act 1 Scene 1. Does this change your feelings about the way these insults are used here?

	Thou slander of thy heavy mother's womb,	**230**
	Thou loathèd issue of thy father's loins,	
	Thou rag of honour, thou detested –	

RICHARD   Margaret!

MARGARET   Richard!

RICHARD   Ha?

MARGARET   I call thee not.

RICHARD   I cry thee mercy then, for I did think
That thou hadst called me all these bitter names.   **235**

MARGARET   Why, so I did, but looked for no reply.
O, let me make the period to my curse!

RICHARD   'Tis done by me, and ends in 'Margaret'.

ELIZABETH   Thus have you breathed your curse against yourself.

MARGARET   Poor painted queen, vain flourish of my fortune!   **240**
Why strew'st thou sugar on that bottled spider
Whose deadly web ensnareth thee about?
Fool, fool! Thou whet'st a knife to kill thyself!
The day will come that thou shalt wish for me
To help thee curse this poisonous bunch-backed toad!   **245**

HASTINGS   False-boding woman, end thy frantic curse,
Lest to thy harm thou move our patience.

MARGARET   Foul shame upon you! You have all moved mine.

RIVERS   Were you well served, you would be taught your duty.

MARGARET   To serve me well you all should do *me* duty –   **250**
Teach me to be your queen and you my subjects.
O, serve me well, and teach yourselves that duty!

DORSET   Dispute not with her. She is lunatic!

The cursing and quarrelling continues. Buckingham tries to calm the situation and Margaret is friendly towards him.

254 **malapert**: disrespectful and rude

255 **fire-new … current**: brand-new badge of rank is so new it's barely valid

258 **blasts**: winds

260 **marry**: indeed

261 **touches**: applies to

263 **eyrie buildeth**: eagles' nest is built

264 **dallies**: plays

269 **eyrie … nest**: eagles' nest has been built in the place of ours

270 **suffer**: allow

272 **Peace**: i.e. Be quiet

Think about

- Pick out the images of height, eagles and their nests, and the sun in lines 258 to 270. What is the combined effect of these images?

- Margaret has suffered terribly, but has become eaten up with hatred. Does she deserve pity or disgust?

280 **league and amity**: alliance and friendship

281 **Now … thee**: Good luck to you

283 **compass**: range

MARGARET	Peace, Master Marquis, you are malapert:
	Your fire-new stamp of honour is scarce current. 255
	O, that your young nobility could judge
	What 'twere to lose it and be miserable!
	They that stand high have many blasts to shake them,
	And if they fall they dash themselves to pieces.
RICHARD	Good counsel, marry! Learn it, learn it, Marquis. 260
DORSET	It touches you, my lord, as much as me.
RICHARD	Ay, and much more. But I was born so high:
	Our eyrie buildeth in the cedar's top,
	And dallies with the wind, and scorns the sun.
MARGARET	– And turns the sun to shade – alas! Alas! 265
	Witness my son, now in the shade of death,
	Whose bright out-shining beams thy cloudy wrath
	Hath in eternal darkness folded up.
	Your eyrie buildeth in our eyrie's nest –
	O God that see'st it, do not suffer it! 270
	As it is won with blood, lost be it so!
BUCKINGHAM	Peace, peace – for shame, if not for charity!
MARGARET	Urge neither charity nor shame to me.
	Uncharitably with me have you dealt,
	And shamefully my hopes by you are butchered! 275
	My charity is outrage, life my shame –
	And in that shame still live my sorrow's rage!
BUCKINGHAM	Have done, have done.
MARGARET	O princely Buckingham, I'll kiss thy hand
	In sign of league and amity with thee. 280
	Now fair befall thee and thy noble house!
	Thy garments are not spotted with our blood,
	Nor thou within the compass of my curse.
BUCKINGHAM	Nor no one here – for curses never pass
	The lips of those that breathe them in the air. 285

Buckingham rejects Margaret's advice to beware of Richard and, before leaving, Margaret predicts Buckingham's downfall. Richard expresses false pity for her, and also asks for forgiveness for those who imprisoned Clarence (i.e. himself).

286 not ... but: only believe that

289 Look: Expect that
fawns: behaves flatteringly
290 venom: poisonous
rankle: fester and rot
293 ministers: i.e. devils

295 respect: pay any attention to

296 counsel: advice
297 soothe: i.e. flatter

304 muse: wonder

307 part thereof: share in the wrong

309 all the vantage: reaped all the benefits
310 hot: eager

312 Marry: And indeed
313 franked up to fatting: shut up like an animal in a sty to be fattened for killing

316 scathe: harm

317 well advised: suitably cautious

Think about

- Richard once again pretends to be humble and innocent. We know that he is play-acting, but do you think he fools the other characters?

- Margaret calls herself a 'prophetess' in line 300. Is this a fair summary?

MARGARET	I will not think but they ascend the sky
	And there awake God's gentle-sleeping peace.
	O Buckingham, take heed of yonder dog!
	Look when he fawns, he bites – and when he bites,
	His venom tooth will rankle to the death.
	Have not to do with him, beware of him!
	Sin, death, and hell have set their marks on him,
	And all their ministers attend on him.

Richard (handwritten annotation)

290

RICHARD	What doth she say, my Lord of Buckingham?
BUCKINGHAM	Nothing that I respect, my gracious lord.

295

MARGARET	What, dost thou scorn me for my gentle counsel,
	And soothe the devil that I warn thee from?
	O, but remember this another day,
	When he shall split thy very heart with sorrow –
	And say poor Margaret was a prophetess!
	Live each of you the subjects to his hate,
	And he to yours, and all of you to God's!

300

Exit.

BUCKINGHAM	My hair doth stand on end to hear her curses.
RIVERS	And so doth mine. I muse why she's at liberty.
RICHARD	I cannot blame her. By God's holy Mother,
	She hath had too much wrong – and I repent
	My part thereof that I have done to her.

305

ELIZABETH	I never did her any, to my knowledge.
RICHARD	Yet you have all the vantage of her wrong.
	I was too hot to do somebody good
	That is too cold in thinking of it now.
	Marry, as for Clarence, he is well repaid:
	He is franked up to fatting for his pains.
	God pardon them that are the cause thereof!

310

RIVERS	A virtuous and a Christian-like conclusion,
	To pray for them that have done scathe to us!

315

RICHARD	So do I ever – (*Aside*) being well advised –
	For had I cursed now, I had cursed myself.

All but Richard leave to go to the King. Alone, Richard tells of how he is deceiving the others. He gives the murderers a document to allow them access to the Tower of London, and orders them to be quick and pitiless when they kill Clarence.

323   **brawl**: quarrel
324   **abroach**: in motion
325   **lay … of others**: turn into damaging accusations against others
327   **gulls**: fools

331   **whet**: encourage

336   **holy writ**: the Bible

339   **hardy stout resolvèd**: strong-willed and determined
340   **dispatch this thing**: do this deed

Think about

• When talking in asides that the audience (but no-one else) can hear, Richard is open about his evil motives and plans. What strategies does he reveal? In what different ways might audiences react to this?

344   **repair**: go
       Crosby Place: one of Richard's houses
345   **sudden**: quick
346   **obdurate**: hard-hearted
348   **mark**: take notice of

Enter CATESBY.

CATESBY	Madam, his Majesty doth call for you, And for your Grace, and you, my gracious lords.

320

ELIZABETH	Catesby, I come. Lords, will you go with me?

RIVERS	We wait upon your Grace.

Exit QUEEN ELIZABETH. *All follow, except* RICHARD.

RICHARD   I do the wrong, and first begin to brawl.
The secret mischiefs that I set abroach
I lay unto the grievous charge of others. 325
Clarence, who I indeed have cast in darkness,
I do beweep to many simple gulls –
Namely, to Derby, Hastings, Buckingham –
And tell them 'tis the Queen and her allies
That stir the King against the Duke my brother. 330
Now they believe it, and withal whet me
To be revenged on Rivers, Dorset, Grey.
But then I sigh and, with a piece of scripture,
Tell them that God bids us do good for evil.
And thus I clothe my naked villainy 335
With odd old ends stol'n forth of holy writ,
And seem a saint when most I play the devil!

Enter two MURDERERS.

But, soft, here come my executioners.
How now, my hardy stout resolvèd mates!
Are you now going to dispatch this thing? . 340

MURDERER 1   We are, my lord, and come to have the warrant,
That we may be admitted where he is.

RICHARD   Well thought upon; I have it here about me.

He gives them the warrant.

When you have done, repair to Crosby Place.
But, sirs, be sudden in the execution – 345
Withal obdurate. Do not hear him plead:
For Clarence is well-spoken, and perhaps
May move your hearts to pity, if you mark him.

The first murderer reassures Richard that they will do as he wishes. Richard sends the murderers to their work.

349 **prate**: chat

352 **millstones**: rocks used for grinding grain ('Crying millstones' was a well-known saying meaning 'hard-hearted'.)
fall: drip

354 **Go, go, dispatch**: 1 Get on with it; 2 Go and kill

---**Think about**

• To what extent does Richard trust the murderers? Would this affect how you would ask the actors to deliver these lines, if you were the director?

MURDERER 1   Tut, tut, my lord, we will not stand to prate.
Talkers are no good doers. Be assured   350
We go to use our hands and not our tongues.

RICHARD   Your eyes drop millstones when fools' eyes fall tears.
I like you, lads. About your business straight:
Go, go, dispatch.

MURDERER 1   We will, my noble lord.

Exeunt.

In this scene ...

- In the Tower, Clarence wakes from a nightmare, in which he was accidently killed by Richard, and tells the details to his jailer.
- Clarence sleeps and Brakenbury, the officer in charge of the Tower, considers the worries of being a Prince.
- Brakenbury leaves Clarence with the murderers, who debate whether or not to kill him.
- Clarence wakes up and, although he begs for mercy, they kill him.

Imprisoned in the Tower of London, Clarence tells his jailer about the terrible dream he had during the night. He dreamt he was escaping by ship, but Richard accidently knocked him overboard.

1   **heavily**: sadly

9   **Methoughts**: I thought
    broken: broken out (i.e. escaped)
10 **embarked**: on a ship
    Burgundy: an area which is in modern day Belgium and France. This was a place of safety for the York family.
13 **hatches**: decks on ship
14 **cited up**: talked about
17 **giddy**: dizzy / unsteady, i.e. the deck was difficult to walk on
19 **that ... him**: who intended to stop him falling
20 **main**: ocean

Think about

- Clarence's dream expresses his fears and uncertainty about his future. Which images do you find particularly vivid and effective in showing the depth of his feelings?

26 **Wedges**: bars
27 **Inestimable**: 1 countless; 2 invaluable
    unvalued: priceless

32 **wooed**: looked seductively at

Inside the Tower of London.

Enter CLARENCE *and* KEEPER.

KEEPER	Why looks your Grace so heavily today?
CLARENCE	O, I have passed a miserable night –
	So full of fearful dreams, of ugly sights,
	That, as I am a Christian faithful man,
	I would not spend another such a night 5
	Though 'twere to buy a world of happy days –
	So full of dismal terror was the time!
KEEPER	What was your dream, my lord? I pray you tell me.
CLARENCE	Methoughts that I had broken from the Tower
	And was embarked to cross to Burgundy – 10
	And in my company my brother Gloucester,
	Who from my cabin tempted me to walk
	Upon the hatches. Thence we looked toward England,
	And cited up a thousand heavy times,
	During the wars of York and Lancaster, 15
	That had befall'n us. As we paced along
	Upon the giddy footing of the hatches,
	Methought that Gloucester stumbled, and in falling
	Struck me, that thought to stay him, overboard,
	Into the tumbling billows of the main. 20
	O Lord, methought what pain it was to drown –
	What dreadful noise of waters in my ears,
	What sights of ugly death within my eyes!
	Methoughts I saw a thousand fearful wrecks,
	A thousand men that fishes gnawed upon, 25
	Wedges of gold, great anchors, heaps of pearl,
	Inestimable stones, unvalued jewels –
	All scattered in the bottom of the sea!
	Some lay in dead men's skulls, and in the holes
	Where eyes did once inhabit there were crept – 30
	As 'twere in scorn of eyes – reflecting gems,
	That wooed the slimy bottom of the deep
	And mocked the dead bones that lay scattered by.

Continuing the story of his dream, Clarence tells of the terrible pain of drowning and of arriving in hell. There he was accused of betrayal and murder by the spirits of Warwick and Prince Edward for his part in their deaths.

37   **yield the ghost**: die
     envious: spiteful

40   **panting bulk**: gasping body

45   **melancholy flood**: the River Styx, the river of Death
46   **sour ferryman**: Charon, the ferryman on the River Styx, who takes souls from the living world into the afterlife
50   **scourge**: punishment
     perjury: breaking oaths
51   **afford**: give to
53   **shadow**: spirit / ghost (This is the murdered Edward Prince of Wales, son of King Henry VI.)
55   **fleeting**: inconstant
     perjured: lying
57   **furies**: mythic spirits of revenge
58   **legion**: huge group
59   **Environed**: surrounded
61   **season**: while

---Think about---

• It was Richard's plotting that led to Clarence's imprisonment, but Clarence played a violent part in the civil wars. What evidence is there that Clarence might have a guilty conscience?

68   **Edward**: King Edward IV (Clarence's brother)
     requites: repays
69   **appease**: satisfy

KEEPER	Had you such leisure in the time of death	
	To gaze upon these secrets of the deep?	35
CLARENCE	Methought I had. And often did I strive	
	To yield the ghost: but still the envious flood	
	Stopped in my soul and would not let it forth	
	To find the empty, vast, and wandering air –	
	But smothered it within my panting bulk,	40
	Who almost burst to belch it in the sea.	
KEEPER	Awaked you not in this sore agony?	
CLARENCE	No, no, my dream was lengthened after life.	
	O, then began the tempest to my soul!	
	I passed, methought, the melancholy flood	45
	With that sour ferryman which poets write of,	
	Unto the kingdom of perpetual night.	
	The first that there did greet my stranger soul	
	Was my great father-in-law, renownèd Warwick,	
	Who spake aloud 'What scourge for perjury	50
	Can this dark monarchy afford false Clarence?'	
	And so he vanished. Then came wandering by	
	A shadow like an angel, with bright hair	
	Dabbled in blood, and he shrieked out aloud	
	'Clarence is come – false, fleeting, perjured Clarence,	55
	That stabbed me in the field by Tewkesbury.	
	Seize on him, furies, take him unto torment!'	
	With that, methoughts, a legion of foul fiends	
	Environed me, and howlèd in mine ears	
	Such hideous cries that, with the very noise,	60
	I trembling waked – and for a season after	
	Could not believe but that I was in hell,	
	Such terrible impression made my dream.	
KEEPER	No marvel, lord, though it affrighted you:	
	I am afraid, methinks, to hear you tell it.	65
CLARENCE	Ah, Keeper, Keeper, I have done these things	
guilt	That now give evidence against my soul	
	For Edward's sake, and see how he requites me!	
	O God! If my deep prayers cannot appease Thee,	
	But Thou wilt be avenged on my misdeeds,	70
	Yet execute Thy wrath in me alone.	

Clarence sleeps. Brakenbury considers the outward happiness and inner restlessness of those in authority. He receives Richard's warrant from the murderers and leaves them alone with Clarence.

74 **heavy**: sad
    fain would: want to

79 **toil**: labour
80 **unfelt imaginations**: things imagined but not actually experienced
82 **low name**: common people

85 **wouldst thou**: do you want
    hither: here

88 **brief**: abrupt

93 **reason**: question

96 **signify to him**: let him know

Think about

- Look at lines 76 to 83. What does Brakenbury say about the nature of power and glory?

- Do you think that Brakenbury knows what is going to happen to Clarence? Look at lines 91 to 97.

O, spare my guiltless wife and my poor children!
Keeper, I prithee sit by me awhile.
My soul is heavy, and I fain would sleep.

KEEPER   I will, my lord. God give your Grace good rest.   75

CLARENCE *sleeps. Enter* BRAKENBURY *(Lieutenant of the Tower).*

BRAKENBURY   Sorrow breaks seasons and reposing hours,
Makes the night morning and the noontide night.
Princes have but their titles for their glories,
An outward honour for an inward toil –
And for unfelt imaginations   80
They often feel a world of restless cares,
So that between their titles and low name
There's nothing differs but the outward fame.

Enter the two MURDERERS.

MURDERER 1   Ho! Who's here?

BRAKENBURY   What wouldst thou, fellow? And how cam'st thou hither?   85

MURDERER 1   I would speak with Clarence, and I came hither on my
legs.

BRAKENBURY   What, so brief?

MURDERER 2   'Tis better, sir, than to be tedious. Let him see our
commission and talk no more.   90

BRAKENBURY *reads the warrant.*

BRAKENBURY   I am, in this, commanded to deliver
The noble Duke of Clarence to your hands.
I will not reason what is meant hereby,
Because I will be guiltless from the meaning.
There lies the Duke asleep – and there the keys.   95
I'll to the King and signify to him
That thus I have resigned to you my charge.

MURDERER 1   You may, sir – 'tis a point of wisdom. Fare you well.

Exit BRAKENBURY, *with the* KEEPER.

MURDERER 2   What, shall I stab him as he sleeps?

MURDERER 1   No. He'll say 'twas done cowardly, when he wakes.   100

The murderers discuss how they will kill Clarence. The second murderer begins to have doubts, but when the other murderer tells him to think of the reward, he is persuaded to go through with the killing.

101 great judgment day: the last day of the world, on which Christ will return to earth to judge every individual
103 urging: mentioning in the argument
104 remorse: pity

108 resolute: determined

111–12 passionate humour: merciful mood
112 wont: usual
113 but … twenty: only as long as it takes to count to twenty

118 Zounds: God's wounds (an exclamation like 'My God')

124 entertain: receive

126 meddle: bother

128 checks him: makes him stop

130 shamefaced: ashamed
mutinies: rebels
bosom: heart

Think about
- The murderers' debate contains elements of both comedy and horror. If you were the director, would you want this scene to contain some humour? How would you stage this scene to make it particularly funny or horrific?

MURDERER 2   Why, he shall never wake until the great judgement day.

MURDERER 1   Why, *then* he'll say we stabbed him sleeping.

MURDERER 2   The urging of that word 'judgement' hath bred a kind of remorse in me.

MURDERER 1   What, art thou afraid?   105

MURDERER 2   Not to kill him, having a warrant – but to be damned for killing him, from the which no warrant can defend me.

MURDERER 1   I thought thou hadst been resolute.

MURDERER 2   So I am – to let him live.

MURDERER 1   I'll back to the Duke of Gloucester and tell him so.   110

MURDERER 2   Nay, I prithee, stay a little. I hope this passionate humour of mine will change. It was wont to hold me but while one tells twenty.

MURDERER 1   How dost thou feel thyself now?

MURDERER 2   Faith, some certain dregs of conscience are yet within   115
me.

MURDERER 1   Remember our reward when the deed's done.

MURDERER 2   Zounds, he dies! I had forgot the reward.

MURDERER 1   Where's thy conscience now?

MURDERER 2   O, in the Duke of Gloucester's purse!   120

MURDERER 1   When he open his purse to give us our reward, thy conscience flies out.

MURDERER 2   'Tis no matter. Let it go – there's few or none will entertain it.

MURDERER 1   What if it come to thee again?   125

MURDERER 2   I'll not meddle with it – it makes a man a coward. A man cannot steal, but it accuseth him; a man cannot swear, but it checks him; a man cannot lie with his neighbour's wife, but it detects him. 'Tis a blushing shamefaced spirit that mutinies in a man's bosom: it   130
fills a man full of obstacles. It made me once restore a

The murderers discuss conscience but choose not to follow it. They plan to hit Clarence on the head and throw him into a barrel of wine. Clarence wakes up and guesses that they are going to harm him.

135 endeavours: tries

138 Take ... not: Think of the devil and do not follow your conscience
139 insinuate: make friends
140 prevail: win
141 tall: brave
142 fall to: get down to

143 Take: Hit
    costard: head
    hilts: handle
144 malmsey-butt: barrel of sweet wine
145 device: idea
    sop: a biscuit or cake dipped into wine

148 reason: talk

150 anon: soon

Think about

- Look at Clarence's speech in lines 157 to 159. Do you think the descriptions of the murderers would be a help or a hindrance to the actor and director?

157 darkly: threateningly

purse of gold that by chance I found. It beggars any man that keeps it. It is turned out of towns and cities for a dangerous thing – and every man that means to live well endeavours to trust to himself and live without it. 135

Murderer 1 Zounds, 'tis even now at *my* elbow, persuading me not to kill the Duke!

Murderer 2 Take the devil in thy mind and believe him not. He would insinuate with thee but to make thee sigh.

Murderer 1 I am strong-framed; he cannot prevail with me. 140

Murderer 2 Spoke like a tall man that respects thy reputation. Come, shall we fall to work?

Murderer 1 Take him on the costard with the hilts of thy sword, and then throw him in the malmsey-butt in the next room.

Murderer 2 O excellent device! And make a sop of him! 145

Murderer 1 Soft! He wakes.

Murderer 2 Strike!

Murderer 1 No. We'll reason with him.

Clarence Where art thou, Keeper? Give me a cup of wine.

Murderer 2 You shall have wine enough, my lord, anon. 150

Clarence In God's name, what art thou?

Murderer 2 A man, as you are.

Clarence But not as I am, royal.

Murderer 2 Nor you as we are, loyal.

Clarence Thy voice is thunder, but thy looks are humble. 155

Murderer 1 My voice is now the King's, my looks mine own.

Clarence How darkly and how deadly dost thou speak! Your eyes do menace me. Why look you pale? Who sent you hither? Wherefore do you come?

Murderer 2 To, to, to – 160

Clarence To murder me?

Clarence says that he should not be killed as he has not been convicted of a crime and that only God can judge and punish.

162   **Ay**: Yes

165   **Wherein**: How

167   **reconciled to**: friends with

172   **quest**: jury / group of people holding a legal inquiry

175   **convict**: convicted / proved guilty

177   **redemption**: eternal life in heaven

183   **Erroneous vassals**: Misguided servants
      King of kings: God
184   **tables of his law**: tablets carrying the Ten Commandments
186   **Spurn at His edict**: reject God's command

Think about

- Pick out the arguments Clarence puts forward to try to convince the men not to kill him. How would you direct the murderers to react? Think about the murderers' conversation on the previous page and whether Clarence's plea might appeal to their conscience.

191–2   **Thou ... Lancaster**: Clarence vowed to fight for his father-in-law of the house of Lancaster and then changed his loyalties and returned to the house of York.
195   **thy sovereign's son**: Prince Edward, King Henry VI's son

MURDERERS	Ay, ay.
CLARENCE	You scarcely have the hearts to tell me so,
	And therefore cannot have the hearts to do it.
	Wherein, my friends, have I offended you? 165
MURDERER 1	Offended *us* you have not, but the King.
CLARENCE	I shall be reconciled to him again.
MURDERER 2	Never, my lord. Therefore prepare to die.
CLARENCE	Are you drawn forth among a world of men
	To slay the innocent? What is my offence? 170
	Where is the evidence that doth accuse me?
	What lawful quest have given their verdict up
	Unto the frowning judge, or who pronounced
	The bitter sentence of poor Clarence' death?
	Before I be convict by course of law, 175
	To threaten me with death is most unlawful.
	I charge you, as you hope to have redemption
	By Christ's dear blood shed for our grievous sins,
	That you depart and lay no hands on me.
	The deed you undertake is damnable. 180
MURDERER 1	What we will do, we do upon command.
MURDERER 2	And he that hath commanded is our King.
CLARENCE	Erroneous vassals! The great King of kings
	Hath in the tables of His law commanded
	That thou shalt do no murder. Will you then 185
	Spurn at His edict and fulfil a man's?
	Take heed – for He holds vengeance in His hand
	To hurl upon their heads that break His law!
MURDERER 2	And that same vengeance doth He hurl on thee
	For false forswearing, and for murder too! 190
	Thou didst receive the sacrament to fight
	In quarrel of the house of Lancaster.
MURDERER 1	– And like a traitor to the name of God
	Didst break that vow – and with thy treacherous blade
	Unripped'st the bowels of thy sovereign's son. 195
MURDERER 2	– Whom thou wast sworn to cherish and defend.

The murderers accuse Clarence of being disloyal by killing Prince Edward (King Henry's son). Clarence says that he murdered him for the sake of his brother, King Edward. Clarence claims that Richard will protect him, but the murderers tell him that Richard hates him.

197   **dreadful**: fear and awe-inspiring
198   **dear degree**: an important way

204–7   **He ... His ... Him**: references to God

206   **indirect**: secret

208   **minister**: performer of the crime
209   **gallant-springing brave Plantagenet**: Edward Prince of Wales, son of King Henry VI
210   **novice**: beginner

216   **meed**: reward

Think about

- Richard often play-acts and tries to fool people, but not everyone falls for his tricks. How does his trust in Richard make you feel about Clarence?

224   **his three sons**: Richard, King Edward, and Clarence himself

228   **millstones**: rocks for grinding grain ('Crying millstones' was a saying meaning 'hard-hearted'.)
      lessoned: taught

84

MURDERER 1	How canst thou urge God's dreadful law to us,
	When thou hast broke it in such dear degree?
CLARENCE	Alas! For whose sake did I that ill deed?
	For Edward, for my brother, for his sake.

MURDERER 1 How canst thou urge God's dreadful law to us,
            When thou hast broke it in such dear degree?

CLARENCE   Alas! For whose sake did I that ill deed?
            For Edward, for my brother, for his sake.   200
            He sends you not to murder me for this,
            For in that sin he is as deep as I.
            If God will be avengèd for the deed,
            O, know you yet, He doth it publicly.
            Take not the quarrel from His powerful arm!   205
            He needs no indirect or lawless course
            To cut off those that have offended Him.

MURDERER 1 Who made *thee* then a bloody minister
            When gallant-springing brave Plantagenet,
            That princely novice, was struck dead by thee?   210

CLARENCE   My brother's love, the devil, and my rage.

MURDERER 1 Thy brother's love, our duty, and thy faults,
            Provoke us hither now to slaughter thee.

CLARENCE   If you do love my brother, hate not me:
            I am his brother, and I love him well.   215
            If you are hired for meed, go back again,
            And I will send you to my brother Gloucester,
            Who shall reward you better for my life
            Than Edward will for tidings of my death.

MURDERER 2 You are deceived. Your brother Gloucester hates you.   220

CLARENCE   O no, he loves me, and he holds me dear.
            Go you to him from me.

MURDERER 1   Ay, so we will.

CLARENCE   Tell him, when that our princely father York
            Blessed his three sons with his victorious arm
            And charged us from his soul to love each other,   225
            He little thought of this divided friendship.
            Bid Gloucester think of this, and he will weep.

MURDERER 1 Ay, millstones – as he lessoned us to weep.

CLARENCE   O do not slander him, for he is kind!

Clarence refuses to believe that Richard is his enemy and says that the murderers will face God's judgement if they kill him. While he is begging for mercy the first murderer stabs him. The second murderer immediately regrets his involvement.

230 **as ... harvest**: i.e. Richard is as kind / natural as a blizzard in harvest time

234 **labour my delivery**: work for my freedom

236 **thraldom**: slavery

239 **counsel**: advise

241 **war with God**: defy God
242 **set you on**: encouraged you

244 **Relent**: Stop and be merciful

248 **pent from liberty**: kept from freedom

250 **entreat**: plead

252 **thine ... flatterer**: your appearance is not false

258 **malmsey-butt**: barrel of sweet wine
    within: in the next room
260 **fain**: gladly
    Pilate: Pontius Pilate, the Roman governor who allowed the execution of Jesus Christ

Think about

- Look at the imagery in Clarence's account of his dream (lines 9 to 63). Now look at line 258. Does the way in which Clarence is killed seem particularly significant?

- What do you think are the dramatic effects of making the time leading up to Clarence's death so long drawn-out?

MURDERER 1	Right, as snow in harvest! Come, you deceive yourself. 230 'Tis he that sends us to destroy you here.
CLARENCE	It cannot be! – for he bewept my fortune, And hugged me in his arms, and swore with sobs That he would labour my delivery.
MURDERER 1	Why, so he doth – when he delivers you 235 From this earth's thraldom to the joys of heaven.
MURDERER 2	Make peace with God, for you must die, my lord.
CLARENCE	Have you that holy feeling in your souls To counsel me to make my peace with God, And are you yet to your own souls so blind 240 That you will war with God by murdering me? O, sirs, consider! They that set you on To do this deed will hate you for the deed.
MURDERER 2	What shall we do?
CLARENCE	Relent, and save your souls.
MURDERER 1	Relent! No, 'tis cowardly and womanish. 245
CLARENCE	Not to relent is beastly, savage, devilish! Which of you, if you were a prince's son – Being pent from liberty as I am now – If two such murderers as yourselves came to you, Would not entreat for life? 250 My friend, I spy some pity in thy looks. O, if thine eye be not a flatterer, Come thou on my side and entreat for me – As you would beg were you in my distress. A begging prince what beggar pities not? 255
MURDERER 2	Look behind you, my lord!
MURDERER 1	(*Stabbing* CLARENCE) Take that, and that! If all this will not do, I'll drown you in the malmsey-butt within!

Exit, dragging the body.

MURDERER 2	A bloody deed, and desperately dispatched! How fain, like Pilate, would I wash my hands 260 Of this most grievous murder!

Having put Clarence's body in the barrel, the first murderer complains that the second has been unhelpful. The second murderer wishes that he had saved Clarence.

263   **what ... not**: why didn't you help me

267   **repent me**: am sorry

268   **So do not I**: I am not sorry

271   **meed**: reward
272   **this will out**: this crime will be discovered

Think about

- How would you describe the political world on show in the play so far?

- One murderer regrets killing Clarence and the other is anxious that his part in the murder will be found out. We are not told, but what do you think is likely to happen to them?

Re-enter FIRST MURDERER.

MURDERER 1   How now, what mean'st thou that thou help'st me not?
By heavens, the Duke shall know how slack you have
been!

MURDERER 2   I would he knew that I had saved his brother!   265
Take thou the fee, and tell him what I say –
For I repent me that the Duke is slain.

                                                            Exit.

MURDERER 1   So do not I. Go, coward as thou art.
Well, I'll go hide the body in some hole,
Till that the Duke give order for his burial.   270
And when I have my meed, I will away –
For this will out, and then I must not stay.

                                                            Exit.

Act 2   Scene 1

In this scene ...

- King Edward tries to bring peace to the competing groups at court. Richard plays along with his wishes, claiming to be eager for reconciliation.
- The King is shocked to hear of Clarence's death and blames himself.
- Richard pretends to be grief-stricken too, but suggests to Buckingham that Queen Elizabeth's relatives are to blame.

Edward enters with his court. He has made peace between the competing groups. They swear to remain friends.

Think about

- What do you think might have happened directly before this scene takes place?

- How and why do you think Edward has brought the enemies together?

2 **peers**: Lords
league: alliance
3 **embassage**: message
4 **Redeemer**: Christ (regarded by Christians as saving humanity from sin), i.e. Edward expects to die soon
8 **Dissemble**: Disguise

9 **purged**: cleansed

11 **thrive I**: may I live

12 **dally**: pretend

14 **Confound**: defeat
award: judge / decree

18 **yourself is not exempt**: i.e. you are included
20 **factious**: plotting

22 **unfeignèdly**: without pretending

24 **thrive**: prosper

27 **be inviolable**: never be broken

London: the palace.

Trumpets sound. Enter KING EDWARD *the Fourth (weakened by his illness) and* QUEEN ELIZABETH, *with* DORSET, RIVERS, HASTINGS, BUCKINGHAM, GREY, *and others.*

KING EDWARD	Why, so. Now have I done a good day's work.
	You peers, continue this united league.
	I every day expect an embassage
	From my Redeemer to redeem me hence –
	And more at peace my soul shall part to heaven, 5
	Since I have made my friends at peace on earth.
	Hastings and Rivers, take each other's hand.
	Dissemble not your hatred: swear your love.
RIVERS	By heaven, my soul is purged from grudging hate;
	And with my hand I seal my true heart's love. 10
HASTINGS	So thrive I, as I truly swear the like!
KING EDWARD	Take heed you dally not before your King –
	Lest He that is the supreme King of kings
	Confound your hidden falsehood and award
	Either of you to be the other's end. 15
HASTINGS	So prosper I, as I swear perfect love!
RIVERS	And I, as I love Hastings with my heart!
KING EDWARD	Madam, yourself is not exempt from this –
	Nor you, son Dorset; Buckingham, nor you.
	You have been factious one against the other. 20
	Wife, love Lord Hastings, let him kiss your hand –
	And what you do, do it unfeignèdly.
ELIZABETH	There, Hastings: I will never more remember
	Our former hatred, so thrive I and mine!
KING EDWARD	Dorset, embrace him. Hastings, love Lord Marquis. 25
DORSET	This interchange of love, I here protest,
	Upon my part shall be inviolable.

Buckingham declares a new loving loyalty to the Queen, asking God's punishment if he breaks his promise. Richard enters, also apparently wanting a reconciliation.

Think about

- Look closely at the language used by Buckingham and Richard. Are there any hints that they are hiding something or being insincere?

29 **princely Buckingham**: Buckingham is 'princely' because he is descended from the youngest son of King Edward III.
league: alliance

33–4 **but ... Doth**: and does not treasure you with all respectful love

38 **Deep**: secretive
guile: deceit

41 **cordial**: medicine

43 **There wanteth**: We only need
44 **period ... peace**: ending of this peace-making process

50 **charity**: love
51 **enmity**: hostility
52 **swelling wrong-incensèd**: puffed up with misguided arrogance and anger
54 **princely heap**: high-born group
55 **By false ... surmise**: through false information or wrong calculation
56 **foe**: enemy
58 **aught**: anything
hardly borne: resented

HASTINGS   And so swear I.

They embrace.

KING EDWARD Now princely Buckingham, seal thou this league
               With thy embracements to my wife's allies,   30
               And make me happy in your unity.

BUCKINGHAM (*To the Queen*) Whenever Buckingham doth turn
                 his hate
               Upon your Grace, but with all duteous love
               Doth cherish you and yours, God punish me
               With hate in those where I expect most love!   35
               When I have most need to employ a friend
               And most assurèd that he is a friend,
               Deep, hollow, treacherous and full of guile,
               Be he unto me! This do I beg of God
               When I am cold in love to you or yours.   40

They embrace.

KING EDWARD A pleasing cordial, princely Buckingham,
               Is this thy vow unto my sickly heart.
               There wanteth now our brother Gloucester here
               To make the blessèd period of this peace.

BUCKINGHAM And, in good time,   45
               Here comes Sir Richard Ratcliffe and the Duke.

Enter RICHARD, *with* RATCLIFFE.

RICHARD   Good morrow to my sovereign King and Queen –
               And, princely peers, a happy time of day!

KING EDWARD Happy, indeed, as we have spent the day.
               Gloucester, we have done deeds of charity,   50
               Made peace of enmity, fair love of hate,
               Between these swelling wrong-incensèd peers.

RICHARD   A blessèd labour, my most sovereign lord!
               Among this princely heap, if any here,
               By false intelligence or wrong surmise,   55
               Hold me a foe –
               If I unwittingly, or in my rage,
               Have aught committed that is hardly borne
               To any in this presence – I desire

93

Richard claims to be at peace with everyone. When Elizabeth mentions Clarence, not knowing that he is dead, Richard pretends to be outraged. King Edward and the others are shocked to learn that Clarence has been killed.

63 **madam**: i.e. Queen Elizabeth

68 **desert**: me deserving it

71 **any jot at odds**: the slightest bit in opposition

75 **would**: wish
compounded: sorted out
77 **take … your grace**: include Clarence in your forgiveness

79 **flouted**: insulted

Think about

- The tone of the scene alters when Elizabeth mentions Clarence. Do you think that Richard planned this moment, or has he just taken his opportunity to attack her?

- In either case, what do you think he wants to achieve?

85 **the presence**: i.e. of the King
86 **forsook**: left

89 **wingèd Mercury**: the messenger of the gods, i.e. fast
90 **tardy**: slow moving
bare: carried
countermand: order reversing the previous command
91 **lag**: late

	To reconcile me to his friendly peace.	60
	'Tis death to me to be at enmity:	
	I hate it, and desire all good men's love.	
	First, madam, I entreat true peace of you,	
	Which I will purchase with my duteous service –	
	Of you, my noble cousin Buckingham,	65
	If ever any grudge were lodged between us –	
	Of you, and you, Lord Rivers, and of Dorset,	
	That all without desert have frowned on me –	
	Dukes, earls, lords, gentlemen – indeed, of all.	
	I do not know that Englishman alive	70
	With whom my soul is any jot at odds	
	More than the infant that is born tonight.	
	I thank my God for my humility!	

ELIZABETH	A holy day shall this be kept hereafter.	
	I would to God all strifes were well compounded!	75
	My sovereign lord, I do beseech your Highness	
	To take our brother Clarence to your grace.	

RICHARD	Why, madam, have I offered love for this?	
	– To be so flouted in this royal presence?	
	Who knows not that the gentle Duke is dead?	80

All react with shock.

| | You do him injury to scorn his corpse! | |

| KING EDWARD | Who knows not he is dead! Who knows he *is*? | |

| ELIZABETH | All-seeing heaven, what a world is this! | |

| BUCKINGHAM | Look I so pale, Lord Dorset, as the rest? | |

| DORSET | Ay, my good lord – and no man in the presence | 85 |
| | But his red colour hath forsook his cheeks. | |

| KING EDWARD | Is Clarence dead? The order was reversed. | |

RICHARD	But he, poor man, by your first order died –	
	And that a wingèd Mercury did bear.	
	Some tardy cripple bare the countermand	90
	That came too lag to see him burièd.	
	God grant that some, less noble and less loyal,	

Derby's servant has committed a murder and Derby asks the King to spare the man's life. Edward, feeling guilty about the death of Clarence on his orders, reflects on the irony that he must pardon an undeserving man while the brother who had helped him so much is dead.

Think about

- What elements of King Edward's speech (lines 103 to 126) give it particular emotional power? Look at the large number of questions and exclamations.

- Why do you think Edward blames those who did not ask for mercy on Clarence's behalf?

93 **Nearer ... blood**: more bloody in their thoughts, though not as royal in blood

95 **current**: free

96 **boon**: favour

100–1 **The forfeit ... gentleman**: Derby wants one of his servants who has killed someone in a drunken brawl to be pardoned. By law he should die.

103 **doom**: decree

104 **slave**: servant

105 **fault was thought**: crime was in what he thought, not in what he did

107 **sued ... him**: begged me to spare his life

108 **be advised**: think again

113 **Oxford**: an aristocratic enemy in the battle

116 **lap**: wrap

118 **thin**: thinly dressed

123 **carters ... waiting-vassals**: labourers or your serving men

123–4 **defaced ... Redeemer**: Killing a person is a kind of vandalism, since humans were made in the image of God.

125 **straight**: immediately

Nearer in bloody thoughts, but not in blood,
Deserve not worse than wretched Clarence did –
And yet go current from suspicion!   95

Enter DERBY *(and kneels before the* KING*).*

DERBY   A boon, my sovereign, for my service done!

KING EDWARD   I prithee, peace. My soul is full of sorrow.

DERBY   I will not rise unless your Highness hear me.

KING EDWARD   Then say at once what is it thou requests.

DERBY   The forfeit, sovereign, of my servant's life –   100
                   Who slew today a riotous gentleman
                   Lately attendant on the Duke of Norfolk.

KING EDWARD   Have I a tongue to doom my brother's death,
                   And shall that tongue give pardon to a slave?
                   My brother killed no man – his fault was thought,   105
                   And yet his punishment was bitter death.
                   Who sued to me for him? Who, in my wrath,
                   Kneeled at my feet, and bid me be advised?
                   Who spoke of brotherhood? Who spoke of love?
                   Who told me how the poor soul did forsake   110
                   The mighty Warwick and did fight for me?
                   Who told me, in the field at Tewkesbury,
                   When Oxford had me down, he rescued me
                   And said 'Dear Brother, live, and be a king'?
                   Who told me, when we both lay in the field   115
                   Frozen almost to death, how he did lap me
                   Even in his garments, and did give himself,
                   All thin and naked, to the numb cold night?
                   All this from my remembrance brutish wrath
                   Sinfully plucked, and not a man of you   120
                   Had so much grace to put it in my mind!
                   But when your carters or your waiting-vassals
                   Have done a drunken slaughter and defaced
                   The precious image of our dear Redeemer,
                   You straight are on your knees for pardon, pardon! –   125
                   And I, unjustly too, must grant it you.

DERBY *rises from his knees.*

Edward leaves, greatly distressed. Richard comments that Elizabeth's family looked pale when they heard of the death of Clarence and implies that they are to blame.

130 **been beholding to him**: owed him something

134 **closet**: private room

135 **fruits of rashness**: results of hasty action
136 **kindred**: relations

138 **did urge it still**: constantly pressed for Clarence's death

141 **wait upon**: will come with

Think about

- Look at Richard's lines here and on the previous two pages. How does he pass the blame for Clarence's death onto others?

- From what you have read so far, how long do you think the peace brought about by King Edward will last?

But for my brother not a man would speak –
Nor I, ungracious, speak unto myself
For him, poor soul. The proudest of you all
Have been beholding to him in his life –   **130**
Yet none of you would once beg for his life.
O God, I fear Thy justice will take hold
On me, and you, and mine, and yours, for this!
Come, Hastings, help me to my closet. Ah, poor
   Clarence!

Exit KING EDWARD, *assisted by* HASTINGS.
QUEEN ELIZABETH, RIVERS, GREY, DORSET, *and others follow.*

RICHARD   This is the fruits of rashness. Marked you not   **135**
How that the guilty kindred of the Queen
Looked pale when they did hear of Clarence' death?
O, they did urge it still unto the King!
God will revenge it. Come, lords, will you go
To comfort Edward with our company?   **140**

BUCKINGHAM   We wait upon your Grace.

Exeunt.

In this scene ...

- Richard's mother, the Duchess of York, weeps in front of Clarence's children. Richard has suggested that their father's death is Queen Elizabeth's fault.
- Queen Elizabeth brings the news that King Edward has died.
- Rivers suggests that the young Prince Edward must be crowned King as soon as possible.
- Richard and Buckingham agree, but secretly plan to separate the Queen's family from the Prince.

The Duchess of York mourns for her son, Clarence. She tries to hide his death from her grandchildren, but they see through her and say that their uncle Richard has told them he will protect them.

1 **grandam**: grandmother

8 **cousins**: grandchildren ('cousins' was a general term for relatives)
10 **loath**: very unwilling
11 **lost sorrow to wail**: pointless to cry for

14 **importune**: beg

18 **Incapable ... innocents**: Helpless and unknowing children, unable to understand the depth of what has happened
20 **Gloucester**: i.e. Richard
22 **impeachments**: serious accusations

25 **Bade me**: told me to

Think about

- So far we have seen a lot of corruption and conspiracy in the court. What is the effect of placing two innocent children in this scene?

London: the palace.

Enter the old DUCHESS *of York (mother of King Edward, Richard* **and Clarence), with Clarence's young** SON *and* DAUGHTER.

SON	Good grandam, tell us, is our father dead?
DUCHESS	No, boy.
DAUGHTER	Why do you weep so oft, and beat your breast,
	And cry 'O Clarence, my unhappy son!'?
SON	Why do you look on us, and shake your head,
	And call us orphans, wretches, castaways,
	If that our noble father were alive?
DUCHESS	My pretty cousins, you mistake me both.
	I do lament the sickness of the King,
	As loath to lose *him*, not your father's death.
	It were lost sorrow to wail one that's lost.
SON	Then you conclude, my grandam, he *is* dead.
	The King mine uncle is to blame for it.
	God will revenge it – whom I will importune
	With earnest prayers, all to that effect.
DAUGHTER	And so will I.
DUCHESS	Peace, children, peace! The King doth love you well.
	Incapable and shallow innocents –
	You cannot guess who caused your father's death.
SON	Grandam, we can. For my good uncle Gloucester
	Told me the King, provoked to it by the Queen,
	Devised impeachments to imprison him.
	And when my uncle told me so, he wept,
	And pitied me, and kindly kissed my cheek –
	Bade me rely on him as on my father,
	And he would love me dearly as a child.

5

10

15

20

25

Queen Elizabeth enters, grieving and bringing the news of the death of King Edward. The Duchess says that she has even more reason to mourn.

27 gentle shape: good appearance
28 vizor: mask
    vice: wickedness
29 ay, and therein: yes, and so he is
30 dugs: breasts
31 dissemble: pretend

35 chide: rebuke / scold

37 to myself … enemy: i.e. kill myself

38 rude impatience: wild lack of control

42 want: lack
43 brief: quick

47 interest: right to share
48 title: rights as a mother

50 his images: his sons
51 semblance: appearance
52 malignant: hateful
53 false glass: mirror which shows an untrue reflection. She means Richard, the third son.

Think about

- At the beginning of Act 2 Scene 1 Edward talked of dying and going to heaven, but how does Elizabeth describe the afterlife in line 46? How does this image link with other imagery of darkness in the play?

---

60 moiety … moan: half of my grief
61 overgo: be greater than / outdo

DUCHESS	Ah, that deceit should steal such gentle shape,
	And with a virtuous vizor hide deep vice!
	He is my son – ay, and therein my shame!
	Yet from my dugs he drew not this deceit.	30

SON   Think you my uncle did dissemble, grandam?

DUCHESS Ay, boy.

SON   I cannot think it. Hark! What noise is this?

Enter QUEEN ELIZABETH *(rushing in grief-stricken, her hair hanging loose).* RIVERS *and* DORSET *come after her.*

ELIZABETH Ah, who shall hinder me to wail and weep,
     To chide my fortune, and torment myself? 35
     I'll join with black despair against my soul
     And to myself become an enemy!

DUCHESS What means this scene of rude impatience?

ELIZABETH To make an act of tragic violence.
     Edward, my lord, thy son, our King, is dead! 40
     Why grow the branches when the root is gone?
     Why wither not the leaves that want their sap?
     If you will live, lament – if die, be brief,
     That our swift-wingèd souls may catch the King's,
     Or like obedient subjects follow him 45
     To his new kingdom of ne'er-changing night!

DUCHESS Ah, so much interest have I in thy sorrow
     As I had title in thy noble husband!
     I have bewept a worthy husband's death,
     And lived with looking on his images. 50
     But now two mirrors of his princely semblance
     Are cracked in pieces by malignant death –
     And I for comfort have but one false glass,
     That grieves me when I see my shame in him!
     Thou art a widow, yet thou art a mother 55
     And hast the comfort of thy children left –
     But death hath snatched my husband from mine arms
     And plucked two crutches from my feeble hands –
     Clarence and Edward. O, what cause have I –
     Thine being but a moiety of my moan – 60
     To overgo thy woes and drown thy cries?

The Duchess, Queen Elizabeth and Clarence's children join together in their grief. Dorset tries to comfort his mother, Queen Elizabeth.

64 **unmoaned**: unmourned
65 **widow-dolour**: widow's sadness

67 **not ... complaints**: i.e. able to weep as much as I need to
68 **reduce**: bring
69 **governed ... moon**: controlled by the moon, like ocean tides

74 **stay**: support

77 **dear**: 1 costly; 2 beloved

81 **parcelled**: divided into parts between them

---**Think about**---

• The language of mourning here is very formally patterned. Does the formality make the emotion seem more or less sincere to you? How might the actors use the patterns of language to minimise or magnify the scene's emotional impact?

86 **threefold distressed**: i.e. with grief for her husband and two sons
88 **pamper it**: give it full support

92 **dull**: lacking energy
    a debt: i.e. the life of King Edward IV
93 **bounteous**: generous
94 **opposite with heaven**: hostile towards heaven
95 **For it requires**: because heaven demands payment of

SON	Ah, aunt, you wept not for our father's death!
	How can we aid you with our kindred tears?
DAUGHTER	Our fatherless distress was left unmoaned –
	Your widow-dolour likewise be unwept!	65
ELIZABETH	Give me no help in lamentation:
	I am not barren to bring forth complaints.
	All springs reduce their currents to mine eyes –
	That I, being governed by the watery moon,
	May send forth plenteous tears to drown the world!	70
	Ah, for my husband, for my dear Lord Edward!
CHILDREN	Ah, for our father, for our dear Lord Clarence!
DUCHESS	Alas for both, both mine, Edward and Clarence!
ELIZABETH	What stay had I but Edward? And he's gone.
CHILDREN	What stay had we but Clarence? And he's gone.	75
DUCHESS	What stays had I but they? And they are gone.
ELIZABETH	Was never widow had so dear a loss.
CHILDREN	Were never orphans had so dear a loss.
DUCHESS	Was never mother had so dear a loss.
	Alas, I am the mother of these griefs!	80
	Their woes are parcelled, mine is general.
	She for an Edward weeps, and so do I:
	I for a Clarence weep, so doth not she.
	These babes for Clarence weep, and so do I:
	I for an Edward weep, so do not they.	85
	Alas, you three on me, threefold distressed,
	Pour all your tears! I am your sorrow's nurse,
	And I will pamper it with lamentation!
DORSET	(*To* QUEEN ELIZABETH) Comfort, dear mother. God is
	much displeased
	That you take with unthankfulness His doing.	90
	In common worldly things 'tis called ungrateful
	With dull unwillingness to repay a debt
	Which with a bounteous hand was kindly lent –
	Much more to be thus opposite with heaven,
	For it requires the royal debt it lent you.	95

105

Rivers encourages Elizabeth to think of her son, who is to be the new King, to help her get over her grief. Richard and the other lords enter. They join (and Richard pretends to join) in the grieving. They too focus on Prince Edward and his coronation.

97 **straight**: at once

99 **dead Edward**: i.e. King Edward IV
100 **living Edward**: i.e. Prince Edward

101 **Sister**: i.e. Sister-in-law
102 **shining star**: i.e. King Edward IV
103 **But none ... them**: crying will not make anything better
104 **cry you mercy**: beg your pardon

110 **butt-end**: final part

112 **cloudy**: gloomy
113 **mutual ... moan**: shared weight of grief
115 **spent**: used

117 **rancour ... hearts**: hostility of your proud hearts
118 **splinted**: mended (like a broken bone)
120 **Me seemeth good**: I think it's a good idea
    little train: small group of attendants
121 **Forthwith**: immediately
    Ludlow: Ludlow Castle, on the border with Wales
124–5 **Marry ... break out**: Buckingham says that because peace has only recently been re-established, a large group of attendants might cause a disturbance.
127 **green**: 1 weak; 2 fresh and new
128 **bears ... rein**: is in charge of himself
130 **harm apparent**: actual damage

---Think about ---

• In an extended metaphor, Buckingham develops images of harvest and the natural world. How does the language he uses here (lines 115 to 116, and 127 to 129) compare with similar images in Act 1 Scene 2, line 248 and Act 1 Scene 4, line 230?

• Harvests usually refer to fertility and plenty, but is another pattern developing here?

RIVERS	Madam, bethink you, like a careful mother,
	Of the young Prince your son. Send straight for him.
	Let him be crowned. In him your comfort lives.
	Drown desperate sorrow in dead Edward's grave,
	And plant your joys in living Edward's throne.	100

Enter RICHARD, *with* BUCKINGHAM, DERBY, HASTINGS, *and* RATCLIFFE.

RICHARD	Sister, have comfort. All of us have cause
	To wail the dimming of our shining star;
	But none can help our harms by wailing them.
	Madam, my mother, I do cry you mercy –
	I did not see your Grace. Humbly on my knee	105
	I crave your blessing.

| DUCHESS | God bless thee, and put meekness in thy breast: |
| | Love, charity, obedience, and true duty! |

RICHARD	Amen! (*Aside*) And make me die a good old man!
	That is the butt-end of a mother's blessing:	110
	I marvel that her Grace did leave it out.

BUCKINGHAM	You cloudy princes and heart-sorrowing peers,
	That bear this heavy mutual load of moan,
	Now cheer each other in each other's love.
	Though we have spent our harvest of this king,	115
	We are to reap the harvest of his son.
	The broken rancour of your high-swoll'n hearts,
	But lately splinted, knit, and join'd together,
	Must gently be preserved, cherished, and kept.
	Me seemeth good that, with some little train,	120
	Forthwith from Ludlow the young Prince be fetched
	Hither to London, to be crowned our King.

| RIVERS | Why with some little train, my Lord of Buckingham? |

BUCKINGHAM	Marry, my lord, lest by a multitude
	The new-healed wound of malice should break out –	125
	Which would be so much the more dangerous
	By how much the estate is green and yet ungoverned.
	Where every horse bears his commanding rein
	And may direct his course as please himself,
	As well the fear of harm as harm apparent,	130
	In my opinion, ought to be prevented.

Rivers and Hastings are persuaded that the young King should be brought to London without ceremony. Left alone, Buckingham and Richard agree their plans to separate the Queen's family from the new King.

133   **compact**: agreement

135   **green**: new
136   **apparent ... breach**: obvious possibility of being broken
137   **haply**: perhaps
        urged: incited
139   **meet**: right

141   **determine**: decide
142   **straight shall post**: immediately ride
143   **Madam**: i.e. Duchess of York
        my sister: i.e. Queen Elizabeth
144   **censures**: opinions

148   **by ... occasion**: on the way I'll find an opportunity
149   **index**: introduction

151   **my counsel's consistory**: the meeting place of my advisors
152   **oracle**: source of the best advice
153   **as ... direction**: like a child, I will follow your guidance

---

Think about

• Why do Rivers and Hastings agree so easily to Buckingham's proposal?

• How would you describe Richard's mood at the end of this scene?

RICHARD	I hope the King made peace with all of us;
	And the compact is firm and true in me.
RIVERS	And so in me – and so, I think, in all.
	Yet, since it is but green, it should be put 135
	To no apparent likelihood of breach,
	Which haply by much company might be urged.
	Therefore I say with noble Buckingham
	That it is meet so few should fetch the Prince.
HASTINGS	And so say I. 140
RICHARD	Then be it so. And go we to determine
	Who they shall be that straight shall post to Ludlow.
	Madam, and you, my sister, will you go
	To give your censures in this business?
DUCHESS AND	
ELIZABETH	With all our hearts. 145

Exit QUEEN ELIZABETH, *followed by all*
except RICHARD *and* BUCKINGHAM.

BUCKINGHAM	My lord, whoever journeys to the Prince,
	For God's sake, let not us two stay at home –
	For by the way I'll sort occasion,
	As index to the story we late talked of,
	To part the Queen's proud kindred from the Prince. 150
RICHARD	My other self, my counsel's consistory,
	My oracle, my prophet, my dear cousin –
	I, as a child, will go by thy direction.
	Toward Ludlow then, for we'll not stay behind.

Exeunt.

In this scene ...

- Ordinary citizens meet in the street and discuss King Edward's death.
- Because the Prince is young and unable to rule, some of them are frightened that fighting for power will ruin the country.

A group of citizens are talking about Edward's death and discussing the problem of having a child King, using the example of King Henry the Sixth, who was crowned when he was nine months old.

1   **morrow**: morning
    Whither away: Where are you going
2   **promise**: assure
3   **abroad**: that is going around

4   **Ill**: Bad
    by'r lady: by Our Lady (by the Virgin Mary)
    seldom ... better: better news does not come often
5   **giddy**: mad / unstable
6   **God speed**: short for 'God speed you'. Usually a farewell but used here as a greeting.
7   **Doth ... hold**: Is the news true
8   **God ... while**: God help these times
9   **troublous**: disturbed
10 **his son**: King Edward IV's son, Edward Prince of Wales

13 **in his nonage**: before he comes of age
    council: the King's council of noblemen

18 **wot**: knows

20 **politic grave**: wise and serious

Think about

- Throughout King Henry the Sixth's reign there was bloody civil war, despite his wise uncles. Is the third citizen right to be pessimistic about the future, considering who is to be official Protector to the Princes?

London: a street.

Enter two CITIZENS, *meeting.*

CITIZEN 1	Good morrow, neighbour. Whither away so fast?
CITIZEN 2	I promise you, I scarcely know myself. Hear you the news abroad?
CITIZEN 1	Yes, that the King is dead.
CITIZEN 2	Ill news, by'r lady: seldom comes the better. I fear, I fear 'twill prove a giddy world!

5

Enter a third CITIZEN.

CITIZEN 3	Neighbours, God speed!
CITIZEN 1	Give you good morrow, sir.
CITIZEN 3	Doth the news hold of good King Edward's death?
CITIZEN 2	Ay, sir, it is too true. God help the while!
CITIZEN 3	Then, masters, look to see a troublous world.
CITIZEN 1	No, no. By God's good grace, his son shall reign.

10

CITIZEN 3	Woe to that land that's governed by a child!
CITIZEN 2	In him there is a hope of government – Which, in his nonage, council under him, And, in his full and ripened years, himself, No doubt shall then, and till then, govern well.

15

CITIZEN 1	So stood the state when Henry the Sixth Was crowned in Paris but at nine months old.
CITIZEN 3	Stood the state so? No, no, good friends, God wot – For then this land was famously enriched With politic grave counsel. Then the King Had virtuous uncles to protect his Grace.

20

CITIZEN 1	Why, so hath this, both by his father and mother.

One of the citizens says how
pessimistic he is about Richard,
and what an uncertain state he
feels the kingdom is in.

23–4 Better … at all: It would be better if all
his uncles were from his father's side or
if there were only uncles on his
mother's side (This would avoid rivalry.)

25 emulation: competition
nearest: have most influence over the
Prince

26 touch … near: seriously damage us

28 Queen's sons: i.e. Dorset and Grey
haught: haughty

30 solace: take comfort

35 dearth: shortage of food
36 sort: arranges

40 heavily: mournful

41 still: always
42 mistrust: sense and suspect
43 Ensuing: oncoming
proof: knowledge from experience

46 justices: law courts / judges

47 bear you company: come with you

Think about

• How does this scene differ
from the previous one?
Think about the language
and social status of the
characters.

• How does Citizen 3 use
images of the weather and
the seasons?

CITIZEN 3	Better it were they all came by his father,
	Or by his father there were none at all.
	For emulation who shall now be nearest **25**
℞.	Will touch us all too near, if God prevent not.
	O, full of danger is the Duke of Gloucester!
	And the Queen's sons and brothers haught and proud.
	And were they to be ruled, and not to rule,
	This sickly land might solace as before. **30**
CITIZEN 1	Come, come, we fear the worst! All will be well.
CITIZEN 3	When clouds are seen, wise men put on their cloaks;
	When great leaves fall, then winter is at hand.
	When the sun sets, who doth not look for night?
	Untimely storms make men expect a dearth. **35**
	All *may* be well. But, if God sort it so,
	'Tis more than we deserve or I expect.
CITIZEN 2	Truly, the hearts of men are full of fear.
	You cannot reason almost with a man
	That looks not heavily and full of dread. **40**
CITIZEN 3	Before the days of change, still is it so.
	By a divine instinct men's minds mistrust
	Ensuing danger – as by proof we see
	The water swell before a boisterous storm.
	But leave it all to God. Whither away? **45**
CITIZEN 2	Marry, we were sent for to the justices.
CITIZEN 3	And so was I. I'll bear you company.

Exeunt.

In this scene ...

- Queen Elizabeth and her youngest son, the Duke of York, accompanied by the old Duchess of York and the Archbishop of York, wait for the arrival of the Prince.
- They hear news that Queen Elizabeth's relatives have been imprisoned by Richard and Buckingham.
- Helped by the Archbishop of York, Queen Elizabeth takes the young Duke to a place of safety.

The Archbishop, the old Duchess of York, the young Duke of York, and Queen Elizabeth talk about how fast the princes are growing up.

1 **they**: i.e. the Prince of Wales and his attendants
Stony Stratford: a village in Buckinghamshire

9 **cousin**: grandchild ('cousins' was a general term for relatives)
10 **Grandam**: Grandmother

12 **quoth**: said

13 **grace**: good properties
apace: quickly
14 **methinks ... not**: I don't think I want to

16 **hold**: turn out to be true
17 **object the same**: put this argument

19 **leisurely**: slow

Think about

- Which characters do you think might be compared to weeds and which to flowers, according to Richard's proverb?

- Do the images of nature here have more than one meaning?

23 **been remembered**: remembered
24 **my uncle's Grace**: my uncle his Grace, i.e. Richard
a flout: an insult or tease
25 **touch**: strike at
26 **prithee**: ask you

London: the palace.

Enter the ARCHBISHOP *of York,* QUEEN ELIZABETH, *the young*

Duke of YORK *(her son), and the old* DUCHESS *of York.*

ARCHBISHOP	Last night, I hear, they lay at Stony Stratford,
	And at Northampton they do rest tonight.
	Tomorrow or next day they will be here.

DUCHESS   I long with all my heart to see the Prince.
I hope he is much grown since last I saw him.   5

ELIZABETH   But I hear no. They say my son of York
Has almost overta'en him in his growth.

YORK   Ay, mother. But I would not have it so.

DUCHESS   Why, my good cousin? It is good to grow.

YORK   Grandam, one night as we did sit at supper,   10
My uncle Rivers talked how I did grow
More than my brother. 'Ay,' quoth my uncle
    Gloucester –
'Small herbs have grace: great weeds do grow apace.'
And since, methinks, I would not grow so fast –
Because sweet flowers are slow and weeds make haste.   15

DUCHESS   Good faith, good faith, the saying did not hold
In him that did object the same to thee!
He was the wretched'st thing when he was young,
So long a-growing and so leisurely
That, if his rule were true, he should be gracious.   20

ARCHBISHOP   And so no doubt he is, my gracious madam.

DUCHESS   I hope he is. But yet let mothers doubt.

YORK   Now, by my troth, if I had been remembered,
I could have given my uncle's Grace a flout
To touch *his* growth nearer than he touched mine.   25

DUCHESS   How, my young York? I prithee let me hear it.

York is cheeky about his uncle, Richard. A messenger brings the news that Richard and Buckingham have imprisoned the Queen's relatives.

29 ere: before
30 biting jest: 1 a joke about teeth; 2 an effective (biting) joke

35 parlous: mischievous
Go to: Stop it / Take care
shrewd: sharp-tongued
37 Pitchers have ears: a saying: 'Little jugs have big ears (or handles).' The Queen is suggesting that her son hears more than he should.

42 Pomfret: Pontefract Castle in Yorkshire

44 committed them: sent them to prison

Think about

- Elizabeth and the young Duke are left without protection. How would you direct the scene to emphasise their helplessness?

- Look at Elizabeth's language both before the messenger arrives and after he gives the news. In what different ways does she show her anxiety?

---

47 The sum … disclosed: I've told you everything I can

51 tiger: i.e. Richard
hind: female deer, i.e. its helpless victim
52 jut: intrude / threaten
53 aweless: not awe-inspiring (because the throne is occupied by Prince Edward who is still a child)
55 map: diagram

YORK	Marry, they say my uncle grew so fast
	That he could gnaw a crust at two hours old.
	'Twas full two years ere I could get a tooth.
	Grandam, this would have been a biting jest! 30
DUCHESS	I prithee, pretty York, who told thee this?
YORK	Grandam, his nurse.
DUCHESS	His nurse! Why, she was dead ere thou wast born.
YORK	If 'twere not she, I cannot tell who told me.
ELIZABETH	A parlous boy! Go to, you are too shrewd! 35
ARCHBISHOP	Good madam, be not angry with the child.
ELIZABETH	Pitchers have ears.

Enter a MESSENGER.

ARCHBISHOP	Here comes a messenger. What news?
MESSENGER	Such news, my lord, as grieves me to report.
ELIZABETH	How doth the Prince?
MESSENGER	Well, madam, and in health. 40
DUCHESS	What is thy news?
MESSENGER	Lord Rivers and Lord Grey are sent to Pomfret,
	And with them Sir Thomas Vaughan, prisoners.
DUCHESS	Who hath committed them?
MESSENGER	The mighty Dukes, Gloucester and Buckingham. 45
ARCHBISHOP	For what offence?
MESSENGER	The sum of all I can, I have disclosed.
	Why or for what the nobles were committed
	Is all unknown to me, my gracious lord.
ELIZABETH	Ay me, I see the ruin of my house! 50
	The tiger now hath seized the gentle hind!
	Insulting tyranny begins to jut
	Upon the innocent and aweless throne.
	Welcome, destruction, blood, and massacre!
	I see, as in a map, the end of all. 55

The Duchess cries out in rage and sadness. Elizabeth decides to seek safety for herself and her son. The Duchess and Archbishop decide to go with them.

56 **wrangling**: bickering / fighting

61 **being seated**: having gained the throne
broils: quarrels (The conflicts mentioned in this speech are all part of the civil war which ended before the action of the play begins.)

62 **Clean over-blown**: completely finished / blown right away

64 **preposterous**: ridiculous and absurd

65 **spleen**: spite

67 **sanctuary**: The Church traditionally offered a place of safety to people in danger.

71 **resign**: hand over

72 **seal**: the Great Seal of England (entrusted to him by King Edward IV)

72–3 **so betide … of yours**: let my fortune depend on how well I look after you and your family

Think about

• Elizabeth announces her plan with little hesitation. Do you think this is a spur-of-the-moment decision or has she been planning this escape for a while?

DUCHESS	Accursèd and unquiet wrangling days –
	How many of you have mine eyes beheld!
	My husband lost his life to get the crown –
	And often up and down my sons were tossed,
	For me to joy and weep their gain and loss. 60
	And being seated, and domestic broils
	Clean over-blown, themselves the conquerors
	Make war upon themselves – brother to brother,
	Blood to blood, self against self! O, preposterous
	And frantic outrage, end thy damnèd spleen – 65
	Or let me die, to look on death no more!
ELIZABETH	Come, come, my boy. We will to sanctuary.
	Madam, farewell.
DUCHESS	Stay, I will go with you.
ELIZABETH	You have no cause.
ARCHBISHOP	*(To the* QUEEN*)* My gracious lady, go.
	And thither bear your treasure and your goods. 70
	For my part, I'll resign unto your Grace
	The seal I keep – and so betide to me
	As well I tender you and all of yours!
	Go, I'll conduct you to the sanctuary.

Exeunt.

In this scene ...

- Richard welcomes Prince Edward to London.
- The young Duke of York is brought to join his brother after the Cardinal has persuaded his mother, Queen Elizabeth, to let him leave sanctuary.
- Despite their fear of the place, Richard sends the Princes to stay in the Tower.
- Buckingham and Richard discuss what to do with Hastings and Derby if they are not supportive of Richard's plans.

Buckingham and Richard welcome the Prince to London. The Prince wonders why there are not more people to greet him, but Richard tells him that his other uncles (Queen Elizabeth's relatives) were not to be trusted.

1 **chamber**: royal capital

2 **sovereign**: king

4 **crosses**: troubles
5 **wearisome**: tiresome
6 **want**: 1 lack; 2 need

7 **untainted**: pure

10 **outward show**: appearance
11 **jumpeth**: agrees

16 **they**: i.e. the Prince's uncle, Rivers, and Grey

Think about

- The Prince is isolated and vulnerable. If you were the director, how would you emphasise this fact in this scene?

21 **ere**: before
22 **Fie**: an exclamation of disgust or reproach
slug: slowcoach

London: a street.

Enter the young PRINCE EDWARD *(Prince of Wales), with* RICHARD,
BUCKINGHAM, CATESBY, CARDINAL BOURCHIER (ARCHBISHOP OF
CANTERBURY), *and others.*

BUCKINGHAM	Welcome, sweet Prince, to London, to your chamber.
RICHARD	Welcome, dear cousin, my thoughts' sovereign.
	The weary way hath made you melancholy?
PRINCE	No, uncle. But our crosses on the way
	Have made it tedious, wearisome, and heavy. 5
	I want more uncles here to welcome me.
RICHARD	Sweet Prince, the untainted virtue of your years
	Hath not yet dived into the world's deceit.
	Nor more can you distinguish of a man
	Than of his outward show – which, God He knows, 10
	Seldom or never jumpeth with the heart.
	Those uncles which you want were dangerous.
	Your Grace attended to their sugared words,
	But looked not on the poison of their hearts.
	God keep you from them and from such false friends! 15
PRINCE	God keep me from false friends! But they were none.
RICHARD	My lord, the Mayor of London comes to greet you.

Enter the LORD MAYOR *of London, with attendants.*

MAYOR	God bless your Grace with health and happy days!
PRINCE	I thank you, good my lord, and thank you all.
	I thought my mother and my brother York 20
	Would long ere this have met us on the way.
	Fie, what a slug is Hastings, that he comes not
	To tell us whether they will come or no!

Enter HASTINGS.

BUCKINGHAM	And, in good time, here comes the sweating lord.

Hastings says that Queen Elizabeth and the young Duke of York have gone into church sanctuary for safety. Buckingham asks the Cardinal to persuade the Queen to let the Duke of York come to his brother, and asks Hastings to remove the Duke by force if necessary. They are persuaded to do as Buckingham asks.

26 **On what occasion**: For what reason

28 **tender**: i.e. young
29 **fain**: gladly
30 **perforce withheld**: forcibly prevented

31 **indirect and peevish**: devious and stubborn

34 **presently**: immediately

36 **perforce**: by force

37 **oratory**: speech-making

39 **Anon**: soon
    obdurate: resistant
40 **entreaties**: requests
41 **infringe**: break

44 **senseless**: unreasonably
45 **ceremonious**: precisely formal
46 **Weigh ... age**: Compare it with the disorderly state of the world today
48 **thereof**: i.e. of sanctuary
49 **dealings**: behaviour
50 **wit**: intelligence

53 **Then ... there**: Taking him from a place that is, for him, no sanctuary
54 **charter**: special right

Think about

- What reasons does Buckingham give for removing the Duke of York from sanctuary? Do you think his arguments are convincing?

PRINCE	Welcome, my lord. What, will our mother come? **25**
HASTINGS	On what occasion, God He knows, not I,
	The Queen your mother and your brother York
	Have taken sanctuary. The tender Prince
	Would fain have come with me to meet your Grace,
	But by his mother was perforce withheld. **30**
BUCKINGHAM	Fie, what an indirect and peevish course
	Is this of hers! Lord Cardinal, will your Grace
	Persuade the Queen to send the Duke of York
	Unto his princely brother presently?
	If she deny, Lord Hastings, go with him **35**
	And from her jealous arms pluck him perforce.
CARDINAL	My Lord of Buckingham, if my weak oratory
	Can from his mother win the Duke of York,
	Anon expect him here. But, if she be obdurate
	To mild entreaties, God in heaven forbid **40**
	We should infringe the holy privilege
	Of blessèd sanctuary! Not for all this land
	Would I be guilty of so deep a sin.
BUCKINGHAM	You are too senseless-obstinate, my lord,
	Too ceremonious and traditional. **45**
	Weigh it but with the grossness of this age,
	You break not sanctuary in seizing him.
	The benefit thereof is always granted
	To those whose dealings have deserved the place
	And those who have the wit to claim the place. **50**
	This Prince hath neither claimed it nor deserved it –
	And therefore, in mine opinion, cannot have it.
	Then, taking him from thence that is not there,
	You break no privilege nor charter there.
	Oft have I heard of sanctuary men; **55**
	But sanctuary children never till now!
CARDINAL	My lord, you shall o'errule my mind for once.
	Come on, Lord Hastings, will you go with me?
HASTINGS	I go, my lord.
PRINCE	Good lords, make all the speedy haste you may. **60**

Exit the CARDINAL, *with* HASTINGS.

Richard advises the Prince to stay in the Tower of London for a few days. The Prince does not like the Tower and asks questions about it. In his asides, Richard is secretly threatening.

62 **sojourn**: stay

64 **counsel**: advise
65 **repose you**: stay / rest
66 **fit**: suitable

71 **re-edified**: rebuilt
72 **upon … reported**: written down or spoken of

75 **registered**: written down

77 **retailed**: repeated
    posterity: people coming afterwards
78 **general … day**: the final day of judgement, when Christians believe the world will end
79 **So wise … long**: those who are so wise when they are young rarely live very long
81 **characters**: written records
82 **formal … Iniquity**: a character representing sin or evil in the old morality plays
83 **moralize … word**: i.e. get two meanings out of one word
85–6 **With what … live**: i.e. his brave acts improved his mind; then he used his mind to write down his actions and so made himself famous
92 **our … France**: the long-standing English claim to rule over parts of France

---
Think about

- The audience hears everything that Richard is saying. To what extent should the Prince overhear Richard's asides? How would you stage this?

Say, uncle Gloucester, if our brother come,
Where shall we sojourn till our coronation?

RICHARD   Where it seems best unto your royal self.
               If I may counsel you, some day or two
               Your Highness shall repose you at the Tower –   65
               Then where you please and shall be thought most fit
               For your best health and recreation.

PRINCE   I do not like the Tower, of any place.
               Did Julius Caesar build that place, my lord?

BUCKINGHAM   He did, my gracious lord, begin that place,   70
               Which, since, succeeding ages have re-edified.

PRINCE   Is it upon record, or else reported
               Successively from age to age, he built it?

BUCKINGHAM   Upon record, my gracious lord.

PRINCE   But say, my lord, it were not registered,   75
               Methinks the truth should live from age to age,
               As 'twere retailed to all posterity,
               Even to the general all-ending day.

RICHARD   (Aside) So wise so young, they say, do never live long.

PRINCE   What say you, uncle?   80

RICHARD   I say, without characters, fame lives long.
               (Aside) Thus, like the formal vice, Iniquity,
               I moralize two meanings in one word.

PRINCE   That Julius Caesar was a famous man.
               With what his valour did enrich his wit,   85
               His wit set down to make his valour live.
               Death makes no conquest of this conqueror –
               For now he lives in fame, though not in life.
               I'll tell you what, my cousin Buckingham –

BUCKINGHAM   What, my gracious lord?   90

PRINCE   And if I live until I be a man,
               I'll win our ancient right in France again –
               Or die a soldier, as I lived a king.

125

In an aside, Richard again threatens the Prince. Hastings and the Cardinal bring in the young Duke of York, who talks cheekily with Richard.

94 **lightly**: often
    forward: early

96 **how ... brother**: how are you

97 **dread**: feared

98 **Ay**: Yes

99 **late**: recently
    he: i.e. their father, King Edward IV

103 **idle**: useless

107 **beholding**: indebted / under obligation

108 **sovereign**: King

109 **kinsman**: relative

110 **I pray you**: Please

114 **but a toy**: only a trivial thing

116 **to it**: to go with it

117 **light**: 1 light in weight; 2 of little value

119 **weightier**: 1 heavier; 2 more important

---Think about

• The young Prince is very formal and adult in his language. Look at the words of the Prince on this and previous pages. Is he ready to be King?

• What sort of King do you think he would make?

RICHARD   (*Aside*) Short summers lightly have a forward spring.

Re-enter HASTINGS *and the* CARDINAL, *with the young Duke of*
   YORK.

BUCKINGHAM   Now, in good time, here comes the Duke of York.   **95**

PRINCE   Richard of York, how fares our loving brother?

YORK   Well, my dread lord – so must I call you now.

PRINCE   Ay, brother – to our grief, as it is yours.
                Too late he died that might have kept that title,
                Which by his death hath lost much majesty.   **100**

RICHARD   How fares our cousin, noble lord of York?

YORK   I thank you, gentle uncle. O, my lord,
                You said that idle weeds are fast in growth.
                The Prince my brother hath outgrown me far.

RICHARD   He hath, my lord.

YORK   And therefore is he idle?   **105**

RICHARD   O, my fair cousin, I must not say so!

YORK   Then he is more beholding to you than I.

RICHARD   He may command me as my sovereign –
                But you have power in me as in a kinsman.

YORK   I pray you, uncle, give me this dagger.   **110**

RICHARD   My dagger, little cousin? With all my heart!

PRINCE   A beggar, brother?

YORK   Of my kind uncle, that I know will give –
                And being but a toy, which is no grief to give.

RICHARD   A greater gift than that I'll give my cousin.   **115**

YORK   A greater gift! O, that's the sword to it!

RICHARD   Ay, gentle cousin, were it light enough.

YORK   O, then, I see you will part but with light gifts.
                In weightier things you'll say a beggar nay.

RICHARD   It is too heavy for your Grace to wear.   **120**

York continues to joke with Richard, laughing at his expense. Despite feeling anxious about it, the Prince and York go to the Tower.

121 **I weigh … heavier**: I would think it unimportant even if it weighed more

126 **still be cross**: always be annoying / contradictory
127 **bear**: 1 put up with; 2 carry

129 **mocks**: laughs at

132 **sharp-provided**: quick
133 **mitigate**: lessen

135 **cunning**: clever

136 **pass**: come

138 **entreat**: ask

141 **needs … it**: insists

145 **grandam**: grandmother (i.e. the Duchess of York)

150 **them**: i.e. his dead relatives

Think about

- Look at lines 128 to 131. York is humiliating his hunch-backed uncle and in some productions, he jumps onto Richard's back at line 131. Monkeys sometimes rode on the backs of bears or clowns in fairground shows. How should Richard react in performance?

YORK   I weigh it lightly, were it heavier.

RICHARD   What, would you have my weapon, little lord?

YORK   I would, that I might thank you as you call me.

RICHARD   How?

YORK   Little!   125

PRINCE   My Lord of York will still be cross in talk.
            Uncle, your Grace knows how to bear with him.

YORK   You mean, to bear me, not to bear with me.
            Uncle, my brother mocks both you and me:
            Because that I am little, like an ape,   130
            He thinks that you should bear me on your shoulders!

BUCKINGHAM With what a sharp-provided wit he reasons!
            To mitigate the scorn he gives his uncle
            He prettily and aptly taunts himself.
            So cunning and so young is wonderful.   135

RICHARD   My lord, will't please you pass along?
            Myself and my good cousin Buckingham
            Will to your mother, to entreat of her
            To meet you at the Tower and welcome you.

YORK   (To PRINCE EDWARD) What? Will you go unto the Tower,
                 my lord?   140

PRINCE   My Lord Protector needs will have it so.

YORK   I shall not sleep in quiet at the Tower.

RICHARD   Why, what should you fear?

YORK   Marry, my uncle Clarence' angry ghost!
            My grandam told me he was murdered there.   145

PRINCE   I fear no uncles dead.

RICHARD   Nor none that live, I hope.

PRINCE   And if they live, I hope I need not fear.
            But come, my lord. With a heavy heart,
            Thinking on them, go I unto the Tower.   150

        A trumpet sounds.

Buckingham and Richard comment on York's rudeness. They discuss whether Hastings and Derby can be persuaded to support Richard. Catesby is sent to discover where Hastings' loyalties lie.

151 **prating**: chattering
152 **incensèd**: encouraged
     subtle: cunning
153 **opprobriously**: insultingly
154 **parlous**: dangerous
155 **capable**: intelligent and competent
156 **is ... mother's**: takes after his mother
158 **effect**: carry out
159 **conceal ... impart**: keep secret what we tell you
160 **urged ... the way**: i.e. given on the journey from Ludlow to London
162 **of our mind**: agree with our plans
163 **instalment**: placing
164 **seat royal**: throne

166 **aught**: anything

169 **no more but this**: do nothing more than this
170 **as it ... off**: as a distant possibility
170–1 **sound ... our purpose**: find out how Lord Hastings feels about our plan
173 **sit**: come to a meeting
174 **tractable**: easily persuaded / in agreement

179 **divided councils**: two different meetings
180 **highly**: in a position of importance
181 **Commend me**: Give my respects
182 **knot**: group
     adversaries: enemies
183 **let blood**: will be bled (i.e. killed)
185 **Mistress Shore**: Hastings' lover (previously the lover of King Edward IV)

Think about

• In line 155, Richard calls York 'capable'. Compare this with Act 2 Scene 2, line 18 where the Duchess calls Clarence's children 'incapable'. Are these terms used in the same way? Think about how children have been presented in the play so far. Contrast their behaviour with that of the adults around them.

Exit PRINCE EDWARD *with his brother* YORK.
All follow except RICHARD, BUCKINGHAM, *and* CATESBY.

BUCKINGHAM	Think you, my lord, this little prating York
	Was not incensèd by his subtle mother
	To taunt and scorn you thus opprobriously?

RICHARD	No doubt, no doubt. O, 'tis a parlous boy! –	
	Bold, quick, ingenious, forward, capable.	155
	He is all the mother's, from the top to toe!	

BUCKINGHAM	Well, let them rest. Come hither, Catesby.	
	Thou art sworn as deeply to effect what we intend	
	As closely to conceal what we impart.	
	Thou know'st our reasons urged upon the way.	160
	What think'st thou? Is it not an easy matter	
	To make William Lord Hastings of our mind,	
	For the instalment of this noble Duke	
	In the seat royal of this famous isle?	

CATESBY	He for his father's sake so loves the Prince	165
	That he will not be won to aught against him.	

BUCKINGHAM	What think'st thou then of Stanley? Will not he?

CATESBY	He will do all in all as Hastings doth.

BUCKINGHAM	Well then, no more but this: go, gentle Catesby,	
	And, as it were far off, sound thou Lord Hastings	170
	How he doth stand affected to our purpose.	
	And summon him tomorrow to the Tower,	
	To sit about the coronation.	
	If thou dost find him tractable to us,	
	Encourage him, and tell him all our reasons.	175
	If he be leaden, icy, cold, unwilling,	
	Be thou so too – and so break off the talk,	
	And give us notice of his inclination.	
	For we tomorrow hold divided councils,	
	Wherein thyself shalt highly be employed.	180

RICHARD	Commend me to Lord William. Tell him, Catesby,	
	His ancient knot of dangerous adversaries	
	Tomorrow are let blood at Pomfret Castle.	
	And bid my lord, for joy of this good news,	
	Give Mistress Shore one gentle kiss the more.	185

It is arranged that Buckingham, Catesby and Richard will meet later. Richard says that Hastings may well be beheaded if he will not join them and promises to reward Buckingham for his help.

186   **effect soundly**: carry out effectively

187   **heed**: careful attention

188   **ere**: before

192   **yield to**: join in with
      complots: conspiracies

195   **movables**: personal possessions (rather than land and buildings)

196   **Whereof**: of which

198   **look**: expect

199   **sup betimes**: eat early

200   **digest**: arrange
      some form: an orderly way

Think about

- How close are Buckingham and Richard at this stage in the play? Can you see any potential problems in the future?

BUCKINGHAM	Good Catesby, go effect this business soundly.
CATESBY	My good lords both, with all the heed I can.
RICHARD	Shall we hear from you, Catesby, ere we sleep?
CATESBY	You shall, my lord.
RICHARD	At Crosby House: there shall you find us both.

190

Exit CATESBY.

BUCKINGHAM	Now, my lord, what shall we do if we perceive
	Lord Hastings will not yield to our complots?
RICHARD	Chop off his head, man! *Something* we will do!
	And look – when I am King – claim thou of me
	The earldom of Hereford, and all the movables
	Whereof the King my brother was possessed.

195

BUCKINGHAM	I'll claim that promise at your Grace's hand.
RICHARD	And look to have it yielded with all kindness.
	Come, let us sup betimes, that afterwards
	We may digest our complots in some form.

200

Exeunt.

In this scene ...

- Derby has dreamed that Richard means to harm him and Hastings.
- Hastings dismisses Derby's fears.
- Catesby discovers that Hastings will not support Richard's attempt to become King.
- Hastings goes cheerfully to the Tower, but Catesby and Buckingham hint to the audience that he will not be allowed to leave it.

A message from Derby wakes Hastings in the early hours of the morning. Derby has dreamed that Richard means to harm them, but Hastings dismisses these fears.

Think about

- Derby's dream is one of many in the play which prove accurate in their predictions. Do you think that some sort of supernatural power is implied, or that the dreams reveal otherwise hidden anxieties and knowledge?

4   **is't o'clock**: is the time

6   **tedious**: long

8   **commends him**: sends his greetings

10   **certifies**: assures / swears

11   **boar**: Richard's emblem
     razèd ... helm: torn off his helmet

12   **two councils kept**: two simultaneous and separate meetings of the King's advisers

13   **determined**: decided

14   **rue at**: regret

16   **presently**: at once

17   **post**: ride quickly

18   **shun**: avoid
     divines: suspects

20   **Bid**: Tell

21   **His honour**: i.e. He

23   **toucheth**: affects

24   **intelligence**: secret information

25   **shallow ... instance**: groundless / without motive

26   **simple**: foolish

27   **mockery**: unreality
     unquiet slumbers: disturbed sleep

28   **fly**: run away from

29   **Were to incense**: would be to irritate and cause

London: in front of Lord HASTINGS' *house.*

Enter a MESSENGER *(and knocks at the door).*

MESSENGER   My lord! My lord!

HASTINGS   *(Calling from inside)* Who knocks?

MESSENGER   One from the Lord Stanley.

HASTINGS   *(Coming out of the door)* What is't o'clock?

MESSENGER   Upon the stroke of four.   5

HASTINGS   Cannot my Lord Stanley sleep these tedious nights?

MESSENGER   So it appears by that I have to say.
              First, he commends him to your noble self.

HASTINGS   What then?

MESSENGER   Then certifies your lordship that this night   10
              He dreamt the boar had razèd off his helm.
              Besides, he says there are two councils kept –
              And that may be determined at the one
              Which may make you and him to rue at th' other.
              Therefore he sends to know your lordship's pleasure –   15
              If you will presently take horse with him
              And with all speed post with him toward the north,
              To shun the danger that his soul divines.

HASTINGS   Go, fellow, go. Return unto thy lord.
              Bid him not fear the separated council.   20
              His honour and myself are at the one,
              And at the other is my good friend Catesby –
              Where nothing can proceed that toucheth us
              Whereof I shall not have intelligence.
              Tell him his fears are shallow, without instance.   25
              And for his dreams, I wonder he's so simple
              To trust the mockery of unquiet slumbers!
              To fly the boar before the boar pursues
              Were to incense the boar to follow us,
              And make pursuit where he did mean no chase.   30

Hastings sends the messenger to fetch Derby. As instructed by Richard, Catesby arrives to find out if Hastings will support Richard as King. Hastings will not, but is delighted to discover that the Queen's relatives are due to be executed.

33 use: treat
kindly: 1 gently; 2 as his kind (i.e. a wild boar) would

36 early stirring: up early
37 tott'ring state: unsteady country

38 reeling: whirling

40 garland of the realm: crown

43 this crown: Hastings' head
44 foul misplaced: disgracefully put in the wrong place

46–7 forward ... party: supporting his cause

48 thereupon: for that reason
50 kindred: relations (i.e. Rivers, Grey, and Vaughan)
52 still: always
adversaries: enemies
53 give ... side: support Richard
54 bar: exclude, i.e. from the royal succession
55 to the death: even at the risk of death

58–9 That ... tragedy: i.e. that I live to see the deaths of those who caused King Edward IV to hate me
60 ere: before
61 send some packing: i.e. get rid of some people

Think about

- Catesby seems very friendly towards Hastings here, but what is he doing?

136

Go, bid thy master rise and come to me;
And we will both together to the Tower –
Where, he shall see, the boar will use us kindly.

MESSENGER   I'll go, my lord, and tell him what you say.

Exit.

Enter CATESBY.

CATESBY   Many good morrows to my noble lord!   **35**

HASTINGS   Good morrow, Catesby. You are early stirring.
What news, what news, in this our tott'ring state?

CATESBY   It is a reeling world indeed, my lord –
And I believe will never stand upright
Till Richard wear the garland of the realm.   **40**

HASTINGS   How? Wear the garland! Dost thou mean the crown?

CATESBY   Ay, my good lord.

HASTINGS   I'll have this crown of mine cut from my shoulders
Before I'll see the crown so foul misplaced!
But canst thou guess that he doth aim at it?   **45**

CATESBY   Ay, on my life – and hopes to find you forward
Upon his party for the gain thereof.
And thereupon he sends you this good news:
That this same very day your enemies,
The kindred of the Queen, must die at Pomfret.   **50**

HASTINGS   Indeed, I am no mourner for *that* news,
Because they have been still my adversaries.
But that I'll give my voice on Richard's side
To bar my master's heirs in true descent,
God knows I will not do it – to the death!   **55**

CATESBY   God keep your lordship in that gracious mind!

HASTINGS   But I shall laugh at this a twelve month hence –
That they which brought me in my master's hate,
I live to look upon their tragedy.
Well, Catesby, ere a fortnight make me older,   **60**
I'll send some packing that yet think not on't.

Hastings reflects on the changing fortunes of Rivers, Vaughan and Grey, but cannot understand Catesby's double-edged comments which show the audience that Hastings' own life is in danger. Derby points out that though Hastings is cheerful, so were Rivers, Vaughan and Grey before their arrest.

62 **vile**: horrid

64 **falls it out**: it happens

66 **men else**: other men

69 **make … you**: value you highly
70 **account … bridge**: i.e. look forward to him being executed and his head placed on a spike on London Bridge (where the heads of traitors were displayed to warn others to be loyal)
72 **boar-spear**: a spear for killing a boar (i.e. Richard)
73 **unprovided**: unarmed
75 **jest on**: joke about it
    holy rood: cross on which Christ was crucified
76 **several**: separate

80 **but that**: unless
    state: position
81 **triumphant**: confident

82 **lords at Pomfret**: i.e. Rivers and Grey
83 **jocund**: cheerful

85 **o'ercast**: clouded over
86 **rancour**: bitterness
    misdoubt: suspect / mistrust
87 **needless**: unnecessary
88 **The day is spent**: Time is getting on

89 **have with you**: come along
    Wot: Know
91–2 **They … their hats**: i.e. Their honesty gives them a better right to live than some of those who have accused them
93 **away**: go

Think about

- What do you think of Hastings' behaviour? Is he brave, foolish, or a well-meaning victim?

CATESBY   'Tis a vile thing to die, my gracious lord,
            When men are unprepared and look not for it.

HASTINGS   O monstrous, monstrous! And so falls it out
            With Rivers, Vaughan, Grey. And so 'twill do   65
            With some men else that think themselves as safe
            As thou and I – who, as thou knowest, are dear
            To princely Richard and to Buckingham.

CATESBY   The Princes both make high account of you –
            (*Aside*) For they account his head upon the bridge!   70

HASTINGS   I know they do, and I have well deserved it!

            Enter DERBY *(Lord Stanley).*

            Come on, come on – where is your boar-spear, man?
            Fear you the boar, and go so unprovided?

DERBY   My lord, good morrow. Good morrow, Catesby,
            You may jest on, but, by the holy rood,   75
            I do not like these several councils, I.

HASTINGS   My lord, I hold my life as dear as yours,
            And never in my days, I do protest,
            Was it so precious to me as 'tis now.
            Think you, but that I know our state secure,   80
            I would be so triumphant as I am?

DERBY   The lords at Pomfret, when they rode from London,
            Were jocund, and supposed their states were sure –
            And they indeed had no cause to mistrust.
            But yet you see how soon the day o'ercast.   85
            This sudden stab of rancour I misdoubt.
            Pray God, I say, I prove a needless coward!
            What, shall we toward the Tower? The day is spent.

HASTINGS   Come, come, have with you. Wot you what, my lord?
            Today the lords you talked of are beheaded.   90

DERBY   They, for their truth, might better wear their heads
            Than some that have accused them wear their hats!
            But come, my lord, let's away.

Hastings talks with a royal messenger about his good fortune and the suffering of his enemies. Buckingham finds Hastings talking with a priest and jokes that it is Rivers, Vaughan and Grey who need the priest's spiritual attention.

94 **on before**: ahead

95 **sirrah**: a term of address used to someone of lower status
96 **please**: is pleased

98 **when ... meet**: the last time we met here

103 **e'er**: ever

104 **hold it**: keep it that way

105 **Gramercy**: Many thanks
drink that for me: i.e. spend this money on drink

107 **Well met**: Good to see you

108 **Sir**: a respectful way to address a priest
109 **exercise**: religious service or sermon
110 **sabbath**: Sunday
content: pay

Think about

- Hastings is very cheerful, but is going to be killed soon. If you were the director, how could you make it clear that his good mood is out of place?

114 **shriving ... hand**: need to ask for confession and forgiveness

Enter a PURSUIVANT *(a royal messenger).*

HASTINGS   Go on before. I'll talk with this good fellow.

Exit DERBY, *with* CATESBY.

How now, sirrah! How goes the world with thee?   **95**

PURSUIVANT   The better that your lordship please to ask.

HASTINGS   I tell thee, man, 'tis better with me now
Than when thou met'st me last where now we meet.
Then was I going prisoner to the Tower,
By the suggestion of the Queen's allies.   **100**
But now, I tell thee – keep it to thyself –
This day those enemies are put to death,
And I in better state than e'er I was!

PURSUIVANT   God hold it, to your honour's good content!

HASTINGS   Gramercy, fellow! There, drink that for me.   **105**
(*Throwing him his purse*)

PURSUIVANT   I thank your honour.

Exit.

Enter a PRIEST.

PRIEST   Well met, my lord! I am glad to see your honour.

HASTINGS   I thank thee, good Sir John, with all my heart!
I am in your debt for your last exercise.
Come the next sabbath, and I will content you.   **110**
(*He whispers in his ear.*)

PRIEST   I'll wait upon your lordship.

Enter BUCKINGHAM.

BUCKINGHAM   What, talking with a priest, Lord Chamberlain!
Your friends at Pomfret, *they* do need the priest:
Your honour hath no shriving work in hand!

HASTINGS   Good faith, and when I met this holy man,   **115**
The men you talk of came into my mind.
What, go you toward the Tower?

Hastings goes with Buckingham to the Tower. Buckingham jokes that Hastings will be there longer than he thinks.

119 **thence**: from there

120 **stay**: wait for
dinner: the midday meal (as opposed to supper, the evening meal)

Think about

- Should the audience pity Hastings or share Buckingham's cynical amusement at Hastings' expense here? How might a director push the audience in one direction or another?

BUCKINGHAM   I do, my lord, but long I cannot stay there.
I shall return before your lordship thence.

HASTINGS   Nay, like enough, for I stay dinner there.   **120**

BUCKINGHAM   (*Aside*) And supper too, although thou knowest it not. –
Come, will you go?

HASTINGS   I'll wait upon your lordship.

Exeunt.

In this scene ...

- Rivers, Grey and Vaughan are on their way to be executed.
- They lament their fate and remember how Margaret cursed them.

4 **the Prince**: i.e. Edward Prince of Wales

5 **knot**: gang

6 **cry ... this**: regret this

7 **Dispatch**: Hurry up
The limit ... out: You have reached the end of your lives

9 **ominous**: menacing

12 **for more ... seat**: to increase the disgrace linked to this sad place

14 **Margaret**: widow of King Henry VI (see Act 1 Scene 3)

15 **exclaimed on**: cried out against

---Think about---

- Those who are about to die have been cursed by Margaret. How significant is it that she also cursed Richard and Hastings, and warned Buckingham about Richard?

23 **is expiate**: has come

Yorkshire: the castle of Pomfret (Pontefract).

Enter Sir Richard RATCLIFFE, *with guards, taking* RIVERS, GREY,

and Sir Thomas VAUGHAN *to be put to death.*

RIVERS	Sir Richard Ratcliffe, let me tell thee this:
	Today shalt thou behold a subject die
	For truth, for duty, and for loyalty.
GREY	God bless the Prince from all the pack of you!
	A knot you are of damnèd blood-suckers!

5

VAUGHAN	You live that shall cry woe for this hereafter!
RATCLIFFE	Dispatch! The limit of your lives is out.
RIVERS	O Pomfret, Pomfret! O thou bloody prison,
	Fatal and ominous to noble peers!
	Within the guilty closure of thy walls

10

	Richard the Second here was hacked to death –
	And, for more slander to thy dismal seat,
	We give to thee our guiltless blood to drink!
GREY	Now Margaret's curse is fall'n upon our heads,
	When she exclaimed on Hastings, you, and I,

15

	For standing by when Richard stabbed her son.
RIVERS	Then cursed she Richard, then cursed she Buckingham.
	Then cursed she Hastings. O, remember, God,
	To hear her prayer for them, as now for us!
	And for my sister, and her princely sons,

20

	Be satisfied, dear God, with our true blood,
	Which, as thou know'st, unjustly must be spilt.
RATCLIFFE	Make haste! The hour of death is expiate.
RIVERS	Come, Grey; come, Vaughan – let us here embrace.
	Farewell, until we meet again in heaven.

25

Exeunt.

In this scene ...

- The council of nobles meets to plan the coronation of the young Prince Edward.
- Richard has learned that Hastings will not support him.
- Richard says that Jane Shore and Queen Elizabeth have bewitched him. He accuses Hastings of protecting Jane Shore and orders that he must be beheaded as a traitor.
- Before being taken to execution, Hastings grieves for himself and predicts a terrible future for England.

Those meeting to decide the date of the Prince's coronation want to know Richard's opinion. Hastings says that he will speak for him, but then Richard himself enters.

Think about

- Do you think that Ely and Derby know that Hastings is under threat?

2 **determine of**: decide about
   the coronation: the crowning of Edward Prince of Wales as King Edward V

3 **royal day**: i.e. the day of coronation

5 **wants but nomination**: we only need to name the day

7 **Lord Protector**: i.e. Richard
   herein: about this

8 **inward**: familiar

11 **mine**: i.e. my heart

15 **purpose in**: plans for

16 **sounded him**: asked his opinion
    delivered: spoken about

19 **And in ... voice**: I'll speak for the Duke (i.e. Richard)

20 **take ... part**: willingly accept

24 **doth ... design**: has not delayed any business

25 **concluded**: finished

ACT 3   SCENE 4

London: a council-room in the Tower.

Enter BUCKINGHAM, DERBY, HASTINGS, *the Bishop of* ELY, *the*

Duke of NORFOLK, *Lord* LOVELL, RATCLIFFE, *and others. They sit*

at a table.

HASTINGS	Now, noble peers, the cause why we are met
	Is to determine of the coronation.
	In God's name speak – when is the royal day?
BUCKINGHAM	Is all things ready for the royal time?
DERBY	It is, and wants but nomination.
ELY	Tomorrow then I judge a happy day.
BUCKINGHAM	Who knows the Lord Protector's mind herein?
	Who is most inward with the noble Duke?
ELY	Your Grace, we think, should soonest know his mind.
BUCKINGHAM	We know each other's faces. For our hearts,
	He knows no more of mine than I of yours –
	Or I of his, my lord, than you of mine.
	Lord Hastings, you and he are near in love.
HASTINGS	I thank his Grace, I know he loves me well.
	But for his purpose in the coronation
	I have not sounded him – nor he delivered
	His gracious pleasure any way therein.
	But you, my honourable lords, may name the time –
	And in the Duke's behalf I'll give my voice,
	Which, I presume, he'll take in gentle part.

Enter RICHARD.

ELY	In happy time, here comes the Duke himself.
RICHARD	My noble lords and cousins all, good morrow!
	I have been long a sleeper, but I trust
	My absence doth neglect no great design
	Which by my presence might have been concluded.

5

10

15

20

25

Richard sends the Bishop of Ely away from the meeting. Privately, Richard tells Buckingham that Hastings will not support their plans. Hastings says that Richard looks particularly cheerful and that Richard's appearance is always a true reflection of his thoughts.

26 **cue**: the right time for entrance
27 **pronounced your part**: spoken for you

31 **My lord of Ely**: i.e. the bishop
Holborn: the location of the bishop's house in London
33 **beseech**: beg
34 **Marry and will**: Indeed I will

37 **testy**: strong-willed
hot: angry
38 **ere**: before
39 **His master's child**: Edward Prince of Wales
41 **Withdraw**: Go outside

42 **set down**: decided upon
day of triumph: i.e. the day of the coronation
43 **sudden**: i.e. soon
44 **provided**: prepared
45 **prolonged**: put off

48 **smooth**: calm
49 **conceit**: idea / thought
likes him well: he likes very much
51 **never … Christendom**: no one in any Christian country
53 **straight**: directly

54 **perceive**: see
55 **livelihood**: liveliness

Think about

- Hastings says that Richard cannot hide his thoughts and feelings. We have repeatedly seen Richard acting and being deceitful. What does this tell us about Hastings' judgement?

BUCKINGHAM	Had you not come upon your cue, my lord,
	William Lord Hastings had pronounced your part –
	I mean, your voice for crowning of the King.
RICHARD	Than my Lord Hastings no man might be bolder.
	His lordship knows me well and loves me well.
	My lord of Ely – when I was last in Holborn,
	I saw good strawberries in your garden there.
	I do beseech you send for some of them.
ELY	Marry and will, my lord, with all my heart!

Exit.

RICHARD	Cousin of Buckingham, a word with you.

RICHARD *and* BUCKINGHAM *move aside to speak.*

	Catesby hath sounded Hastings in our business,
	And finds the testy gentleman so hot
	That he will lose his head ere give consent
	His master's child – as worshipfully he terms it –
	Shall lose the royalty of England's throne.
BUCKINGHAM	Withdraw yourself awhile. I'll go with you.

Exit RICHARD, *with* BUCKINGHAM.

DERBY	We have not yet set down this day of triumph.
	Tomorrow, in my judgement, is too sudden –
	For I myself am not so well provided
	As else I would be, were the day prolonged.

Re-enter the Bishop of ELY.

ELY	Where is my lord the Duke of Gloucester?
	I have sent for these strawberries.
HASTINGS	His Grace looks cheerfully and smooth this morning.
	There's some conceit or other likes him well
	When that he bids good morrow with such spirit.
	I think there's never a man in Christendom
	Can lesser hide his love or hate than he –
	For by his face straight shall you know his heart.
DERBY	What of his heart perceive you in his face
	By any livelihood he showed today?

Line numbers: 30, 35, 40, 45, 50, 55

When asked, Hastings tells Richard that those who attack him with witchcraft should be killed. Richard says that Elizabeth and Mistress Shore have bewitched him and Hastings is protecting them. He orders the execution of Hastings. Hastings regrets not believing the danger signs.

56 **Marry**: To be sure

59 **conspire**: secretly plan
60 **prevailed**: used their power

63 **most forward**: bold
64 **doom**: condemn

68 **blasted sapling**: shrunken and thin young tree
69 **Edward's wife**: i.e. Queen Elizabeth
70 **Consorted ... Shore**: i.e. together with that whore and prostitute, Mistress Shore (Hastings' lover)

77 **look ... done**: see that it is done

79 **a whit**: at all
80 **fond**: foolish
81 **raze our helms**: tear off our helmets
82 **disdain to fly**: refuse to run away
83 **foot-cloth**: richly equipped
84 **started**: jolted suddenly
85 **As loath**: as if unwilling
86 **spake**: spoke
87 **pursuivant**: messenger
88 **triumphing**: triumphantly

---Think about---
• Do you think that any of the characters actually believe Richard's claim that Hastings is a traitor?

• Why do you think Richard chooses to condemn Hastings with something as unlikely as witchcraft?

HASTINGS   Marry, that with no man here he is offended –
                For, were he, he had shown it in his looks.

Re-enter RICHARD *and* BUCKINGHAM.

RICHARD   I pray you all, tell me what they deserve
                That do conspire my death with devilish plots
                Of damnèd witchcraft – and that have prevailed   60
                Upon my body with their hellish charms?

HASTINGS   The tender love I bear your Grace, my lord,
                Makes me most forward in this princely presence
                To doom th' offenders – whosoe'er they be.
                I say, my lord, they have deservèd death.   65

RICHARD   Then be your eyes the witness of their evil.
                Look how I am bewitched! Behold, mine arm
                Is like a blasted sapling withered up!
                And this is Edward's wife, that monstrous witch,
                Consorted with that harlot strumpet Shore,   70
                That by their witchcraft thus have markèd me!

HASTINGS   If they have done this deed, my noble lord –

RICHARD   If? – Thou protector of this damnèd strumpet!
                Talk'st thou to me of ifs? Thou art a traitor!
                Off with his head! Now by Saint Paul I swear   75
                I will not dine until I see the same.
                Lovell and Ratcliffe, look that it be done.
                The rest that love me, rise and follow me.

Exit RICHARD. *All follow, except* HASTINGS, RATCLIFFE, *and* LOVELL.

HASTINGS   Woe, woe, for England! Not a whit for me –
                For I, too fond, might have prevented this!   80
                Stanley did dream the boar did raze our helms,
                And I did scorn it and disdain to fly.
                Three times today my foot-cloth horse did stumble,
                And started when he looked upon the Tower,
                As loath to bear me to the slaughter-house.   85
                O, now I need the priest that spake to me!
                I now repent I told the pursuivant,
                As too triumphing, how mine enemies
                Today at Pomfret bloodily were butchered,

Hastings remembers Margaret's curse on him and predicts misery and death for others in the future under Richard's leadership. Ratcliffe and Lovell hurry him off to execution.

90 **secure**: safe

92 **Is lighted:** has fallen

93 **dispatch**: hurry up

94 **short shrift**: brief confession (of his sins, before death)
    He: i.e. Richard

95 **momentary … men**: short-lived good fortune on earth

97 **Who builds … good looks**: Whoever puts his trust in the appearance of earthly good fortune

99 **nod**: sway

100 **deep**: sea

101 **bootless**: useless
     exclaim: protest

105 **block**: execution block for a beheading

Think about

- Who is Hastings' final line (line 106) aimed at? How do you think Ratcliffe and Lovell should react?

- Look at the images of the sea and drowning in lines 98 to 100 and think back over the play, including Clarence's dream. Can you see a significant pattern developing?

	And I myself secure in grace and favour!	90
	O Margaret, Margaret, now thy heavy curse	
	Is lighted on poor Hastings' wretched head!	

RATCLIFFE   Come, come, dispatch! The Duke would be at dinner.
Make a short shrift! He longs to see your head!

HASTINGS   O momentary grace of mortal men,   95
Which we more hunt for than the grace of God!
Who builds his hope in air of your good looks
Lives like a drunken sailor on a mast –
Ready with every nod to tumble down
Into the fatal bowels of the deep.   100

LOVELL   Come, come, dispatch. 'Tis bootless to exclaim.

HASTINGS   O bloody Richard! Miserable England!
I prophesy the fearfull'st time to thee
That ever wretched age hath looked upon!
Come, lead me to the block. Bear him my head.   105
They smile at me who shortly shall be dead!

Exeunt.

In this scene ...

- Richard and Buckingham play-act to persuade the Lord Mayor of London that Hastings was a traitor and had to be executed. Richard pretends to be terrified of attack.
- Richard tells Buckingham to spread lies about King Edward and the Princes to suggest that they were illegitimate.

Buckingham claims that he can convincingly fake any emotion. Richard and Buckingham pretend to be frightened of attack to fool the Lord Mayor.

1 **quake**: shake
2 **Murder**: i.e. stop

5 **counterfeit**: pretend to be
  deep tragedian: serious tragic actor
6 **pry**: look around
7 **start**: jump with shock
  wagging ... straw: any little thing
8 **Intending**: suggesting
  Ghastly: Terrible
10 **offices**: assigned duties
11 **grace my stratagems**: play their part in my tricks

17 **o'erlook**: look out over / inspect

19 **Look ... thee**: Look out, defend yourself

21 **patient**: calm

22 **ignoble**: dishonourable

Think about

- Why do you think Richard and Buckingham are acting in this way in front of the Lord Mayor? Are they enjoying themselves?

- How might Hastings' head be revealed for greatest dramatic effect?

The courtyard of the Tower of London.

Enter RICHARD *and* BUCKINGHAM, *wearing old and very rusty*

pieces of armour (as if hurriedly put on).

RICHARD	Come, cousin, canst thou quake and change thy colour,
	Murder thy breath in middle of a word,
	And then again begin, and stop again,
	As if thou wert distraught and mad with terror?
BUCKINGHAM	Tut, I can counterfeit the deep tragedian!
	Speak and look back, and pry on every side,
	Tremble and start at wagging of a straw,
	Intending deep suspicion. Ghastly looks
	Are at my service, like enforcèd smiles –
	And both are ready in their offices
	At any time to grace my stratagems.
	But what, is Catesby gone?
RICHARD	He is – and see, he brings the mayor along.

Enter CATESBY, *with the* LORD MAYOR *of London.*

BUCKINGHAM	Lord Mayor –
RICHARD	Look to the drawbridge there!
BUCKINGHAM	Hark! A drum.
RICHARD	Catesby, o'erlook the walls!
BUCKINGHAM	Lord Mayor, the reason we have sent –
RICHARD	Look back, defend thee! Here are enemies!
BUCKINGHAM	God and our innocence defend and guard us!

Enter LOVELL *and* RATCLIFFE, *bringing the head of Hastings.*

RICHARD	Be patient. They are friends – Ratcliffe and Lovell.
LOVELL	Here is the head of that ignoble traitor,
	The dangerous and unsuspected Hastings.

5

10

15

20

Richard pretends to be upset at Hastings' death. Buckingham claims that Hastings had planned to kill both himself and Richard, and wishes aloud that the Lord Mayor could have heard Hastings' confession.

25 **plainest**: most straightforward

27 **my book**: my diary, keeper of my secrets
    wherein: in which
29 **daubed**: painted
30 **apparent**: obvious
    omitted: ignored
31 **conversation**: sexual relationship
32 **from ... suspects**: free from all suspicion
33 **covert'st**: most secret
    sheltered: hidden

36 **by great preservation**: being saved by good fortune
37 **subtle**: cunning
39 **Lord of Gloucester**: i.e. Richard

41 **Turks or infidels**: people who don't believe in Christianity
42 **form of law**: letter of the law
43 **rashly**: hastily
44 **peril**: danger

47 **Now ... you**: May good fortune come to you
48 **well proceeded**: done well
49 **the like**: similar
50 **looked ... hands**: expected him to behave well
51 **fell in**: became involved
52 **determined**: decided

55 **meanings**: intentions

57 **timorously**: fearfully
59 **signified**: reported
60 **haply**: perhaps
61 **Misconster ... him**: misunderstand our actions towards him

---

Think about

• Is the Mayor entirely convinced by the story told by Richard and Buckingham? Look at lines 40, and 47 to 49. The Lord Mayor seems to be persuaded that Hastings is guilty, but could these lines be delivered in different ways to show that he either believed or disbelieved their story?

RICHARD	So dear I loved the man that I must weep.
	I took him for the plainest harmless creature **25**
	That breathed upon the earth a Christian:
	Made him my book, wherein my soul recorded
	The history of all her secret thoughts.
	So smooth he daubed his vice with show of virtue
	That, his apparent open guilt omitted – **30**
	I mean his conversation with Shore's wife –
	He lived from all attainder of suspects.
BUCKINGHAM	Well, well, he was the covert'st sheltered traitor
	That ever lived!
	Would you imagine, or almost believe – **35**
	Were't not that by great preservation
	We live to tell it – that the subtle traitor
	This day had plotted, in the council-house,
	To murder me and my good Lord of Gloucester?
MAYOR	Had he done so? **40**
RICHARD	What! Think you we are Turks or infidels?
	Or that we would, against the form of law,
	Proceed thus rashly in the villain's death
	But that the extreme peril of the case,
	The peace of England and our persons' safety, **45**
	Enforced us to this execution?
MAYOR	Now fair befall you! He deserved his death!
	And your good Graces both have well proceeded
	To warn false traitors from the like attempts.
BUCKINGHAM	I never looked for better at his hands **50**
	After he once fell in with Mistress Shore.
	Yet had we not determined he should die
	Until your lordship came to see his end –
	Which now the loving haste of these our friends,
	Something against our meanings, have prevented – **55**
	Because, my lord, I would have had you heard
	The traitor speak, and timorously confess
	The manner and the purpose of his treasons;
	That you might well have signified the same
	Unto the citizens, who haply may **60**
	Misconster us in him and wail his death.

The Mayor is convinced of
Hastings' guilt and goes to tell
the citizens what has happened.
Richard sends Buckingham after
the Mayor, telling him to spread
false rumours about King
Edward and his sons.

65 **acquaint**: tell

66 **just proceedings**: correct actions

67 **to that end**: for that reason

68 **censures**: condemnations
    carping: critical

69–70 **come ... intend**: came too late to see
       what we had planned, tell them what
       you hear we had meant to do

73 **hies ... post**: goes as quickly as he can

74 **your ... time**: the time you think is best

75 **Infer**: suggest
    bastardy: illegitimacy

77–9 **make ... termèd so**: i.e. the citizen's
      son would inherit the building whose
      sign said it was called 'the Crown'

80 **urge**: put forward
    luxury: sexual lust

81 **bestial**: animal-like
    lust: sexual partners

82 **stretched unto**: included

84 **lusted ... prey**: wanted to find a victim

85 **for ... person**: if you have to, mention
    me as follows

86 **went with child**: was pregnant

87 **insatiate**: never satisfied

89 **true computation**: accurate working out

90 **issue ... begot**: child was not fathered
    by him

91 **lineaments**: features

93 **touch this sparingly**: just mention this
    in passing

94 **my mother lives**: my mother is still alive

95 **orator**: speech-maker

96 **golden fee**: golden prize / the crown of
    England

---Think about

• Are there any patterns to
  the different ways Richard is
  using to clear his path to
  the throne? Are some tactics
  more effective than others?

MAYOR	But, my good lord, your Graces' words shall serve
	As well as I had seen and heard him speak.
	And do not doubt, right noble Princes both,
	But I'll acquaint our duteous citizens
	With all your just proceedings in this cause.

65

| RICHARD | And to that end we wished your lordship here, |
| | T' avoid the censures of the carping world. |

BUCKINGHAM	Which, since you come too late of our intent,
	Yet witness what you hear we did intend.
	And so, my good Lord Mayor, we bid farewell.

70

Exit LORD MAYOR.

RICHARD	Go, after, after, cousin Buckingham!
	The Mayor towards Guildhall hies him in all post.
	There, at your meetest vantage of the time,
	Infer the bastardy of Edward's children.
	Tell them how Edward put to death a citizen
	Only for saying he would make his son
	Heir to the crown – meaning indeed his house,
	Which by the sign thereof was termèd so.
	Moreover, urge his hateful luxury
	And bestial appetite in change of lust,
	Which stretched unto their servants, daughters, wives,
	Even where his raging eye or savage heart
	Without control lusted to make a prey.
	Nay, for a need, thus far come near *my* person:
	Tell them, when that my mother went with child
	Of that insatiate Edward, noble York
	My princely father then had wars in France
	And, by true computation of the time,
	Found that the issue was not his begot –
	Which well appearèd in his lineaments,
	Being nothing like the noble Duke my father.
	Yet touch this sparingly, as 'twere far off;
	Because, my lord, you know my mother lives.

75

80

85

90

BUCKINGHAM	Doubt not, my lord, I'll play the orator
	As if the golden fee for which I plead
	Were for myself. And so, my lord, adieu.

95

Richard arranges to meet Buckingham later. He then sends for two churchmen and plans to hide away Clarence's children and the two Princes.

98 **thrive well**: succeed
Baynard's Castle: Richard's London mansion

102 **that … affords**: from the Guildhall (the place where the Lord Mayor and other officials met)
103–4 **Shaw … Penker**: two churchmen who were supporters of Richard

106 **privy order**: secret arrangement

108 **no manner person**: no one
109 **Have … recourse**: should have access at any time

Think about

- Richard sends for two churchmen. How do you think they might be useful to him?

RICHARD   If you thrive well, bring them to Baynard's Castle –
           Where you shall find me well accompanied
           With reverend fathers and well-learnèd bishops.   **100**

BUCKINGHAM I go – and towards three or four o'clock
           Look for the news that the Guildhall affords.

                                                        Exit.

RICHARD   Go, Lovell, with all speed to Doctor Shaw.
           (*To* RATCLIFFE) Go thou to Friar Penker. Bid them both
           Meet me within this hour at Baynard's Castle.   **105**

                              Exit LOVELL, *with* RATCLIFFE.

           Now will I go to take some privy order
           To draw the brats of Clarence out of sight,
           And to give order that no manner person
           Have any time recourse unto the Princes.

                                                        Exit.

In this scene ...

- A legal clerk makes it clear that Richard acted illegally in having Hastings killed.

1 **indictment**: written legal accusation
2 **in a ... engrossed**: clearly written out in formal handwriting
3 **Paul's**: St. Paul's Cathedral
4 **sequel**: the series of events
6 **yesternight**: yesterday night
7 **precedent ... a-doing**: original document took at least as long to draft
9 **Untainted**: unaccused
10 **Here's ... while**: That's how good the world is nowadays
  gross: stupid
11 **palpable device**: obvious trick
12 **Yet ... it not**: i.e. But who is brave enough to go against this accusation
13 **nought**: nothing (and wordplay on 'naught': bad)
14 **ill dealing**: wicked actions
  seen in thought: thought about (i.e. not discussed)

Think about

- This scene is often cut in performance. What do you think we gain and what do we lose if it is? What would you do if you were the director?

- Think about the last two lines of the scene. What is the moral they give, and how can this be applied to the play as a whole?

London: a street.

Enter a SCRIVENER *(legal clerk), carrying papers.*

SCRIVENER   Here is the indictment of the good Lord Hastings;
Which in a set hand fairly is engrossed
That it may be today read o'er in Paul's.
And mark how well the sequel hangs together:
Eleven hours I have spent to write it over,   5
For yesternight by Catesby was it sent me.
The precedent was full as long a-doing:
And yet within these five hours Hastings lived –
Untainted, unexamined, free, at liberty!
Here's a good world the while! Who is so gross   10
That cannot see this palpable device?
Yet who so bold but *says* he sees it not?
Bad is the world – and all will come to nought,
When such ill dealing must be seen in thought.

                                                    Exit.

In this scene ...

- Buckingham tells Richard that he has not been able to persuade the citizens of London to support his claim to be King.
- Richard and Buckingham play-act a scene where Richard pretends to be unwilling, but is eventually persuaded, to take on the duty of ruling the country as King.
- Richard's coronation is arranged for the next day.

Buckingham tells how the citizens did not respond to his speech, and gives details of all the ways he praised Richard and attacked Edward. He reports that he bullied the Mayor, asking why the citizens were silent.

Think about

- List the things for which Buckingham praised Richard when talking to the citizens. Do you think truth and falsehood are mixed together here?

- Why do you think the citizens were silent and looked pale?

2 **Mother of our Lord**: Mary, mother of Jesus Christ

3 **mum**: silent

4 **Touched you**: Did you mention **bastardy**: illegitimacy

5–6 **Lady ... France**: When he married Elizabeth, King Edward had already made arrangements to marry both Lady Elizabeth Lucy and Lady Bona of France.

7 **insatiate**: never satisfied

8 **enforcement**: rape

9 **tyranny for trifles**: cruelty about unimportant things

10 **got**: conceived

11 **resemblance**: appearance

12 **Withal ... lineaments**: Also, I reminded them of your features **right idea**: true image

14 **form**: shape

15 **Laid open**: clearly displayed (like a book)

17 **bounty**: generosity

18 **fitting**: useful

19 **handled in discourse**: dealt with in my words

20 **oratory**: speech

24 **spake**: spoke

27 **reprehended**: told off

28 **wilful**: obstinate

30 **but ... Recorder**: except by the chief magistrate

32 **inferred**: alleged

London: Baynard's Castle (Richard's mansion by the Thames).

Enter RICHARD *and* BUCKINGHAM, *meeting.*

RICHARD   How now, how now? What say the citizens?

BUCKINGHAM   Now, by the holy Mother of our Lord,
              The citizens are mum, say not a word.

RICHARD   Touched you the bastardy of Edward's children?

BUCKINGHAM   I did – with his contract with Lady Lucy,   5
              And his contract by deputy in France;
              Th' insatiate greediness of his desire,
              And his enforcement of the city wives;
              His tyranny for trifles; his own bastardy –
              As being got, your father then in France,   10
              And his resemblance, being not like the Duke.
              Withal I did infer your lineaments –
              Being the right idea of your father,
              Both in your form and nobleness of mind;
              Laid open all your victories in Scotland,   15
              Your discipline in war, wisdom in peace,
              Your bounty, virtue, fair humility –
              Indeed, left nothing fitting for your purpose
              Untouched or slightly handled in discourse.
              And when mine oratory drew toward end   20
              I bid them that did love their country's good
              Cry 'God save Richard, England's royal King!'

RICHARD   And did they so?

BUCKINGHAM   No, so God help me, they spake not a word!
              But, like dumb statues or breathing stones,   25
              Stared each on other, and looked deadly pale.
              Which when I saw, I reprehended them,
              And asked the Mayor what meant this wilful silence.
              His answer was, the people were not used
              To be spoke to but by the Recorder.   30
              Then he was urged to tell my tale again:
              'Thus saith the Duke, thus hath the Duke inferred' –

Buckingham says he used the cries of his men to pretend that the whole crowd supported Richard. He advises Richard to appear before the Mayor with a prayer book and two clergymen.

33   **in warrant from himself**: on his own responsibility

37   **vantage**: opportunity
38   **quoth**: said

41   **even here**: at that point
     brake off: stopped

43   **brethren**: fellow citizens
44   **here at hand**: close by
     Intend some fear: Pretend to be fearful

45   **Be not ... suit**: Speak to them only after great persuasion
48   **on that ... descant**: to that tune I'll add a holy accompaniment
49   **be not easily won**: don't be easily persuaded
50   **maid**: woman
     still ... take it: say no and mean yes. (A reference to the sexist saying that women say 'no' to sexual invitations when they mean 'yes'.)
53   **issue**: outcome
54   **leads**: flat roof covered in lead

55   **dance attendance**: am waiting eagerly (for Richard)
56   **spoke withal**: spoken with

57   **your lord**: i.e. Richard
58   **entreat**: plead with
60   **within**: inside
61   **Divinely bent**: prayerfully focused
62   **suits**: arguments
     moved: persuaded
63   **draw**: take
     holy exercise: prayers and meditations

---Think about---

• Are Buckingham and Richard fearful that their plans will not work, or are they excited by the challenge?

But nothing spoke in warrant from himself.
When he had done, some followers of mine own
At lower end of the hall hurled up their caps,   35
And some ten voices cried 'God save King Richard!'
And thus I took the vantage of those few –
'Thanks, gentle citizens and friends,' quoth I,
'This general applause and cheerful shout
Argues your wisdoms and your love to Richard'.   40
And even here brake off and came away.

RICHARD   What, tongueless blocks were they? Would they not
                     speak?
                 Will not the Mayor then and his brethren come?

BUCKINGHAM   The Mayor is here at hand. Intend some fear.
                 Be not you spoke with but by mighty suit.   45
                 And look you get a prayer-book in your hand,
                 And stand between two churchmen, good my lord –
                 For on that ground I'll make a holy descant.
                 And be not easily won to our requests:
                 Play the maid's part – still answer nay, and take it.   50

RICHARD   I go. And if you plead as well for them
                 As I can say nay to thee for myself,
                 No doubt we bring it to a happy issue.

BUCKINGHAM   Go, go, up to the leads! The Lord Mayor knocks.

                                              Exit RICHARD.

Enter the LORD MAYOR, *and citizens.*

                 Welcome, my lord. I dance attendance here.   55
                 I think the Duke will not be spoke withal.

Enter CATESBY.

                 Now, Catesby, what says your lord to my request?

CATESBY   He doth entreat your Grace, my noble lord,
                 To visit him tomorrow or next day.
                 He is within, with two right reverend fathers,   60
                 Divinely bent to meditation –
                 And in no worldly suits would he be moved,
                 To draw him from his holy exercise.

Buckingham and Catesby try to make Richard seem as holy as possible. Catesby reports that Richard is fearful of the citizens' intentions towards him.

66 **deep designs**: complex issues
   moment: importance
67 **no less importing**: concerning nothing less
68 **conference**: discussion
69 **signify**: tell

71 **lolling**: lying around
   lewd: lustful
73 **dallying ... courtezans**: playing around with a pair of prostitutes
74 **deep divines**: serious holy men
75 **engross**: fatten

78 **Take ... thereof**: agree to be King

80 **Marry**: Why (an exclamation)
   defend: forbid

83 **to what end**: for what reason

85 **thereof**: about this

87 **my noble cousin**: Richard and Buckingham are relatives

Think about

• How convincing is Buckingham's performance? Is he overdoing his praise of Richard?

---

91 **devout**: sincere
92 **at their beads**: i.e. praying
   'tis ... thence: it is difficult to distract them
93 **zealous**: holy / devoted

BUCKINGHAM	Return, good Catesby, to the gracious Duke.
	Tell him, myself, the Mayor and aldermen,
	In deep designs, in matter of great moment,
	No less importing than our general good,
	Are come to have some conference with his Grace.

65

CATESBY	I'll signify so much unto him straight.

Exit.

BUCKINGHAM	Ah ha, my lord, this prince is not an Edward!
	He is not lolling on a lewd love-bed,
	But on his knees at meditation!
	Not dallying with a brace of courtezans,
	But meditating with two deep divines –
	Not sleeping, to engross his idle body,
	But praying, to enrich his watchful soul.
	Happy were England, would this virtuous prince
	Take on his Grace the sovereignty thereof!
	But, sure, I fear we shall not win him to it.

70

75

MAYOR	Marry, God defend his Grace should say us nay!

80

BUCKINGHAM	I fear he will. Here Catesby comes again.

Re-enter CATESBY.

Now, Catesby, what says his Grace?

CATESBY	My lord,
	He wonders to what end you have assembled
	Such troops of citizens to come to him.
	His Grace not being warned thereof before,
	He fears, my lord, you mean no good to him.

85

BUCKINGHAM	Sorry I am my noble cousin should
	Suspect me that I mean no good to him.
	By heaven, we come to him in perfect love! –
	And so once more return and tell his Grace.

90

Exit CATESBY.

When holy and devout religious men
Are at their beads, 'tis much to draw them thence,
So sweet is zealous contemplation.

Pretending to have been praying, Richard appears with two Bishops. He agrees to listen to the citizens and Buckingham puts forward a number of reasons to persuade Richard to take the throne.

95 **props of virtue**: good / effective supporters
96 **stay**: protect
98 **ornaments**: signs
99 **Plantagenet**: Richard's family name

102 **zeal**: holiness

106 **Deferred the visitation**: postponed visiting
107 **leaving this**: leaving that aside

111 **disgracious**: displeasing
112 **reprehend**: find fault with
my ignorance: the error I do not know of
114 **entreaties**: pleas
amend: put right
115 **Else wherefore**: Why else
116 **resign**: give up
118 **sceptred office**: position as king
119 **due of birth**: birthright
120 **lineal**: inherited
121 **blemished stock**: illegitimate family
124 **want … limbs**: is lacking her own true and attractive parts
125 **infamy**: public disgrace
126 **graft**: joined
ignoble: unworthy (The 'ignoble plants' are Edward and his sons, who Buckingham claims are illegitimate.)

Think about

- Richard's appearance between the Bishops is loaded with the message that he is holy. In what different ways might it be staged?

- Look at and list the images in Buckingham's speech (lines 116 to 139). How do the images combine ideas of family, land and nature?

RICHARD *appears on an upper balcony, standing between two*
BISHOPS *of the church (all three holding prayer-books).* CATESBY
re-enters below.

MAYOR	See where his Grace stands, 'tween two clergymen!	
BUCKINGHAM	Two props of virtue for a Christian prince,	95
	To stay him from the fall of vanity!	
	And, see, a book of prayer in his hand –	
	True ornaments to know a holy man!	
	Famous Plantagenet, most gracious Prince,	
	Lend favourable ear to our requests,	100
	And pardon us the interruption	
	Of thy devotion and right Christian zeal.	
RICHARD	My lord, there needs no such apology.	
	I do beseech your Grace to pardon me –	
	Who, earnest in the service of my God,	105
	Deferred the visitation of my friends.	
	But, leaving this, what is your Grace's pleasure?	
BUCKINGHAM	Even that, I hope, which pleaseth God above,	
	And all good men of this ungoverned isle	
RICHARD	I do suspect I have done some offence	110
	That seems disgracious in the city's eye,	
	And that you come to reprehend my ignorance.	
BUCKINGHAM	You have, my lord. Would it might please your Grace,	
	On our entreaties, to amend your fault!	
RICHARD	Else wherefore breathe I in a Christian land?	115
BUCKINGHAM	Know then, it is your fault that you resign	
	The supreme seat, the throne majestical,	
	The sceptred office of your ancestors,	
	Your state of fortune and your due of birth,	
	The lineal glory of your royal house,	120
	To the corruption of a blemished stock –	
	Whiles in the mildness of your sleepy thoughts,	
	Which here we waken to our country's good,	
	The noble isle doth want her proper limbs –	
	Her face defaced with scars of infamy,	125
	Her royal stock graft with ignoble plants,	

Buckingham claims that it is the citizens' wish that Richard becomes King. Richard responds by saying that he is not good enough to be King and that King Edward has left his son as an heir.

127 **shouldered in**: pushed into
    gulf: abyss / hole
129 **recure**: make healthy again
    solicit: beg

133 **lowly factor**: unimportant representative
134 **successively**: by inheritance
135 **empery**: complete power
136 **consorted**: in company
137 **worshipful**: distinguished and respectful
138 **vehement instigation**: insistent suggestion
139 **move**: persuade

141 **in your reproof**: to tell you off
142 **degree**: status
143–6 **If not … on me**: If I don't answer, you may think that secretly I am ambitious for the golden crown you are foolishly trying to put on me
147 **reprove you**: tell you off
    suit: request
148 **seasoned**: made pleasant
149 **checked**: rebuked
151 **incur**: bring about
152 **Definitively**: authoritatively
153–4 **desert … shuns**: unworthiness pushes away

156 **even**: straight and smooth
157 **revenue … birth**: possession by right of my birth

161 **bark … sea**: ship that cannot face a great ocean
162 **covet**: desire
163 **vapour**: mist
165 **much I need**: I am inadequate
166 **royal fruit**: i.e. Edward Prince of Wales

─ **Think about** ─

• Look at lines 127 to 128. How is the imagery of the sea and drowning used in the play developed here?

• Look closely at Richard's speech (lines 140 to 172). How do we know that his modesty is false?

And almost shouldered in the swallowing gulf
Of dark forgetfulness and deep oblivion!
Which to recure, we heartily solicit
Your gracious self to take on you that charge   **130**
And kingly government of this your land –
Not as protector, steward, substitute,
Or lowly factor for another's gain –
But as successively, from blood to blood,
Your right of birth, your empery, your own!   **135**
For this – consorted with the citizens,
Your very worshipful and loving friends,
And by their vehement instigation –
In this just cause come I to move your Grace.

RICHARD   I cannot tell if to depart in silence   **140**
Or bitterly to speak in your reproof
Best fitteth my degree or your condition.
If not to answer, you might haply think
Tongue-tied ambition, not replying, yielded
To bear the golden yoke of sovereignty,   **145**
Which fondly you would here impose on me.
If to reprove you for this suit of yours,
So seasoned with your faithful love to me,
Then, on the other side, I checked my friends.
Therefore – to speak, and to avoid the first,   **150**
And then, in speaking, not to incur the last –
Definitively thus I answer you:
Your love deserves my thanks, but my desert
Unmeritable shuns your high request.
First, if all obstacles were cut away,   **155**
And that my path were even to the crown,
As the ripe revenue and due of birth,
Yet so much is my poverty of spirit,
So mighty and so many my defects,
That I would rather hide me from my greatness –   **160**
Being a bark to brook no mighty sea –
Than in my greatness covet to be hid,
And in the vapour of my glory smothered.
But, God be thanked, there is no need of me –
And much I need, to help you, were there need.   **165**
The royal tree hath left us royal fruit

Buckingham reminds Richard of the sinful ways of King Edward and the supposed illegitimacy of his sons. The Mayor and Catesby support Buckingham.

167   **stealing**: softly moving
168   **become**: suit

172   **defend**: forbid
       wring: snatch

174   **respects**: points in your argument
       nice: unimportant

182   **put off**: brushed aside
       petitioner: pleader

186   **Made ... eye**: i.e. Queen Elizabeth set out to win his sexual attention
187   **pitch**: importance
       degree: status
188   **base declension**: shameful decline
       bigamy: having two wives at once
189   **got**: fathered
190   **our manners**: we politely
191   **expostulate**: argue
193   **give ... limit**: restrain
195   **proffered**: offered
       benefit of dignity: royal power
196   **withal**: with your kingship
197   **draw forth**: rescue / extract
199   **Unto ... course**: to the true family line

202   **suit**: petition

Think about

- Buckingham seems to be addressing Richard, but who is he really talking to, and why?

Which, mellowed by the stealing hours of time,
Will well become the seat of majesty
And make, no doubt, us happy by his reign.
On him I lay that you would lay on me –   170
The right and fortune of his happy stars,
Which God defend that I should wring from him!

BUCKINGHAM   My lord, this argues conscience in your Grace;
But the respects thereof are nice and trivial,
All circumstances well considered.   175
You say that Edward is your brother's son.
So say we too – but not by Edward's wife.
For first was he contract to Lady Lucy –
Your mother lives a witness to his vow –
And afterward by substitute betrothed   180
To Bona, sister to the King of France.
These both put off – a poor petitioner,
A care-crazed mother to a many sons,
A beauty-waning and distressèd widow,
Even in the afternoon of her best days –   185
Made prize and purchase of his wanton eye,
Seduced the pitch and height of his degree
To base declension and loathèd bigamy.
By her, in his unlawful bed, he got
This Edward – whom our manners call the Prince.   190
More bitterly could I expostulate,
Save that, for reverence to some alive,
I give a sparing limit to my tongue.
Then, good my lord, take to your royal self
This proffered benefit of dignity –   195
If not to bless us and the land withal,
Yet to draw forth your noble ancestry
From the corruption of abusing times
Unto a lineal true-derivèd course!

MAYOR   Do, good my lord! Your citizens entreat you.   200

BUCKINGHAM   Refuse not, mighty lord, this proffered love!

CATESBY   O, make them joyful! Grant their lawful suit!

Buckingham says that if Richard will not accept, someone else will be placed on the throne. After pretending to refuse again, Richard finally agrees to take the crown, but says that it is not his choice.

205 **amiss**: badly

207 **zeal**: concern
208 **Loath**: very unwilling
   depose: remove from the throne
210 **effeminate remorse**: womanly sorrow
211 **kindred**: family
212 **estates**: ranks
213 **whe'er**: whether

218 **Zounds**: By God's wounds (a strong oath)

220 **their suit**: what they ask of you
221 **rue**: regret

224 **penetrable**: vulnerable
225 **Albeit**: even though

226 **sage**: wise
   grave: serious

231 **Attend … imposition**: come after you've forced me to become king
232–3 **Your … thereof**: the simple fact that you forced this on me will free me from any mark of wrongdoing that follows

---

Think about

• As the play-acting of Richard and Buckingham comes to a climax, do you believe that the Mayor and citizens are fooled, forced into acceptance through fear, or a combination of the two?

176

RICHARD	Alas, why would you heap this care on me?
	I am unfit for state and majesty.
	I do beseech you, take it not amiss:	205
	I cannot nor I will not yield to you.

BUCKINGHAM	If you refuse it – as, in love and zeal,
	Loath to depose the child, your brother's son –
	As well we know your tenderness of heart
	And gentle, kind, effeminate remorse,	210
	Which we have noted in you to your kindred
	And equally indeed to all estates –
	Yet know, whe'er you accept our suit or no,
	Your brother's son shall never reign our king –
	But we will plant some other in the throne	215
	To the disgrace and downfall of your house.
	And in this resolution here we leave you.
	Come, citizens. Zounds, I'll entreat no more!

| RICHARD | O, do not swear, my lord of Buckingham! |

Exit BUCKINGHAM, *followed by the* LORD MAYOR *and citizens.*

| CATESBY | Call him again, sweet Prince. Accept their suit. | 220 |
| | If you deny them, all the land will rue it. |

RICHARD	Will you enforce me to a world of cares?
	Call them again. I am not made of stones,
	But penetrable to your kind entreaties –
	Albeit against my conscience and my soul.	225

Re-enter BUCKINGHAM, LORD MAYOR, *and citizens.*

	Cousin of Buckingham, and sage grave men,
	Since you will buckle fortune on my back,
	To bear her burden, whe'er I will or no,
	I must have patience to endure the load.
	But if black scandal or foul-faced reproach	230
	Attend the sequel of your imposition,
	Your mere enforcement shall acquittance me
	From all the impure blots and stains thereof.
	For God doth know, and you may partly see,
	How far I am from the desire of this!	235

| MAYOR | God bless your Grace! We see it, and will say it. |

Buckingham proclaims Richard King. The coronation is set for the following day and Richard pretends to return to prayer with the Bishops.

238 **salute**: greet / honour

242 **Even when**: Whenever

Think about

- In what different ways might you stage the closing moments of this scene? How would you choose to stage it, if you were the director?

- On the evidence of what you have seen so far, what kind of King do you think Richard will make?

RICHARD	In saying so, you shall but say the truth.
BUCKINGHAM	Then I salute you with this royal title – Long live King Richard, England's worthy King!
ALL	Amen.
BUCKINGHAM	Tomorrow may it please you to be crowned?
RICHARD	Even when you please, for you will have it so.
BUCKINGHAM	Tomorrow, then, we will attend your Grace. And so, most joyfully, we take our leave.
RICHARD	(*To the* BISHOPS *beside him*) Come, let us to our holy work again. Farewell, my cousin. Farewell, gentle friends.

240

245

Exeunt.

National Theatre, 1990

Shakespeare's Globe, 2003

RSC, 1995

In this scene ...

- Elizabeth, the Duchess of York, and Lady Anne try to visit the Princes in the Tower but Richard has given orders to stop them.
- The women are horrified to learn that Richard is to be crowned King, with Anne as his Queen.
- Elizabeth tells her son Dorset to escape and, after she has expressed concern and fears for the Princes in the Tower, the women leave the stage.

A small group, mainly women of the royal family, meets outside the Tower. They have come to see the Princes but Brakenbury, following Richard's orders, will not allow them inside.

1 **niece**: female relative (here meaning grand-daughter)
2 **Gloucester**: i.e. Anne (who has this title now that she is married to Richard, Duke of Gloucester)
4 **the tender Princes**: the young brothers Edward, Prince of Wales, and Richard, Duke of York
5 **Daughter**: Daughter-in-law
7 **sister**: sister-in-law
Whither away: Where are you going
9 **like devotion**: same loving purpose
10 **gratulate**: greet

16 **may not suffer**: cannot allow
17 **charged**: ordered

Think about

- Why is there confusion about the title of King?

- Is the real centre of power still uncertain at this stage?

18 **Lord Protector**: i.e. Richard (his title as the Prince's guardian and ruler on Prince Edward's behalf)
20 **bounds**: walls
21 **bar**: keep

Outside the Tower of London.

Enter QUEEN ELIZABETH, DORSET, *and the old* DUCHESS *of York.*

Meeting them, Lady ANNE (RICHARD'S *wife, Duchess of*

Gloucester), leading Clarence's young DAUGHTER.

DUCHESS	Who meets us here? My niece Plantagenet,
	Led in the hand of her kind aunt of Gloucester?
	Now, for my life, she's wandering to the Tower,
	On pure heart's love, to greet the tender Princes.
	Daughter, well met.

ANNE   God give your Graces both   5
A happy and a joyful time of day!

ELIZABETH   As much to you, good sister! Whither away?

ANNE   No farther than the Tower – and, as I guess,
Upon the like devotion as yourselves,
To gratulate the gentle Princes there.   10

ELIZABETH   Kind sister, thanks. We'll enter all together.

Enter BRAKENBURY.

And in good time, here the Lieutenant comes.
Master Lieutenant, pray you, by your leave,
How doth the Prince, and my young son of York?

BRAKENBURY   Right well, dear madam. By your patience,   15
I may not suffer you to visit them.
The King hath strictly charged the contrary.

ELIZABETH   The King! Who's that?

BRAKENBURY   I mean the Lord Protector.

ELIZABETH   The Lord protect him from that kingly title!
Hath he set bounds between their love and me?   20
I am their mother! Who shall bar me from them?

DUCHESS   I am their father's mother. I will see them!

Derby announces the intended coronation of Richard and Anne. The news shocks and upsets the women. Elizabeth advises her son Dorset to run away and join Richmond.

Think about

- Look at line 45 and back at Margaret's cursing in Act 1 Scene 3. Do you think that the characters are slaves of Margaret's evil words?

23 **in law**: by marriage
24 **bring ... sights**: let me see them
24–5 **bear ... my peril**: i.e. take responsibility
26 **leave it so**: let that happen

30 **looker-on**: observer
two fair queens: i.e. Elizabeth and Anne (the Duchess is mother-in-law to both)
31 **straight**: immediately
Westminster: Westminster Abbey (the place where Kings and Queens of England are crowned)
33 **cut ... asunder**: cut open the lace of my clothes (her bodice would have been tight-fitting)
34 **pent**: confined
scope: space
35 **swoon**: faint
36 **Despiteful**: Cruel
39 **dogs**: pursues
40 **ominous**: a menacing sign
41 **outstrip**: escape
42 **Richmond**: Henry Tudor, Earl of Richmond
from: away from
43 **hie thee**: hurry
45 **thrall**: slave / victim
46 **Nor**: neither
England's counted Queen: acknowledged as England's queen
47 **counsel**: advice

49 **my son**: my stepson, i.e. Richmond
51 **ta'en tardy**: caught late

52 **ill-dispersing**: evil scattering
54 **cockatrice**: mythical monster which could kill with a look
55 **eye**: glance

ANNE	Their aunt I am in law, in love their mother.
	Then bring me to their sights. I'll bear thy blame,
	And take thy office from thee, on my peril. 25
BRAKENBURY	No, madam, no! I may not leave it so.
	I am bound by oath, and therefore pardon me.

Exit.

Enter DERBY.

DERBY	Let me but meet you, ladies, one hour hence,
	And I'll salute your Grace of York as mother
	And reverend looker-on of two fair queens! 30
	(*To* ANNE) Come, madam, you must straight to
	Westminster,
	There to be crownèd Richard's royal queen.
ELIZABETH	Ah, cut my lace asunder! –
	That my pent heart may have some scope to beat,
	Or else I swoon with this dead-killing news! 35
ANNE	Despiteful tidings! O unpleasing news!
DORSET	Be of good cheer, mother. How fares your Grace?
ELIZABETH	O Dorset, speak not to me! Get thee gone!
	Death and destruction dogs thee at thy heels!
	Thy mother's name is ominous to children. 40
	If thou wilt outstrip death, go cross the seas,
	And live with Richmond, from the reach of hell.
	Go, hie thee, hie thee from this slaughter-house! –
	Lest thou increase the number of the dead,
	And make me die the thrall of Margaret's curse – 45
	Nor mother, wife, nor England's counted Queen.
DERBY	Full of wise care is this your counsel, madam.
	(*To* DORSET) Take all the swift advantage of the hours.
	You shall have letters from me to my son
	In your behalf, to meet you on the way. 50
	Be not ta'en tardy by unwise delay!
DUCHESS	O ill-dispersing wind of misery!
	O my accursèd womb, the bed of death!
	A cockatrice hast thou hatched to the world,
	Whose unavoided eye is murderous! 55

Anne says that she would rather be dead than be Queen. She remembers Richard's wooing and her curses, which are now falling upon herself. She predicts that Richard will soon kill her.

58–9 inclusive … golden metal: enclosing circle of gold (i.e. the crown)

60 sear: burn

62 ere: before

64 feed my humour: please me

68 issued: came
my … husband: Edward, son of King Henry VI
69 that dear saint: Henry VI
72 so young … widow: though so young, also experienced as a widow
74–6 And be … lord's death: if anyone is mad enough to marry you, may she be made more miserable by your life than you have made me by killing my husband

79 Grossly: stupidly
honey: sweet
81 hitherto … rest: until now has stopped me sleeping
84 timorous: fearful
still: always
85 Warwick: the powerful lord who first supported and then turned against Richard's family during the Wars of the Roses
87 adieu: goodbye

89 woeful … glory: sorrowful greeter of the news that Anne is to be Queen

—**Think about** —

• Is the force of the curses magical or psychological? Think about whether Anne is being attacked by mysterious outside forces or is punishing herself.

• On the evidence of this scene and the play so far, do you think the women should be described as strong, weak, or a mixture of the two? Do they have any power in this society?

DERBY	Come, madam, come. I in all haste was sent.	
ANNE	And I with all unwillingness will go.	
	O, would to God that the inclusive verge	
	Of golden metal that must round my brow	
	Were red-hot steel, to sear me to the brains!	**60**
	Anointed let me be with deadly venom,	
	And die ere men can say 'God save the Queen!'	
ELIZABETH	Go, go, poor soul. I envy not thy glory.	
	To feed my humour, wish thyself no harm.	
ANNE	No? Why? When he that is my husband now	**65**
	Came to me, as I followed Henry's corpse –	
	When scarce the blood was well washed from his hands	
	Which issued from my other angel husband,	
	And that dear saint which then I weeping followed –	
	O, when, I say, I looked on Richard's face,	**70**
	This was my wish: 'Be thou' quoth I 'accursed	
	For making me, so young, so old a widow.	
	And when thou wed'st, let sorrow haunt thy bed;	
	And be thy wife, if any be so mad,	
	More miserable by the life of thee	**75**
	Than thou hast made me by my dear lord's death'.	
	Lo, ere I can repeat this curse again,	
	Within so small a time, my woman's heart	
	Grossly grew captive to his honey words	
	And proved the subject of mine own soul's curse,	**80**
	Which hitherto hath held my eyes from rest.	
	For never yet one hour in his bed	
	Did I enjoy the golden dew of sleep,	
	But with his timorous dreams was still awaked.	
	Besides, he hates me for my father Warwick –	**85**
	And will, no doubt, shortly be rid of me.	
ELIZABETH	Poor heart, adieu! I pity thy complaining.	
ANNE	No more than with my soul I mourn for yours.	
DORSET	Farewell, thou woeful welcomer of glory!	
ANNE	Adieu, poor soul, that tak'st thy leave of it!	**90**

The Duchess sends the others
on their way with her blessing.
Everyone leaves after Elizabeth
begs the Tower to take pity on
the Princes.

96 **teen**: grief

97 **Stay**: Wait
98 **tender babes**: the Princes in the Tower
99 **immured**: imprisoned

101 **Rude ragged**: Rough
     sullen: gloomy

Think about

- Elizabeth describes and
  personifies the Tower with a
  range of different
  characteristics. How
  relevant and effective are
  the images she chooses?

- Why does Elizabeth
  describe her lamentations
  as 'foolish' (line 103)?

DUCHESS	(*To* **DORSET**) Go thou to Richmond, and good fortune guide thee!
	(*To* **ANNE**) Go thou to Richard, and good angels tend thee!
	(*To* **QUEEN ELIZABETH**) Go thou to sanctuary, and good thoughts possess thee!
	I to my grave – where peace and rest lie with me!
	Eighty-odd years of sorrow have I seen,
	And each hour's joy wrecked with a week of teen.
ELIZABETH	Stay, yet look back with me unto the Tower.
	Pity, you ancient stones, those tender babes
	Whom envy hath immured within your walls –
	Rough cradle for such little pretty ones.
	Rude ragged nurse, old sullen playfellow
	For tender princes, use my babies well!
	So foolish sorrows bids your stones farewell.

95

100

Exeunt.

In this scene ...

- Richard, now King, wants the Princes killed, but Buckingham will not co-operate, which infuriates Richard.
- Richard hires Tyrrel to murder the Princes and orders Catesby to spread rumours that Anne is seriously ill.
- Richard makes plans to kill Anne and marry Queen Elizabeth's daughter to secure the kingdom.
- Richard angrily refuses Buckingham the rewards he had promised him.
- Fearing for his life, Buckingham decides to escape to Wales.

Sitting on the throne, Richard hints that Buckingham should agree to having the Princes killed. Buckingham does not take the hint and Richard asks him directly.

1 **apart**: aside

7 **Still**: For ever

8 **play the touch**: check if something is genuine
9 **try**: test
   current: genuine

13 **thrice-renownèd**: i.e. extremely famous

14 **Edward**: i.e. Prince Edward

17 **thou wast ... dull**: you used not to be so slow on the uptake
18 **bastards**: i.e. Prince Edward and the Duke of York
19 **suddenly**: immediately

---Think about

- There is no coronation in this play, but many productions open this scene with Richard being crowned. What do you think would be the advantages and disadvantages of showing this moment?

London: the palace.

Trumpets sound. Enter RICHARD, *newly crowned as King, in*

procession. Attending him, BUCKINGHAM, CATESBY, RATCLIFFE *and*

LOVELL, *with a boy* PAGE, *and others.*

KING RICHARD Stand all apart! Cousin of Buckingham!

BUCKINGHAM   My gracious sovereign?

KING RICHARD Give me thy hand.

> RICHARD *ascends to the royal throne, and sits.*
> *Trumpets sound a fanfare.*
> *All kneel to him as King, then stand back from the throne as*
> *he speaks with* BUCKINGHAM.

Thus high, by thy advice	
And thy assistance, is King Richard seated.	
But shall we wear these glories for a day? –	5
Or shall they last, and we rejoice in them?	

BUCKINGHAM   Still live they, and for ever let them last!

KING RICHARD Ah, Buckingham, now do I play the touch,
To try if thou be current gold indeed.
Young Edward lives – think now what I would speak.   10

BUCKINGHAM   Say on, my loving lord.

KING RICHARD Why, Buckingham – I say I would be King.

BUCKINGHAM   Why, so you are, my thrice-renownèd lord.

KING RICHARD Ha! Am I King? 'Tis so – but Edward lives.

BUCKINGHAM   True, noble Prince.

KING RICHARD   O bitter consequence!   15
That Edward still should live – 'true noble Prince!'
Cousin, thou wast not wont to be so dull.
Shall I be plain? I wish the bastards dead!
And I would have it suddenly performed.
What say'st thou now? Speak suddenly, be brief.   20

Buckingham asks for time to think. Richard is angry, saying that he will no longer trust Buckingham with his secrets. He sends for Tyrrel.

21   **your pleasure**: as you wish

26   **resolve ... presently**: give you my answer about this shortly

28   **iron-witted**: stupid
29   **unrespective**: disrespectful / unresponsive
30   **considerate**: thoughtful
31   **High-reaching**: i.e. ambitious
     circumspect: cautious

35   **close exploit**: secret act

37   **humble means**: lack of money
     haughty: proud
38   **orators**: persuasive speech makers

Think about

- Look at line 21. Why do you think Buckingham won't answer Richard's questions directly?

- Are there any instructions on this page of the text that actors and directors cannot ignore? Look at Richard's reactions and how others describe them.

41   **partly**: slightly

42   **deep-revolving witty**: thoughtful and crafty
43   **neighbour to my counsels**: let in on my secrets
44   **held out**: kept up

BUCKINGHAM   Your Grace may do your pleasure.

KING RICHARD Tut, tut, thou art all ice. Thy kindness freezes.
Say, have I thy consent that they shall die?

BUCKINGHAM   Give me some little breath, some pause, dear lord,
Before I positively speak in this.   25
I will resolve you herein presently.

Exit.

CATESBY   (*Aside to another*) The King is angry. See, he gnaws
his lip.

KING RICHARD (*Aside*) I will converse with iron-witted fools
And unrespective boys – none are for me
That look into me with considerate eyes!   30
High-reaching Buckingham grows circumspect.
(*To the* PAGE) Boy!

PAGE   (*Coming close to the throne*) My lord?

KING RICHARD Know'st thou not any whom corrupting gold
Will tempt unto a close exploit of death?   35

PAGE   I know a discontented gentleman
Whose humble means match not his haughty spirit.
Gold were as good as twenty orators,
And will, no doubt, tempt him to anything.

KING RICHARD What is his name?

PAGE   His name, my lord, is Tyrrel.   40

KING RICHARD I partly know the man. Go, call him hither, boy.

Exit PAGE.

(*Aside*) The deep-revolving witty Buckingham
No more shall be the neighbour to my counsels.
Hath he so long held out with me, untired,
And stops he now for breath? Well, be it so!   45

Enter DERBY, *and kneels before* RICHARD.

How now, Lord Stanley! What's the news?

Derby tells Richard that Dorset has joined Richmond. Richard plans to get his wife Anne and Clarence's daughter out of the way, and then to marry Queen Elizabeth's daughter. Richard orders Tyrrel to kill the Princes.

50 **Rumour it abroad**: Spread the rumour
51 **very grievous**: extremely
52 **take … close**: make arrangements for her to be shut away
53 **Inquire me out**: Find me
    mean: unimportant
55 **boy**: i.e. Clarence's son
56 **give out**: announce
58 **About it**: Get on with it
    it stands … upon: it's very important to me

60 **my brother's daughter**: Princess Elizabeth, daughter of King Edward IV and Queen Elizabeth
63 **Uncertain**: Risky
64 **pluck on**: bring on more

Think about

• Look at Richard's speech (lines 50 to 59). How do we know that Catesby now seems shocked at Richard's instructions?

68 **Prove**: Test

• What do the blood and tear images (lines 63 to 65) tell us about Richard's attitude to violence and his emotions at this stage?

70 **Please you**: If it pleases you

73 **Foes**: enemies
74 **upon**: with

DERBY Know, my loving lord,
The Marquis Dorset, as I hear, is fled
To Richmond, in the parts where he abides.

DERBY *rises and stands back (as* RICHARD *calls* CATESBY *to him).*

KING RICHARD Come hither, Catesby. Rumour it abroad   50
That Anne, my wife, is very grievous sick.
I will take order for her keeping close.
Inquire me out some mean poor gentleman,
Whom I will marry straight to Clarence' daughter –
The boy is foolish, and I fear not him.   55
Look how thou dream'st! I say again, give out
That Anne, my queen, is sick and like to die.
About it! For it stands me much upon
To stop all hopes whose growth may damage me.

Exit CATESBY.

(*Aside*) I must be married to my brother's daughter,   60
Or else my kingdom stands on brittle glass.
Murder her brothers, and then marry her!
Uncertain way of gain! But I am in
So far in blood that sin will pluck on sin.
Tear-falling pity dwells not in this eye!   65

Re-enter the PAGE, *with Sir James* TYRREL.

Is thy name Tyrrel?

TYRREL James Tyrrel, and your most obedient subject.

KING RICHARD Art thou, indeed?

TYRREL   Prove me, my gracious lord.

KING RICHARD Dar'st thou resolve to kill a friend of mine?

TYRREL Please you –   70
But I had rather kill two enemies.

KING RICHARD Why, then thou hast it. Two deep enemies,
Foes to my rest, and my sweet sleep's disturbers,
Are they that I would have thee deal upon.
Tyrrel, I mean those bastards in the Tower.   75

Buckingham asks for the
rewards Richard promised him
in exchange for his help.
Richard ignores the request and
remembers King Henry the
Sixth's prediction that Richmond
will become King.

76   open means: easy access

79   this token: a sign to give him authority
to go into the Tower
80   There ... but so: That is all
81   prefer: promote

82   dispatch it straight: do it right away

84   late: recent
sound me in: ask me about
85   let that rest: put that out of your mind

87   he: i.e. Richmond
look unto it: deal with it

89   pawned: pledged / promised
90   movables: personal property

92   look to: keep an eye on
93   answer: be held responsible for

97   peevish: silly / irritating

Think about

- Some printed versions of
the play do not include
lines 99 to 116. Are they
important? Do you think
that they should be used in
a production or not?

100   chance: did it happen
101   I being by: since I was there at the
time

| TYRREL | Let me have open means to come to them, |
| | And soon I'll rid you from the fear of them. |

KING RICHARD	Thou sing'st sweet music. Hark, come hither, Tyrrel.
	Go by this token. Rise, and lend thine ear.
	(*He whispers instructions.*)
	There is no more but so. Say it is done,
	And I will love thee and prefer thee for it.

80

| TYRREL | I will dispatch it straight. |

Exit.

Re-enter BUCKINGHAM.

| BUCKINGHAM | My lord, I have considered in my mind |
| | The late request that you did sound me in. |

| KING RICHARD | Well, let that rest. Dorset is fled to Richmond. |

85

| BUCKINGHAM | I hear the news, my lord. |

| KING RICHARD | Stanley, he is your wife's son! Well, look unto it. |

BUCKINGHAM	My lord, I claim the gift, my due by promise,
	For which your honour and your faith is pawned:
	Th' earldom of Hereford and the movables
	Which you have promisèd I shall possess.

90

| KING RICHARD | Stanley, look to your wife! If she convey |
| | Letters to Richmond, you shall answer it. |

| BUCKINGHAM | What says your Highness to my just request? |

KING RICHARD	I do remember me: Henry the Sixth
	Did prophesy that Richmond should be King,
	When Richmond was a little peevish boy.
	A king! – perhaps –

95

| BUCKINGHAM | My lord – |

| KING RICHARD | How chance the prophet could not at that time |
| | Have told me, I being by, that I should kill him? |

100

| BUCKINGHAM | My lord, your promise for the earldom – |

Buckingham continues to ask for his reward, but Richard refuses him again. Buckingham decides to flee to his home in Wales.

105 **started**: jumped in shock (because Rougemont sounds like Richmond)

106 **bard**: mystic poet

109 **o'clock**: the time

110 **thus ... in mind**: being assertive in order to remind you

114 **Jack**: the mechanical man who strikes the bell on the outside of some old clocks

116 **vein**: mood

117 **resolve ... suit**: answer my request

122 **Brecon**: Buckingham's estates in Wales

---**Think about**---

• Look at Buckingham's last speech (lines 119 to 122). He is angry and fearful. Do you think he has been foolish to trust Richard?

King Richard Richmond! When last I was at Exeter,
The mayor in courtesy showed me the castle
And called it Rougemont – at which name I started,   **105**
Because a bard of Ireland told me once
I should not live long after I saw Richmond.

Buckingham My lord –

King Richard Ay – what's o'clock?

Buckingham I am thus bold to put your Grace in mind   **110**
Of what you promised me.

King Richard   Well – but what's o'clock?

Buckingham Upon the stroke of ten.

King Richard   Well, let it strike.

Buckingham Why let it strike?

King Richard Because that like a Jack thou keep'st the stroke
Betwixt thy begging and my meditation!   **115**
I am not in the giving vein today.

Buckingham May it please you to resolve me in my suit?

King Richard Thou troublest me. I am not in the vein!

                    Exit Richard. *All follow, except* Buckingham.

Buckingham And is it thus? Repays he my deep service
With such contempt? Made I him King for *this*?   **120**
O, let me think on Hastings, and be gone
To Brecon while my fearful head is on!

                                                            Exit.

RSC, 2003

RSC, 1992

Richard III, 1995 (directed by R. Loncraine)

RSC, 1988

In this scene ...

- Tyrrel describes the murder of the Princes in the Tower.
- Richard tells how Clarence's children have been removed as a threat to the throne, that Anne is dead, and that he plans to marry Queen Elizabeth's daughter.
- Ratcliffe brings news that the Bishop of Ely has joined Richmond and that Buckingham plans to attack.
- Richard is determined to fight them.

Tyrrel describes the murder of the Princes and the remorse the murderers felt. He tells Richard that the Princes are dead.

1   **act**: the murder of the Princes
2   **arch**: grave and important
4   **suborn**: hire / persuade
5   **ruthful**: 1 pitiful; 2 ruthless
6   **Albeit**: even though
    fleshed: used to violence
    their ... story: telling how the Princes died
10 **girdling**: wrapping
11 **alabaster**: white and smooth

15 **once**: for a moment

18 **replenishèd**: perfect
19 **prime creation**: world's beginning
    she: nature

Think about

- The murders of the Princes happen off-stage. What do you think is gained and what is lost by having their murders described rather than staged?

- Consider the innocence and beauty of the boys and the effect they have on their murderers. Do you think this is the worst of Richard's crimes so far?

25 **gave in charge**: ordered
26 **Beget**: brings about

London: the palace.

Enter TYRREL.

TYRREL	The tyrannous and bloody act is done –	
	The most arch deed of piteous massacre	
	That ever yet this land was guilty of!	
	Dighton and Forrest, who I did suborn	
	To do this piece of ruthful butchery,	5
	Albeit they were fleshed villains, bloody dogs,	
	Melted with tenderness and mild compassion,	
	Wept like two children in their deaths' sad story.	
	'O, thus,' quoth Dighton 'lay the gentle babes' –	
	'Thus, thus,' quoth Forrest 'girdling one another	10
	Within their alabaster innocent arms.	
	Their lips were four red roses on a stalk,	
	And in their summer beauty kissed each other.	
	A book of prayers on their pillow lay –	
	Which once,' quoth Forrest 'almost changed my mind.	15
	But, O, the devil! –' There the villain stopped –	
	When Dighton thus told on: 'We smothered	
	The most replenishèd sweet work of nature	
	That from the prime creation e'er she framed!'	
	Hence both are gone. With conscience and remorse	20
	They could not speak. And so I left them both,	
	To bear this tidings to the bloody King.	

Enter KING RICHARD.

And here he comes. All health, my sovereign lord!

KING RICHARD Kind Tyrrel, am I happy in thy news?

TYRREL	If to have done the thing you gave in charge	25
	Beget your happiness, be happy then –	
	For it is done.	

KING RICHARD   But didst thou see them dead?

TYRREL I did, my lord.

KING RICHARD   And buried, gentle Tyrrel?

Richard tells Tyrrel to return after supper so that he can hear details of the murders. Anne is dead too and Richard plans to marry Queen Elizabeth's daughter. He hears that the Bishop of Ely has joined Richmond and that Buckingham has raised an army. Richard is determined to fight.

32 process: story

34 be … desire: get whatever you want

36 pent up close: imprisoned
37 meanly … marriage: I have forced to marry a low-ranking man
38 sleep … bosom: are dead and in heaven
40 Breton: from Brittany in France (Richmond's place of exile)
40–1 Richmond … Elizabeth: Richmond intends to marry Princess Elizabeth.
42 by that knot: through that marriage
proudly on: ambitiously toward

46 Morton: the Bishop of Ely
47 hardy: courageous and strong
48 in the field: ready for battle
50 rash-levied strength: hastily gathered army
51 fearful commenting: nervously discussing things
52 leaden servitor: slow servant
53 impotent: powerless
beggary: ruin
54 fiery expedition: fierce urgency
55 Jove's Mercury: messenger of the gods
56 muster men: gather armed men
My … shield: i.e. It is best to fight
57 be brief: act quickly
brave the field: face us on the battlefield

Think about

• This is the first bad news Richard has faced. His words are brave, but do you think his thoughts and feelings match his words?

• If you were the director, in what different ways could you ask the actor playing Richard to react?

TYRREL	The chaplain of the Tower hath buried them.	
	But where, to say the truth, I do not know.	**30**

KING RICHARD	Come to me, Tyrrel, soon at after-supper,	
	When thou shalt tell the process of their death.	
	Meantime, but think how I may do thee good	
	And be inheritor of thy desire.	
	Farewell till then.	

TYRREL	I humbly take my leave.	**35**

Exit.

KING RICHARD	The son of Clarence have I pent up close.	
	His daughter meanly have I matched in marriage.	
	The sons of Edward sleep in Abraham's bosom –	
	And Anne my wife hath bid this world good night.	
	Now – for I know the Breton Richmond aims	**40**
	At young Elizabeth, my brother's daughter,	
	And by that knot looks proudly on the crown –	
	To her go I, a jolly thriving wooer!	

Enter RATCLIFFE.

RATCLIFFE	My lord!	

KING RICHARD	Good or bad news, that thou com'st in so bluntly?	**45**

RATCLIFFE	Bad news, my lord! Morton is fled to Richmond.	
	And Buckingham, backed with the hardy Welshmen,	
	Is in the field, and still his power increaseth!	

KING RICHARD	Ely with Richmond troubles me more near	
	Than Buckingham and his rash-levied strength.	**50**
	Come, I have learned that fearful commenting	
	Is leaden servitor to dull delay.	
	Delay leads impotent and snail-paced beggary.	
	Then fiery expedition be my wing –	
	Jove's Mercury, and herald for a king!	**55**
	Go, muster men. My counsel is my shield.	
	We must be brief when traitors brave the field!	

Exeunt.

In this scene ...

- Elizabeth, Margaret and the Duchess of York join together in mourning.
- Elizabeth and the Duchess confront and curse Richard, but when alone with him Elizabeth seems to agree to allow him to marry her daughter.
- Richard does not trust Derby and takes his son hostage.
- Messengers bring conflicting reports. Buckingham's rebellion is scattered and he has been captured, but Richmond's forces have landed in Wales. Richard sets out to fight.

Margaret tells how she has watched the downfall of her enemies, and hopes for further misfortunes to befall them. Queen Elizabeth and the Duchess mourn for their dead families, particularly the Princes in the Tower. Margaret sees the deaths as payment for her own sufferings.

1   **mellow**: ripen
3   **slily**: cunningly
4   **waning**: fading
5   **dire induction**: terrible beginning
6   **will**: will go
     the consequence: what happens next
8   **Withdraw thee**: Step back

10   **unblown flowers**: flowers that never blossomed
      sweets: sweet-smelling flowers
11   **yet**: still
12   **not ... perpetual**: not yet in heaven or hell
15   **right**: justice
16   **morn**: morning
17   **crazed**: cracked
18   **mute**: silent
19   **Edward Plantaganet**: probably the dead King Edward
20–1   **Plantaganet ... debt**: The death of one Edward (Elizabeth's son) pays for the death of another (Margaret's son)
22   **gentle lambs**: i.e. the Princes
23   **entrails**: guts
      wolf: i.e. Richard
25   **holy Harry**: King Henry VI

—**Think about**—

- Margaret speaks as if she is watching a play (lines 1 to 8). If you were the director, how could you reflect this feature of her language in the staging of the scene?

London: outside the palace.

Enter old QUEEN MARGARET.

MARGARET	So now prosperity begins to mellow
	And drop into the rotten mouth of death!
	Here in these confines slily have I lurked
	To watch the waning of mine enemies.
	A dire induction am I witness to,
	And will to France, hoping the consequence
	Will prove as bitter, black, and tragical.
	Withdraw thee, wretched Margaret. Who comes here?
	(She moves aside.)

Enter QUEEN ELIZABETH *and the old* DUCHESS OF YORK

ELIZABETH	Ah, my poor princes! Ah, my tender babes!
	My unblown flowers, new-appearing sweets!
	If yet your gentle souls fly in the air
	And be not fixed in doom perpetual,
	Hover about me with your airy wings
	And hear your mother's lamentation!

MARGARET	*(Aside)* Hover about her! Say that right for right
	Hath dimmed your infant morn to aged night.

DUCHESS	So many miseries have crazed my voice
	That my woe-wearied tongue is still and mute.
	Edward Plantagenet, why art thou dead?

MARGARET	*(Aside)* Plantagenet doth quit Plantagenet:
	Edward for Edward pays a dying debt.

ELIZABETH	Wilt thou, O God, fly from such gentle lambs
	And throw them in the entrails of the wolf?
	When didst Thou sleep when such a deed was done?

MARGARET	*(Aside)* When holy Harry died, and my sweet son!

Line numbers: 5, 10, 15, 20, 25

The three women list their sorrows. They sit down on the ground, a sign of extreme grief. Margaret blames the Duchess for giving birth to Richard. The Duchess asks Margaret for sympathy.

Think about

- What is the dramatic effect of the women's speeches here, in which they list Edwards and Richards? Look at the repetitions and echoes. What effect might this have in performance?

26 **mortal living ghost**: deathly living person (The Duchess of York is referring to herself)
27 **Woe's scene**: the stage of sadness
grave's ... usurped: i.e. almost dead but still, unfairly, alive
28 **abstract**: summary

31 **thou**: i.e the earth
afford: give space for
32 **yield**: offer
melancholy seat: i.e throne
35 **most reverend**: worthy of respect
36 **seniory**: seniority

38 **society**: company

39–43 **Tell ... him**: The dead victims are (in order): Margaret's son, Prince Edward; Margaret's husband, King Henry VI; and Elizabeth's sons, the young princes Edward and Richard.
44–5 **I ... him**: The Duchess names her husband, Richard Duke of York, and her son, Rutland, as victims, blaming Margaret.
45 **holp'st**: helped
46 **Thou**: i.e. the Duchess of York
48 **hell-hound**: i.e. Richard
50 **worry**: bite and kill
lap: drink
52 **excellent**: extreme
53 **gallèd**: painfully smarting
56 **carnal cur**: flesh-eating murderous dog
57 **Preys**: feeds
issue: children
58 **pew-fellow**: person who sits beside (as in church)
59 **Harry's wife**: i.e. Queen Margaret

DUCHESS	Dead life, blind sight, poor mortal living ghost,
	Woe's scene, world's shame, grave's due by life usurped,
	Brief abstract and record of tedious days –
	Rest thy unrest on England's lawful earth – (*She sits*
	down on the ground.)
	Unlawfully made drunk with innocent blood! **30**
ELIZABETH	Ah, that thou wouldst as soon afford a grave
	As thou canst yield a melancholy seat!
	Then would I hide my bones, not rest them here.
	Ah, who hath any cause to mourn but we? (*She sits*
	beside the DUCHESS.)
MARGARET	(*Coming forward*) If ancient sorrow be most reverend, **35**
	Give mine the benefit of seniory,
	And let my griefs frown on the upper hand.
	If sorrow can admit society, (*Sitting down with them*)
	Tell o'er your woes again by viewing mine.
	I had an Edward, till a Richard killed him; **40**
	I had a husband, till a Richard killed him.
	Thou hadst an Edward, till a Richard killed him;
	Thou hadst a Richard, till a Richard killed him.
DUCHESS	I had a Richard too, and thou didst kill him;
	I had a Rutland too: thou holp'st to kill him. **45**
MARGARET	Thou hadst a Clarence too, and Richard killed him.
	From forth the kennel of thy womb hath crept
	A hell-hound that doth hunt us all to death!
	That dog, that had his teeth before his eyes
	To worry lambs and lap their gentle blood – **50**
	That foul defacer of God's handiwork,
	That excellent grand tyrant of the earth
	That reigns in gallèd eyes of weeping souls –
	Thy womb let loose to chase us to our graves.
	O upright, just, and true-disposing God, **55**
	How do I thank Thee that this carnal cur
	Preys on the issue of his mother's body
	And makes her pew-fellow with others' moan!
DUCHESS	O Harry's wife, triumph not in my woes!
	God witness with me, I have wept for thine. **60**

Margaret enjoys her feelings of revenge. Elizabeth remembers Margaret's prediction that she would ask her to help curse Richard. Margaret compares Elizabeth's current situation with her past.

62   **cloy … beholding it**: fully satisfy myself by watching it happen

63   **Thy Edward**: the Duchess of York's son
my Edward: Queen Margaret's son

64   **Thy other Edward**: the Duchess of York's grandson
to quit my Edward: to pay for the death of Queen Margaret's son

65   **Young York**: Queen Elizabeth's son, the Duke of York
but boot: unimportant

66   **Matched not … my loss**: i.e. the deaths of the young princes do not equal the great loss I have suffered

68   **beholders**: watchers

69   **adulterate**: sexually unfaithful

71   **intelligencer**: secret agent

72   **Only … factor**: kept on earth to do the work of hell

73   **at hand**: soon

74   **Ensues piteous**: Will come his dreadful

77   **Cancel … life**: End his life

81   **bottled**: swollen
bunch-backed: hunch-backed

82   **vain flourish**: worthless decoration

84   **presentation**: mere copy

85   **index**: introduction
direful pageant: terrible spectacle

87   **mocked with**: given the illusion of

88   **garish**: very brightly coloured

91   **in jest**: joke / pretend
fill the scene: make up the numbers

93   **Wherein dost thou**: In what do you have

94   **sues**: asks favours

95   **bending**: bowing

97   **Decline**: Go carefully through

98   **For**: instead of
a … widow: i.e. what Elizabeth has become

Think about

- Margaret seems to take pleasure in the pain of others. Does she remind you of another character in the play?

MARGARET	Bear with me. I am hungry for revenge,
	And now I cloy me with beholding it.
	Thy Edward he is dead, that killed my Edward;
	Thy other Edward dead, to quit my Edward.
	Young York he is but boot, because both they
	Matched not the high perfection of my loss.
	Thy Clarence he is dead that stabbed my Edward –
	And the beholders of this frantic play,
	Th' adulterate Hastings, Rivers, Vaughan, Grey,
	Untimely smothered in their dusky graves.
	Richard yet lives, hell's black intelligencer! –
	Only reserved their factor to buy souls
	And send them thither. But at hand, at hand,
	Ensues his piteous and unpitied end.
	Earth gapes, hell burns, fiends roar, saints pray,
	To have him suddenly conveyed from hence!
	Cancel his bond of life, dear God, I pray,
	That I may live and say 'The dog is dead'!
ELIZABETH	O, thou didst prophesy the time would come
	That I should wish for thee to help me curse
	That bottled spider, that foul bunch-backed toad!
MARGARET	I called thee then vain flourish of my fortune;
	I called thee then poor shadow, painted queen,
	The presentation of but what I was,
	The flattering index of a direful pageant,
	One heaved a-high to be hurled down below,
	A mother only mocked with two fair babes,
	A dream of what thou wast, a garish flag
	To be the aim of every dangerous shot,
	A sign of dignity, a breath, a bubble,
	A queen in jest, only to fill the scene.
	Where is thy husband now? Where be thy brothers?
	Where be thy two sons? Wherein dost thou joy?
	Who sues, and kneels, and says 'God save the Queen'?
	Where be the bending peers that flattered thee?
	Where be the thronging troops that followed thee?
	Decline all this, and see what now thou art:
	For happy wife, a most distressèd widow;
	For joyful mother, one that wails the name;

Line numbers in margin: 65, 70, 75, 80, 85, 90, 95

Margaret continues her list of before-and-after comparisons and Elizabeth asks Margaret to teach her how to curse. Margaret advises her to concentrate on her sufferings.

100 **For**: instead of
101 **caitiff**: miserable wretch
102 **of**: by
103 **one**: i.e. Richard

106 **prey**: victim

109 **usurp my place**: wrongfully take my position as Queen
110 **just proportion**: rightful part
111 **burdened yoke**: heavy collar (worn by horses)
112 **here**: i.e. as I speak

114 **mischance**: disaster

118 **Forbear to**: Do not
     fast: starve through

122 **Bett'ring**: Exaggerating
     bad causer: causer of your suffering
123 **Revolving**: Thinking this over
124 **dull**: blunt
     quicken: sharpen

---Think about---

• How would you summarise Margaret's advice to Elizabeth? Do you think her words are helpful to Elizabeth?

127 **Windy attorneys**: Long-winded lawyers
128 **Airy … joys**: i.e. happiness has died without leaving a will and will only be remembered in empty words
129 **orators**: speech makers
130 **scope**: space to speak
130–1 **Though … heart**: Even though words do little except make it easier to bear troubles

	For one being sued to, one that humbly sues;	**100**
	For Queen, a very caitiff crowned with care;	
	For she that scorned at me, now scorn'd of me;	
	For she being feared of all, now fearing one;	
	For she commanding all, obeyed of none.	
	Thus hath the course of justice whirled about	**105**
	And left thee but a very prey to time,	
	Having no more but thought of what thou wast	
	To torture thee the more, being what thou art.	
	Thou didst usurp my place, and dost thou not	
	Usurp the just proportion of my sorrow?	**110**
	Now thy proud neck bears half my burdened yoke,	
	From which even here I slip my weary head	
	And leave the burden of it all on thee.	

She stands.

	Farewell, York's wife, and queen of sad mischance!	
	These English woes shall make me smile in France.	**115**
ELIZABETH	O thou well skilled in curses, stay awhile	
	And teach me how to curse mine enemies!	
MARGARET	Forbear to sleep the nights, and fast the days;	
	Compare dead happiness with living woe.	
	Think that thy babes were sweeter than they were –	**120**
	And he that slew them fouler than he is.	
	Bett'ring thy loss makes the bad causer worse.	
	Revolving this will teach thee how to curse.	
ELIZABETH	My words are dull. O, quicken them with thine!	
MARGARET	Thy woes will make them sharp and pierce like mine.	**125**

Exit.

DUCHESS	Why should calamity be full of words?	
ELIZABETH	Windy attorneys to their client woes,	
	Airy succeeders of intestate joys,	
	Poor breathing orators of miseries,	
	Let them have scope. Though what they will impart	**130**
	Help nothing else, yet do they ease the heart.	

Elizabeth and the Duchess intend to complain bitterly to Richard. When he enters, they do so. Richard tries to drown them out but the Duchess continues to demand to be heard.

135 **Be copious in exclaims**: Use many bitter exclamations

136 **expedition**: departure for war

142 **owed**: owned
143 **dire**: terrible

146 **Ned**: short for Edward

149 **flourish**: fanfare
     alarum: i.e. call to arms
151 **Rail ... anointed**: criticise God's chosen King

152 **entreat me fair**: treat me politely
153 **clamorous report**: noisy sound

Think about

- Rather than argue with the women, Richard tries to drown them out with trumpets and drums. Do you think that this suggests that he is weakening?

158 **condition**: personality
159 **brook ... reproof**: bear to be told off

DUCHESS   If so, then be not tongue-tied. Go with me,
            And in the breath of bitter words let's smother
            My damnèd son that thy two sweet sons smothered!
            The trumpet sounds! Be copious in exclaims.   135

Sounds of trumpet and drum. Enter KING RICHARD, *in armour,
marching with soldiers.*
The DUCHESS *and* QUEEN ELIZABETH *stand and confront him.*

KING RICHARD Who intercepts me in my expedition?

DUCHESS   O, she that might have intercepted thee,
            By strangling thee in her accursèd womb,
            From all the slaughters, wretch, that thou hast done!

ELIZABETH   Hid'st thou that forehead with a golden crown   140
            Where should be branded, if that right were right,
            The slaughter of the Prince that owed that crown,
            And the dire death of my poor sons and brothers?
            Tell me, thou villain slave! Where are my children?

DUCHESS   Thou toad, thou toad! – where is thy brother Clarence? 145
            And little Ned Plantagenet, his son?

ELIZABETH   Where is the gentle Rivers, Vaughan, Grey?

DUCHESS   Where is kind Hastings?

KING RICHARD A flourish, trumpets! Strike alarum, drums!
            Let not the heavens hear these tell-tale women   150
            Rail on the Lord's anointed! Strike, I say!

Trumpets sound and drums beat.

            Either be patient and entreat me fair,
            Or with the clamorous report of war
            Thus will I drown your exclamations!

DUCHESS   Art thou my son?   155

KING RICHARD Ay, I thank God, my father, and yourself.

DUCHESS   Then patiently hear my impatience.

KING RICHARD Madam, I have a touch of your condition,
            That cannot brook the accent of reproof.

DUCHESS   O, let me speak!

The Duchess says that since his birth Richard has brought her nothing but pain and suffering. She predicts that she will never see him again and curses him to defeat in battle.

163 **stayed**: waited

166 **holy rood**: the cross on which Christ was crucified

169 **Tetchy**: Bad-tempered
     wayward: wild
170 **frightful**: alarming
171 **prime**: first stage
172 **age confirmed**: full maturity
     subtle: cunning
173 **kind**: also means 'natural'
174 **comfortable**: pleasant
176 **Humphrey Hower**: This probably refers to a person or saying which is now lost or forgotten.
177 **forth of**: away from
178 **disgracious**: offensive

180 **prithee**: ask you

Think about

- Look at the Duchess's curses on Richard and think back on all the curses in the play so far. Is it significant that even Richard's mother does not have a good word for him?

184 **ordinance**: law
185 **Ere**: before
     turn: return

189 **tire**: 1 tire you out; 2 clothe (in his mother's curse as well as his armour)
191 **adverse party**: other side (i.e. Richard's enemies)

| KING RICHARD | Do, then. But I'll not hear. | **160** |

DUCHESS   I will be mild and gentle in my words.

KING RICHARD And brief, good mother – for I am in haste.

DUCHESS   Art thou so hasty? I have stayed for thee,
            God know, in torment and in agony.

KING RICHARD And came I not at last to comfort you?   **165**

DUCHESS   No, by the holy rood, thou know'st it well –
            Thou cam'st on earth to make the earth my hell!
            A grievous burden was thy birth to me.
            Tetchy and wayward was thy infancy;
            Thy school-days frightful, desperate, wild, and furious;   **170**
            Thy prime of manhood daring, bold, and venturous;
            Thy age confirmed, proud, subtle, sly, and bloody –
            More mild, but yet more harmful, kind in hatred.
            What comfortable hour canst thou name
            That ever graced me with thy company?   **175**

KING RICHARD Faith, none but Humphrey I lower, that called your
                 Grace
            To breakfast once, forth of my company.
            If I be so disgracious in your eye,
            Let me march on and not offend you, madam.
            Strike up the drum!

DUCHESS   I prithee hear me speak!   **180**

KING RICHARD You speak too bitterly.

DUCHESS   Hear me a word –
            For I shall never speak to thee again.

KING RICHARD So.

DUCHESS   Either thou wilt die by God's just ordinance
            Ere from this war thou turn a conqueror –   **185**
            Or I with grief and extreme age shall perish
            And never more behold thy face again.
            Therefore take with thee my most grievous curse! –
            Which in the day of battle tire thee more
            Than all the complete armour that thou wear'st!   **190**
            My prayers on the adverse party fight –

Elizabeth supports the Duchess's curses. She says that she will do anything to protect her daughter and blames Richard for the death of her sons.

196   **attend**: wait for

198   **Abides**: lives
        say amen to: agree with and support

203   **level**: aim

208   **Slander myself ... Edward's bed**: tell the lie that I was unfaithful to my husband, King Edward
209   **infamy**: disgrace
210   **So**: So that

216   **good ... opposite**: the stars were unfavourable
217   **ill**: evil
218   **All unavoided**: Unavoidable
        the doom of destiny: fate
219   **avoided grace**: the absence of God's grace
220   **fairer**: better
222   **cousins**: nephews

Think about

- When Richard mentions Elizabeth's daughter, she thinks he means to kill her. Is this a fair assumption?

And there the little souls of Edward's children
Whisper the spirits of thine enemies
And promise them success and victory.
Bloody thou art. Bloody will be thy end!   195
Shame serves thy life and doth thy death attend.

Exit.

ELIZABETH   Though far more cause, yet much less spirit to curse
                 Abides in me. I say amen to her.

KING RICHARD Stay, madam. I must talk a word with you.

ELIZABETH   I have no more sons of the royal blood   200
                 For thee to slaughter! For my daughters, Richard,
                 They shall be praying nuns, not weeping queens –
                 And therefore level not to hit their lives.

KING RICHARD You have a daughter called Elizabeth,
                 Virtuous and fair, royal and gracious.   205

ELIZABETH   And must she die for this? O, let her live,
                 And I'll corrupt her manners, stain her beauty,
                 Slander myself as false to Edward's bed,
                 Throw over her the veil of infamy!
                 So she may live unscarred of bleeding slaughter,   210
                 I will confess she was not Edward's daughter.

KING RICHARD Wrong not her birth. She is a royal Princess.

ELIZABETH   To save her life I'll say she is not so.

KING RICHARD Her life is safest only in her birth.

ELIZABETH   And only in that safety died her brothers.   215

KING RICHARD Lo, at their birth good stars were opposite.

ELIZABETH   No – to their lives ill friends were contrary.

KING RICHARD All unavoided is the doom of destiny.

ELIZABETH   True, when avoided grace makes destiny.
                 My babes were destined to a fairer death,   220
                 If grace had blessed *thee* with a fairer life.

KING RICHARD You speak as if that I had slain my cousins.

Elizabeth wishes she could die while attacking Richard. Richard professes his love for Princess Elizabeth.

223 **cozened**: cheated
224 **kindred**: family
225 **lanced**: pierced
226 **Thy head ... direction**: you cunningly gave the orders
228 **whetted**: sharpened
229 **revel ... entrails**: play in the guts
230 **But ... grief**: Except that continual grieving

233 **bay**: a bay at sea
234 **bark ... reft**: ship which has lost its sails and rigging

236 **thrive**: succeed
237 **success**: outcome

243 **scaffold**: place of execution

245 **type**: symbol

248 **demise**: give

250 **Will ... endow**: I will give
251 **So**: so long as
Lethe: the river of forgetfulness in classical legend

254 **process**: story
255 **than ... date**: than the kindness itself lasts

Think about

- Richard is King of England and used to commanding. Why is he trying to reason calmly with Elizabeth?

ELIZABETH	Cousins, indeed! And by their uncle cozened –
	Of comfort, kingdom, kindred, freedom, life!
	Whose hand soever lanced their tender hearts,
	Thy head, all indirectly, gave direction.
	No doubt the murderous knife was dull and blunt
	Till it was whetted on thy stone-hard heart
	To revel in the entrails of my lambs!
	But that still use of grief makes wild grief tame,
	My tongue should to thy ears not name my boys
	Till that my nails were anchored in thine eyes –
	And I, in such a desperate bay of death,
	Like a poor bark, of sails and tackling reft,
	Rush all to pieces on thy rocky bosom.

225

230

235

KING RICHARD Madam, so thrive I in my enterprise
And dangerous success of bloody wars,
As I intend more good to you or yours
Than ever you or yours by me were harmed!

ELIZABETH What good is covered with the face of heaven, 240
To be discovered, that can do me good?

KING RICHARD Th' advancement of your children, gentle lady.

ELIZABETH Up to some scaffold, there to lose their heads?

KING RICHARD Unto the dignity and height of fortune,
The high imperial type of this earth's glory! 245

ELIZABETH Flatter my sorrow with report of it.
Tell me what state, what dignity, what honour,
Canst thou demise to any child of mine?

KING RICHARD Even all I have – ay, and myself and all
Will I withal endow a child of thine – 250
So in the Lethe of thy angry soul
Thou drown the sad remembrance of those wrongs
Which thou supposest I have done to thee.

ELIZABETH Be brief, lest that the process of thy kindness
Last longer telling than thy kindness' date. 255

KING RICHARD Then know, that from my soul I love thy daughter.

ELIZABETH My daughter's mother thinks it with her soul.

Richard makes it clear that he wishes to marry Elizabeth's daughter. Elizabeth laughs at him and mocks him.

259 **'from'**: i.e. it is far 'from' your soul to love my daughter

262 **confound**: misunderstand

268 **woo her**: persuade her to marry you

269 **humour**: character

273 **haply**: perhaps
274 **sometime**: once
275 **steeped**: soaked

277 **purple sap**: blood
278 **withal**: with it
279 **inducement**: persuasion

281 **mad'st away**: murdered

283 **conveyance with**: removal of

Think about

- Look at Elizabeth's speech from line 271 to 283. What do you think of Richard's reaction to her violent sarcasm? How would you direct this moment?

KING RICHARD What do you think?

ELIZABETH   That thou dost love my daughter 'from' thy soul.
             So from thy soul's love didst thou love her brothers,   **260**
             And from my heart's love I do thank thee for it!

KING RICHARD Be not so hasty to confound my meaning.
             I mean that with my soul I love thy daughter
             And do intend to make her Queen of England.

ELIZABETH   Well, then, who dost thou mean shall be her king?   **265**

KING RICHARD Even he that makes her Queen. Who else should be?

ELIZABETH   What, *thou*?

KING RICHARD   Even so. How think you of it?

ELIZABETH   How canst *thou* woo her?

KING RICHARD   That would I learn of you,
             As one being best acquainted with her humour.

ELIZABETH   And wilt thou learn of me?

KING RICHARD   Madam, with all my heart.   **270**

ELIZABETH   Send to her, by the man that slew her brothers,
             A pair of bleeding hearts. Thereon engrave
             'Edward' and 'York'. Then haply will she weep.
             Therefore present to her – as sometime Margaret
             Did to thy father, steeped in Rutland's blood –   **275**
             A handkerchief: which, say to her, did drain
             The purple sap from her sweet brother's body,
             And bid her wipe her weeping eyes withal.
             If this inducement move her not to love,
             Send her a letter of thy noble deeds.   **280**
             Tell her thou mad'st away her uncle Clarence,
             Her uncle Rivers – ay, and for her sake
             Mad'st quick conveyance with her good aunt Anne.

KING RICHARD You mock me, madam. This is not the way
             To win your daughter.

ELIZABETH   There is no other way –   **285**
             Unless thou couldst put on some other shape
             And not be Richard that hath done all this!

Richard promises that the marriage will be compensation for all his crimes. He gives details of all the good that will come to Elizabeth and her family after the marriage, and asks her to prepare her daughter for his attentions.

290 **spoil**: destruction

291 **amended**: put right

292 **deal unadvisedly**: act thoughtlessly

293 **after-hours gives leisure**: afterwards have time

296 **issue**: children

297 **quicken your increase**: expand your family

297–8 **beget ... issue**: father more children

299 **grandam**: grandmother

300 **doting**: tender and loving

301 **They**: i.e. Grandchildren

302 **your metal**: the same substance as you

303 **Of ... pain**: cause the same amount of pain

save ... groans: i.e. except for the time it takes to give birth

304 **of**: by

bid like sorrow: suffered similar pain

305 **vexation**: worry and annoyance

307 **but**: only not having

309 **amends**: compensation

310 **I can**: I can give

312 **Leads discontented steps**: is exiled and unhappy

316 **Familiarly**: as part of the family

317 **mother**: mother-in-law

319 **content**: happiness

322 **orient**: shining

323 **Advantaging**: increasing

Think about

- Richard is trying very hard to be persuasive, but can his words overcome past events?

- How should Elizabeth be reacting to Richard during this long speech?

KING RICHARD Say that I did all this for love of her.

ELIZABETH Nay, then indeed she cannot choose but hate thee,
Having bought love with such a bloody spoil! 290

KING RICHARD Look what is done cannot be now amended!
Men shall deal unadvisedly sometimes,
Which after-hours gives leisure to repent.
If I did take the kingdom from your sons,
To make amends I'll give it to your daughter. 295
If I have killed the issue of your womb,
To quicken your increase I will beget
Mine issue of your blood upon your daughter.
A grandam's name is little less in love
Than is the doting title of a mother. 300
They are as children but one step below,
Even of your metal, of your very blood –
Of all one pain, save for a night of groans
Endured of her, for whom you bid like sorrow.
Your children were vexation to your youth; 305
But mine shall be a comfort to your age.
The loss you have is but a son being King,
And by that loss your daughter is made Queen.
I cannot make you what amends I would,
Therefore accept such kindness as I can. 310
Dorset your son, that with a fearful soul
Leads discontented steps in foreign soil,
This fair alliance quickly shall call home
To high promotions and great dignity.
The King, that calls your beauteous daughter wife, 315
Familiarly shall call thy Dorset brother.
Again shall you be mother to a king,
And all the ruins of distressful times
Repaired with double riches of content.
What! We have many goodly days to see! 320
The liquid drops of tears that you have shed
Shall come again, transformed to orient pearl,
Advantaging their loan with interest
Of ten times double gain of happiness!
Go, then, my mother – to thy daughter go. 325
Make bold her bashful years with your experience.
Prepare her ears to hear a wooer's tale.

Richard says that he will marry
Elizabeth after defeating
Buckingham. Elizabeth
continues to mock Richard's
marriage plans and has an
answer for every point he tries
to make in his favour.

328 aspiring flame: ambitious hope

331 chastisèd: punished
332 petty: insignificant
333 triumphant garlands: signs of victory
(Roman military heroes wore wreaths
of laurel in victory processions.)
335 retail: retell
336 Caesar's Caesar: i.e. ruler over Richard

343 Infer: Suggest

345 entreats: begs
346 King's King: i.e. God (who forbids
marriage between uncle and niece as
incest)
348 wail: lament

---Think about

• Contrast the quick
exchanges here with
Richard's previous long
speech (lines 291 to 336).
Who is in control?

358 speeds: succeeds

Put in her tender heart th' aspiring flame
Of golden sovereignty! Acquaint the Princess
With the sweet silent hours of marriage joys.   330
And when this arm of mine hath chastisèd
The petty rebel, dull-brained Buckingham,
Bound with triumphant garlands will I come,
And lead thy daughter to a conqueror's bed –
To whom I will retail my conquest won,   335
And she shall be sole victoress, Caesar's Caesar!

ELIZABETH   What were I best to say? Her father's brother
Would be her lord? Or shall I say her uncle?
Or he that slew her brothers and her uncles?
Under what title shall I woo for thee   340
That God, the law, my honour, and her love
Can make seem pleasing to her tender years?

KING RICHARD Infer fair England's peace by this alliance.

ELIZABETH   Which she shall purchase with still lasting war!

KING RICHARD Tell her the King, that may command, entreats.   345

ELIZABETH   That at her hands which the King's King forbids!

KING RICHARD Say she shall be a high and mighty queen.

ELIZABETH   To wail the title, as her mother doth!

KING RICHARD Say I will love her everlastingly.

ELIZABETH   But how long shall that title 'ever' last?   350

KING RICHARD Sweetly in force unto her fair life's end.

ELIZABETH   But how long fairly shall her sweet life last?

KING RICHARD As long as heaven and nature lengthens it.

ELIZABETH   As long as hell and Richard likes of it!

KING RICHARD Say I, her sovereign, am her subject low.   355

ELIZABETH   But she, your subject, loathes such sovereignty.

KING RICHARD Be eloquent in my behalf to her.

ELIZABETH   An honest tale speeds best being plainly told.

KING RICHARD Then plainly to her tell my loving tale.

Elizabeth will not allow Richard
to swear he is telling the truth.

364 Harp … string: Don't keep returning to
that subject
365 heartstrings: tendons of the heart (i.e.
till my heart breaks)
366 George … garter: symbols of
England's highest order of knighthood
367 Profaned: Dirtied / devalued
usurped: wrongfully taken

370 pawned: given up

─ **Think about** ─
• Elizabeth completes many
of Richard's lines. How
might you direct this scene
to emphasise that it is
increasingly she who seems
in charge?

• Until this point Richard has
killed all those he sees as a
threat. What do you think
has enabled Elizabeth to be
so bold in challenging him?

379 unity: reconciliation (a reference to
King Edward IV's attempts at
peacemaking in Act 2 Scene 1)
382 imperial metal: the crown

385 bedfellows: sleeping companions
386 prey: victims

ELIZABETH	Plain and not honest is too harsh a style.	**360**

KING RICHARD Your reasons are too shallow and too quick.

ELIZABETH O, no, my reasons are too deep and dead –
Too deep and dead, poor infants, in their graves!

KING RICHARD Harp not on that string, madam. That is past.

ELIZABETH	Harp on it still shall I till heartstrings break!	**365**

KING RICHARD Now, by my George, my garter, and my crown –

ELIZABETH Profaned, dishonoured, and the third usurped.

KING RICHARD I swear –

ELIZABETH	By nothing – for this is no oath.	
	Thy George, profaned, hath lost his holy honour;	
	Thy garter, blemished, pawned his knightly virtue;	**370**
	Thy crown, usurped, disgraced his kingly glory.	

If something thou wouldst swear to be believed,
Swear then by something that thou hast not wronged.

KING RICHARD Then, by my self –

ELIZABETH   Thy self is self-misused.

KING RICHARD Now, by the world –

ELIZABETH	'Tis full of thy foul wrongs.	**375**

KING RICHARD My father's death –

ELIZABETH   Thy life hath it dishonoured.

KING RICHARD Why, then, by God –

ELIZABETH	God's wrong is most of all!	
	If thou didst fear to break an oath with Him,	
	The unity the King my husband made	
	Thou hadst not broken, nor my brothers died.	**380**
	If thou hadst feared to break an oath by Him,	
	Th' imperial metal, circling now thy head,	
	Had graced the tender temples of my child!	
	And both the Princes had been breathing here,	
	Which now, two tender bedfellows for dust,	**385**
	Thy broken faith hath made the prey for worms!	
	What canst thou swear by now?	

Richard says that he will be a reformed character if he wins in battle and that England will be destroyed if he cannot marry Elizabeth's daughter.

Think about

- Richard finally seems to win over Elizabeth. Do you think she has really been persuaded to agree to his idea?

- Look closely at the language of force, threat and destruction Richard uses in his speech (lines 397 to 417). What do you think it shows about Richard's state of mind at this point?

388 **time o'erpast**: past

390 **Hereafter time**: the future

392 **Ungoverned**: fatherless

395–6 **Swear not ... o'erpast**: Do not swear by the future, for you ruined that hope before it came by your evil in the past

398 **thrive I**: may I succeed
399 **Myself myself confound**: May I destroy myself
400 **bar**: deny

403 **proceeding**: successful action
404 **Immaculate**: perfect
405 **tender**: feel tenderly for

410 **but**: except

413 **attorney**: representative
414 **Plead**: Put my case for

416 **Urge ... times**: Use the difficult political situation as a reason
417 **peevish-fond ... designs**: childish in spoiling great plans

420 **myself to be myself**: i.e. all that has happened to me in the past in order to become the mother to a king again
421 **Ay ... wrong yourself**: Yes, if your memory of the past damages you in the present

KING RICHARD	The time to come.	

ELIZABETH	That thou hast wrongèd in the time o'erpast –	
	For I myself have many tears to wash	
	Hereafter time, for time past wronged by thee.	390
	The children live whose fathers thou hast slaughtered,	
	Ungoverned youth, to wail it in their age.	
	The parents live whose children thou hast butchered,	
	Old barren plants, to wail it with their age.	
	Swear not by time to come – for that thou hast	395
	Misused ere used, by times ill-used o'erpast.	

KING RICHARD	As I intend to prosper and repent,	
	So thrive I in my dangerous affairs	
	Of hostile arms! Myself myself confound!	
	Heaven and fortune bar me happy hours!	400
	Day, yield me not thy light; nor, night, thy rest!	
	Be opposite all planets of good luck	
	To my proceeding! – if, with dear heart's love,	
	Immaculate devotion, holy thoughts,	
	I tender not thy beauteous princely daughter.	405
	In her consists my happiness and thine.	
	Without her, follows to myself and thee,	
	Herself, the land, and many a Christian soul,	
	Death, desolation, ruin, and decay.	
	It cannot be avoided but by this.	410
	It *will* not be avoided but by this!	
	Therefore, dear mother – I must call you so –	
	Be the attorney of my love to her.	
	Plead what I will be, not what I have been –	
	Not my deserts, but what I will deserve.	415
	Urge the necessity and state of times,	
	And be not peevish-fond in great designs.	

| ELIZABETH | Shall I be tempted of the devil thus? | |

| KING RICHARD | Ay, if the devil tempt you to do good. | |

| ELIZABETH | Shall I forget myself to be myself? | 420 |

| KING RICHARD | Ay, if your self's remembrance wrong yourself. | |

| ELIZABETH | Yet thou didst kill my children. | |

Elizabeth finally says that she will go to her daughter and will report to Richard later. Ratcliffe brings news of an invasion and says that Richard's soldiers are not reliable. Catesby is sent on an urgent errand to the Duke of Norfolk.

424 nest of spicery: a reference to the nest of the phoenix, a magical bird which is born again from its own ashes
425 recomforture: renewed happiness

431 Relenting: Forgiving

434 puissant: powerful
435 doubtful: unreliable
 hollow-hearted: cowardly

438 hull: wait
 expecting but: only waiting for

440 light-foot: fast
 post: go quickly

Think about

• Look at line 431. Does this accurately express Richard's feelings towards women in general?

• What is Richard's state of mind when he hears the news about Richmond? Think about his short-tempered treatment of Catesby.

447 liege: lord

KING RICHARD But in your daughter's womb I bury them –
　　　　　　　Where, in that nest of spicery, they will breed
　　　　　　　Selves of themselves, to your recomforture.　　　　425

ELIZABETH　　Shall I go win my daughter to thy will?

KING RICHARD And be a happy mother by the deed.

ELIZABETH　　I go. Write to me very shortly,
　　　　　　　And you shall understand from me her mind.

KING RICHARD Bear her my true love's kiss *(Kissing her)*
　　　　　　　– and so, farewell.　　　　　　　　　　　　430

　　　　　　　　　　　　　　　Exit QUEEN ELIZABETH.

　　　　　　　Relenting fool, and shallow, changing woman!

　　　Enter RATCLIFFE, *with* CATESBY *following.*

　　　　　　　How now? What news?

RATCLIFFE　　Most mighty sovereign, on the western coast
　　　　　　　Rideth a puissant navy. To our shores
　　　　　　　Throng many doubtful hollow-hearted friends,　　435
　　　　　　　Unarmed, and unresolved to beat them back.
　　　　　　　'Tis thought that Richmond is their admiral;
　　　　　　　And there they hull, expecting but the aid
　　　　　　　Of Buckingham to welcome them ashore.

KING RICHARD Some light-foot friend post to the Duke of Norfolk.　440
　　　　　　　Ratcliffe, thyself – or Catesby. Where is he?

CATESBY　　　Here, my good lord.

KING RICHARD　　　　　　　　　　　　Catesby, fly to the Duke.

CATESBY　　　I will, my lord, with all convenient haste.

KING RICHARD Ratcliffe, come hither. Post to Salisbury.
　　　　　　　When thou com'st thither – *(To* CATESBY*)* Dull,
　　　　　　　　unmindful villain!　　　　　　　　　　　445
　　　　　　　Why stay'st thou here, and go'st not to the Duke?

CATESBY　　　First, mighty liege, tell me your Highness' pleasure,
　　　　　　　What from your Grace I shall deliver to him.

Richard seems confused in his orders to Catesby and Ratcliffe. Derby brings more news of Richmond's approach to claim the crown.

449 **levy straight**: gather (troops) immediately

450 **make**: assemble

451 **suddenly**: as quickly as possible

455 **post before**: go in advance

459 **Hoyday**: an exclamation of impatience

461 **nearest**: simplest

464 **White-livered runagate**: Cowardly rebel

Think about

• How does the way that Richard speaks and behaves suggest that he is losing control?

469 **chair**: throne
    unswayed: not in use

470 **empire unpossessed**: kingdom unruled

473 **makes he**: is he doing

474 **Unless**: Except

KING RICHARD O, true, good Catesby. Bid him levy straight
The greatest strength and power that he can make   450
And meet me suddenly at Salisbury.

CATESBY   I go.

Exit.

RATCLIFFE   What, may it please you, shall I do at Salisbury?

KING RICHARD Why, what wouldst thou do there before I go?

RATCLIFFE   Your Highness told me I should post before.   455

KING RICHARD My mind is changed.

Enter DERBY.

Stanley, what news with you?

DERBY   None good, my liege, to please you with the hearing –
Nor none so bad but well may be reported.

KING RICHARD Hoyday, a riddle! Neither good nor bad!
What need'st thou run so many miles about   460
When thou mayst tell thy tale the nearest way?
Once more, what news?

DERBY   Richmond is on the seas.

KING RICHARD There let him sink, and be the seas on him!
White-livered runagate! What doth he there?

DERBY   I know not, mighty sovereign, but by guess.   465

KING RICHARD Well, as you guess?

DERBY   Stirred up by Dorset, Buckingham, and Morton,
He makes for England here to claim the crown.

KING RICHARD Is the chair empty? Is the sword unswayed?
Is the King dead? The empire unpossessed?   470
What heir of York is there alive but we?
And who is England's King but great York's heir?
Then tell me what makes he upon the seas!

DERBY   Unless for that, my liege, I cannot guess.

Richard makes it clear that he does not trust Derby and orders that his son be kept as a hostage. A messenger brings news of more support for Richmond.

476 **wherefore**: why
     the Welshman: i.e. Richmond

479 **power**: army

482 **Safe-conducting**: helping

488 **muster up**: gather

Think about

- Where do Derby's loyalties lie? Is Richard right to be suspicious of him?

- We do not know George Stanley's age, but he is made to sound young (in an early scene in the McKellen film, George sits on his father's knee). How might an audience react to the fact that Richard has another child under his control?

495–6 **Look … frail**: i.e. Stay loyal or I will cut off his head

499 **advertisèd**: informed
500 **haughty prelate**: proud priest

502 **confederates**: allies

KING RICHARD Unless for that he comes to be *your* liege,   475
You cannot guess wherefore the Welshman comes.
Thou wilt revolt and fly to him, I fear.

DERBY No, my good lord! Therefore mistrust me not.

KING RICHARD Where is thy power then, to beat him back?
Where be thy tenants and thy followers?   480
Are they not now upon the western shore,
Safe-conducting the rebels from their ships?

DERBY No, my good lord! My friends are in the north.

KING RICHARD Cold friends to me! What do they in the north,
When they should serve their sovereign in the west?   485

DERBY They have not been commanded, mighty King.
Pleaseth your Majesty to give me leave,
I'll muster up my friends and meet your Grace
Where and what time your Majesty shall please.

KING RICHARD Ay, ay, thou wouldst be gone, to join with Richmond.   490
But I'll not trust thee.

DERBY   Most mighty sovereign,
You have no cause to hold my friendship doubtful.
I never was nor never will be false.

KING RICHARD Go, then, and muster men. But leave behind
Your son, George Stanley. Look your heart be firm,   495
Or else his head's assurance is but frail!

DERBY So deal with him as I prove true to you.

                                                        Exit.

Enter a MESSENGER.

MESSENGER My gracious sovereign, now in Devonshire,
As I by friends am well advertisèd,
Sir Edward Courtney and the haughty prelate,   500
Bishop of Exeter, his elder brother,
With many more confederates, are in arms.

Messengers report that
Buckingham's army has broken
up and dispersed and that
Richmond's ships have been
scattered by a storm.

504   competitors: allies

507   owls: The cries of owls were supposed
to predict death.

513   whither: where
cry thee mercy: beg your pardon

515   well-advisèd: sensible

Think about

- What does Richard's hitting
  of the messenger tell us?
  Think about what it might
  show about Richard's state
  of mind.

- The pace of the scene gets
  faster as it comes to an end.
  How might a production
  emphasise the increased
  speed and tension?

521   Breton: from Brittany (i.e. Richmond's
men)

524   his assistants: on his side

526   Upon his party: to join his side

Enter a second MESSENGER.

MESSENGER 2   In Kent, my liege, the Guilfords are in arms –
    And every hour more competitors
    Flock to the rebels, and their power grows strong.   **505**

Enter a third MESSENGER.

MESSENGER 3   My lord, the army of great Buckingham –

KING RICHARD Out on you, owls! Nothing but songs of death?

He strikes him.

    There, take thou that till thou bring better news!

MESSENGER 3   The news I have to tell your Majesty
    Is that by sudden floods and fall of waters   **510**
    Buckingham's army is dispersed and scattered;
    And he himself wandered away alone,
    No man knows whither.

KING RICHARD   I cry thee mercy!
    There is my purse to cure that blow of thine.
    Hath any well-advisèd friend proclaimed   **515**
    Reward to him that brings the traitor in?

MESSENGER 3   Such proclamation hath been made, my lord.

Enter a fourth MESSENGER.

MESSENGER 4   Sir Thomas Lovell and Lord Marquis Dorset,
    'Tis said, my liege, in Yorkshire are in arms.
    But this good comfort bring I to your Highness –   **520**
    The Breton navy is dispersed by tempest.
    Richmond in Dorsetshire sent out a boat
    Unto the shore, to ask those on the banks
    If they were his assistants, yea or no;
    Who answered him they came from Buckingham   **525**
    Upon his party. He, mistrusting them,
    Hoist sail, and made his course again for Brittany.

KING RICHARD March on, march on, since we are up in arms!
    If not to fight with foreign enemies,
    Yet to beat down these rebels here at home!   **530**

Catesby brings news that Buckingham has been captured and that Richmond and his army have landed. Richard orders that Buckingham be brought to him, and departs.

533 **Milford**: Milford Haven, in Wales
534 **tidings**: news

535 **reason**: talk

Think about

- How might you describe Richard's mood as this scene ends with both good and bad news? In what different ways might an actor play Richard at this point?

Re-enter CATESBY.

CATESBY   My liege, the Duke of Buckingham is taken –
                 That is the best news. That the Earl of Richmond
                 Is with a mighty power landed at Milford
                 Is colder tidings, but yet they must be told.

KING RICHARD Away towards Salisbury! While we reason here   535
                 A royal battle might be won and lost.
                 Some one take order Buckingham be brought
                 To Salisbury. The rest march on with me!

Trumpet sounds: drums beat again.

Exeunt.

In this scene ...

- Derby reveals that Elizabeth has agreed to allow Richmond to marry her daughter, and Urswick tells of all the noblemen who are joining Richmond.
- Derby cannot openly support Richmond, as Richard has taken his son hostage, but sends Urswick to Richmond with a secret message of support.

2   **deadly boar**: i.e. Richard
3   **franked up in hold**: imprisoned

5   **holds ... aid**: stops me sending immediate help
6   **Commend me**: Give my best wishes
7   **Withal**: Also
8   **espouse**: marry

10   **Ha'rfordwest**: Haverfordwest

11   **men ... resort to**: honourable and important men join

14   **redoubted**: brave and feared
15   **Rice ap Thomas**: an important Welsh lord
17   **bend their power**: direct their army
18   **by the way**: on the way

19   **hie ... lord**: hurry back to Richmond
20   **resolve ... mind:** tell him what I plan to do

Think about

- Look back at lines 426 to 430 of Act 4 Scene 4 where Elizabeth apparently agreed to marry her daughter to Richard. Here we learn that she is to marry Richmond. Is this a surprise, or do you think Elizabeth had planned it all along?

The house of Lord Stanley, Earl of Derby.

Enter DERBY, *with Sir Christopher* URSWICK, *a priest.*

DERBY	Sir Christopher, tell Richmond this from me:
	That in the sty of the most deadly boar
	My son George Stanley is franked up in hold.
	If I revolt, off goes young George's head.
	The fear of that holds off my present aid. 5
	So, get thee gone. Commend me to thy lord.
	Withal say that the Queen hath heartily consented
	He should espouse Elizabeth her daughter.
	But tell me, where is princely Richmond now?
URSWICK	At Pembroke, or at Ha'rfordwest, in Wales. 10
DERBY	What men of name resort to him?
URSWICK	Sir Walter Herbert, a renownèd soldier;
	Sir Gilbert Talbot, Sir William Stanley,
	Oxford, redoubted Pembroke, Sir James Blunt,
	And Rice ap Thomas, with a valiant crew; 15
	And many other of great name and worth –
	And towards London do they bend their power,
	If by the way they be not fought withal.
DERBY	Well, hie thee to thy lord. I kiss his hand.
	My letter will resolve him of my mind. 20
	Farewell.

Exeunt.

In this scene ...

- The captured Buckingham wants to speak to Richard, but is led away to execution.
- Before he dies Buckingham remembers his crimes and the curses laid upon him.

4 **Holy King Henry**: King Henry VI
thy: i.e. King Henry's
5 **miscarried**: been killed
7 **moody**: angry

10 **All Soul's day**: 2nd November, a special day of prayer for the dead

12 **my body's doomsday**: day I face death and God's judgement

16 **wherein**: on which

19 **determined ... wrongs**: the chosen time, delayed until now, for the punishment of my crimes
20 **All-Seer**: God
dallied with: played with
21 **feignèd**: false
22 **in earnest**: seriously
in jest: as a joke
24 **bosoms**: hearts
28 **block of shame**: beheading block

---Think about ---

- Buckingham was an important contributor to Richard's evil plots, but he also remained faithful to Richard until Richard wanted him to kill the princes and until denied the rewards he had been promised. Do you think he deserves to be executed?

- In what different ways could Buckingham's exit to his execution be staged?

ACT 5   SCENE 1

Salisbury.

Enter the SHERIFF *of Wiltshire, with guards, leading* BUCKINGHAM *to his execution.*

BUCKINGHAM	Will not King Richard let me speak with him?
SHERIFF	No, my good lord. Therefore be patient.
BUCKINGHAM	Hastings, and Edward's children, Grey, and Rivers,
	Holy King Henry, and thy fair son Edward,
	Vaughan, and all that have miscarried

5

	By underhand corrupted foul injustice,
	If that your moody discontented souls
	Do through the clouds behold this present hour,
	Even for revenge mock my destruction!
	This is All Souls' day, fellow, is it not?

10

SHERIFF	It is, my lord.
BUCKINGHAM	Why, then All Souls' day is my body's doomsday.
	This is the day which, in King Edward's time,
	I wished might fall on me when I was found
	False to his children and his wife's allies.

15

	This is the day wherein I wished to fall
	By the false faith of him whom most I trusted.
	This, this All Souls' day to my fearful soul
	Is the determined respite of my wrongs.
	That high All-Seer which I dallied with

20

	Hath turned my feignèd prayer on my head,
	And given in earnest what I begged in jest.
	Thus doth He force the swords of wicked men
	To turn their own points in their masters' bosoms.
	Thus Margaret's curse falls heavy on my neck.

25

	'When he' quoth she 'shall split thy heart with sorrow,
	Remember Margaret was a prophetess!'
	Come lead me, officers, to the block of shame!
	Wrong hath but wrong, and blame the due of blame.

Exeunt.

In this scene ...

- Richmond receives Derby's letter of support. He is confident of defeating Richard and bringing peace to England.
- Richmond's army marches towards Richard's forces.

2 **yoke**: burden
3 **bowels**: central part
4 **impediment**: obstacle
5 **father**: i.e. stepfather
6 **Lines**: a letter
7 **usurping**: wrongfully crowned
   boar: i.e. Richard
9 **Swills**: greedily drinks
   wash: pig food
10 **embowelled bosoms**: disembowelled bodies

14 **cheerly**: cheerfully
15 **perpetual**: everlasting

18 **homicide**: murderer

19 **doubt not but**: am sure that

21 **dearest**: greatest

22 **vantage**: advantage

24 **meaner**: less important

Think about

- Look at the images of the natural world in Richmond's speech (lines 1 to 16). How have such images been used before in the play?

- This is the first time we have seen Richmond. What are your impressions of him?

Act 5   Scene 2

Camp of Richmond's forces near Tamworth (Staffordshire).
A drum beats: soldiers carry Richmond's banner. Enter the
Earl of RICHMOND, *with the Earl of* OXFORD, *Sir James* BLUNT,
Sir Walter HERBERT, *and others.*

RICHMOND   Fellows in arms, and my most loving friends,
    Bruised underneath the yoke of tyranny:
    Thus far into the bowels of the land
    Have we marched on without impediment –
    And here receive we from our father Stanley   5
    Lines of fair comfort and encouragement.
    The wretched, bloody, and usurping boar,
    That spoiled your summer fields and fruitful vines,
    Swills your warm blood like wash, and makes his trough
    In your embowelled bosoms – this foul swine   10
    Is now even in the centre of this isle,
    Near to the town of Leicester, as we learn.
    From Tamworth thither is but one day's march.
    In God's name cheerly on, courageous friends! –
    To reap the harvest of perpetual peace   15
    By this one bloody trial of sharp war.

OXFORD   Every man's conscience is a thousand men,
    To fight against this guilty homicide.

HERBERT   I doubt not but his friends will turn to us.

BLUNT   He hath no friends but what are friends for fear,   20
    Which in his dearest need will fly from him.

RICHMOND   All for our vantage. Then in God's name march!
    True hope is swift and flies with swallow's wings:
    Kings it makes gods, and meaner creatures kings!

                                      Exeunt.

In this scene ...

- Richard and Richmond place their armies on opposite sides of Bosworth Field.
- Richard and Richmond sleep in their tents, and both are visited by the ghosts of Richard's victims.
- The ghosts curse and condemn Richard and encourage Richmond, making Richard fearful and Richmond full of hope.
- Richmond and Richard prepare for battle, both making speeches to their men.
- Derby refuses to bring his troops to support Richard.

Richard sets up camp and says that his army is three times the size of Richmond's. He begins to make plans for battle.

5 **have knocks**: suffer blows

8 **all's ... that**: that does not matter
9 **descried**: counted

Think about

- The rest of the scene moves quickly between the two camps. How could this be staged to ensure that the action moves clearly and quickly?

11 **battalia**: army
    account: number
13 **adverse faction**: other side
    want: haven't got
15 **vantage**: advantage
16 **sound direction**: skilled military tactics and leadership

Bosworth Field (Leicestershire).

Enter KING RICHARD, *in armour, with the Duke of* NORFOLK, *the*
Earl OF SURREY, RATCLIFFE, *and others.*

KING RICHARD Here pitch our tent, even here in Bosworth field.

> *Soldiers bring King Richard's tent, to be set up at one side of*
> *the field (stage).*

My Lord of Surrey, why look you so sad?

SURREY My heart is ten times lighter than my looks.

KING RICHARD My Lord of Norfolk!

NORFOLK   Here, most gracious liege.

KING RICHARD Norfolk, we must have knocks – ha, must we not?   5

NORFOLK We must both give and take, my loving lord.

KING RICHARD Up with my tent! Here will I lie tonight.

> *Soldiers set up the tent. King Richard's banner is set up*
> *beside it.*

But where tomorrow? Well, all's one for that.
Who hath descried the number of the traitors?

NORFOLK Six or seven thousand is their utmost power.   10

KING RICHARD Why, our battalia trebles that account!
Besides, the King's name is a tower of strength,
Which they upon the adverse faction want.
Up with the tent! Come, noble gentlemen,
Let us survey the vantage of the ground.   15
Call for some men of sound direction.
Let's lack no discipline, make no delay –
For, lords, tomorrow is a busy day!

Exeunt.

Richmond enters and sets up his camp. Richmond plans his battle tactics and asks Blunt to take an important message to Derby.

20 **tract**: track
   car: chariot
22 **standard**: flag

24 **form and model**: shape
25 **Limit ... charge**: appoint particular command
26 **part ... proportion**: carefully divide and deploy
   power: army
29 **keeps**: stays with

34 **quartered**: camped

35 **colours**: flag / banner

40 **make ... means**: try your best
41 **needful**: important / necessary

Think about

• What do you think might be in the note Richmond sends to Derby?

Enter, to the other side of the field (stage), RICHMOND,
OXFORD, HERBERT, BLUNT, *Sir William* BRANDON, *and others.*
Soldiers bring Richmond's tent and set it up, with his banner,
across the field (stage) from King Richard's.

RICHMOND	The weary sun hath made a golden set,
	And by the bright tract of his fiery car **20**
	Gives token of a goodly day tomorrow.
	Sir William Brandon, you shall bear my standard.
	Give me some ink and paper in my tent.
	I'll draw the form and model of our battle,
	Limit each leader to his several charge, **25**
	And part in just proportion our small power.
	My Lord of Oxford – you, Sir William Brandon –
	And you, Sir Walter Herbert – stay with me.
	The Earl of Pembroke keeps his regiment.
	Good Captain Blunt, bear my good night to him, **30**
	And by the second hour in the morning
	Desire the Earl to see me in my tent.
	Yet one thing more, good Captain, do for me –
	Where is Lord Stanley quartered, do you know?
BLUNT	Unless I have mista'en his colours much – **35**
	Which well I am assured I have not done –
	His regiment lies half a mile at least
	South from the mighty power of the King.
RICHMOND	If without peril it be possible,
	Sweet Blunt, make some good means to speak with him **40**
	And give him from me this most needful note.
BLUNT	Upon my life, my lord, I'll undertake it.
	And so, God give you quiet rest tonight!
RICHMOND	Good night, good Captain Blunt. Come, gentlemen,
	Let us consult upon tomorrow's business. **45**
	Into my tent: the dew is raw and cold.

Exit BLUNT.

RICHMOND *and the others withdraw into his tent.*
A soldier remains as guard.

Richard checks that he is ready for battle. He sends a message to Derby to be ready with his forces before dawn, threatening to kill his son otherwise.

47 **is't o'clock**: time is it

50 **beaver**: helmet
easier: more comfortable

53 **hie thee**: hurry
charge: post
54 **sentinels**: guards

56 **Stir ... lark**: Get up by dawn

57 **warrant**: guarantee

59 **pursuivant-at-arms**: military messenger
60 **power**: troops
61–2 **lest ... night**: i.e. otherwise his son will be killed

63 **watch**: 1 a bodyguard; or 2 a watch-candle (with which to tell the time)
64 **white Surrey**: a particular horse
65 **staves**: spears

68 **melancholy**: sad and gloomy

70 **cock-shut time**: twilight

Think about

- In the past Richard's words have been enough to give him confidence. Is there anything about his behaviour that tells us that he is not so confident now?

- How would you direct the battle preparation scenes to show similarities and differences in the two camps?

Enter, on the other side, KING RICHARD, NORFOLK, RATCLIFFE *and* CATESBY, *with soldiers.*

KING RICHARD What is't o'clock?

CATESBY   It's supper-time, my lord;
                    It's nine o'clock.

KING RICHARD   I will not sup tonight.
                    Give me some ink and paper.
                    What, is my beaver easier than it was   50
                    And all my armour laid into my tent?

CATESBY   It is, my liege; and all things are in readiness.

KING RICHARD Good Norfolk, hie thee to thy charge.
                    Use careful watch, choose trusty sentinels.

NORFOLK   I go, my lord.   55

KING RICHARD Stir with the lark tomorrow, gentle Norfolk.

NORFOLK   I warrant you, my lord.

                                                               Exit.

KING RICHARD Catesby!

CATESBY   My lord?

KING RICHARD   Send out a pursuivant-at-arms
                    To Stanley's regiment. Bid him bring his power   60
                    Before sunrising, lest his son George fall
                    Into the blind cave of eternal night.

                                                    Exit CATESBY.

                    Fill me a bowl of wine. Give me a watch.
                    Saddle white Surrey for the field tomorrow.
                    Look that my staves be sound, and not too heavy.   65
                    Ratcliffe!

RATCLIFFE   My lord?

KING RICHARD Saw'st thou the melancholy Lord Northumberland?

RATCLIFFE   Thomas the Earl of Surrey and himself,
                    Much about cock-shut time, from troop to troop   70
                    Went through the army, cheering up the soldiers.

Richard orders wine and complains that his normal good mood has gone. Derby promises to help Richmond in battle as far as it is possible, as his son George is still at risk.

73   **alacrity**: liveliness
74   **wont**: accustomed

79   **helm**: helmet

81   **father-in-law**: stepfather

83   **by attorney**: on her behalf

86   **flaky**: flecked with the light of dawn

88   **battle**: soldiers
89   **arbitrement**: test
90   **mortal-staring**: 1 able to kill with a look; 2 looking at the face of death
91   **that ... would**: what I would like to do
92   **With best ... time**: at the best opportunity will deceive expectations
93   **doubtful shock**: uncertain clash
94   **forward**: obvious
95   **brother**: i.e. George Stanley, Richmond's stepbrother
       tender: young
97   **leisure**: available time
99   **ample ... discourse**: full and pleasant conversation
100   **sundered**: separated
101   **leisure**: time
102   **speed**: succeed

Think about

- What are the particular signs that Richmond has goodness and right on his side?

- How do the preparations for battle of Richard and Richmond differ?

KING RICHARD So, I am satisfied. Give me a bowl of wine.
I have not that alacrity of spirit
Nor cheer of mind that I was wont to have.
Set it down. Is ink and paper ready?   **75**

RATCLIFFE It is, my lord.

KING RICHARD   Bid my guard watch. Leave me.
Ratcliffe, about the mid of night come to my tent
And help to arm me. Leave me, I say.

Exit RATCLIFFE, *with soldiers.*

RICHARD *lies down to sleep in his tent.*

Enter DERBY *on the other side, to Richmond's tent.*

DERBY (*To* RICHMOND) Fortune and victory sit on thy helm!

RICHMOND All comfort that the dark night can afford   **80**
Be to thy person, noble father-in-law!
Tell me, how fares our loving mother?

DERBY I, by attorney, bless thee from thy mother,
Who prays continually for Richmond's good.
So much for that. The silent hours steal on,   **85**
And flaky darkness breaks within the east.
In brief, for so the season bids us be,
Prepare thy battle early in the morning,
And put thy fortune to th' arbitrement
Of bloody strokes and mortal-staring war.   **90**
I, as I may – that which I would I cannot –
With best advantage will deceive the time
And aid thee in this doubtful shock of arms.
But on thy side I may not be too forward,
Lest, being seen, thy brother, tender George,   **95**
Be executed in his father's sight.
Farewell. The leisure and the fearful time
Cuts off the ceremonious vows of love
And ample interchange of sweet discourse
Which so-long-sundered friends should dwell upon.   **100**
God give us leisure for these rites of love!
Once more, adieu. Be valiant, and speed well!

Left alone, Richmond prays for victory. The first of the ghosts of Richard's victims visit Richard and Richmond as they sleep, each cursing Richard and offering praise and support to Richmond.

Think about

- Look at the language with which Richmond prays for God's support. In what ways does this language differ from the way in which other characters in the play call upon God?

- How would you choose to stage the ghosts if you were the director? Think about their appearance, including such things as costume, special effects, and fake blood.

104 **strive with**: struggle against
105 **peise**: weigh

108 **Thou**: i.e. God

110 **irons of wrath**: weapons of anger

113 **chastisement**: punishment

116 **windows**: eyelids
117 **still**: always

118 **sit heavy**: weigh down

123 **issue**: son

124 **anointed**: blessed (with holy oil at his coronation)

126 **the Tower**: where Richard murdered King Henry VI
127 **Harry**: Henry

RICHMOND   Good lords, conduct him to his regiment.
             I'll strive with troubled thoughts to take a nap –
             Lest leaden slumber peise me down tomorrow   105
             When I should mount with wings of victory.
             Once more, good night, kind lords and gentlemen.

                        Exit DERBY *(from Richmond's tent),*
                   with OXFORD, HERBERT, BRANDON, *and others.*

     RICHMOND *kneels to pray alone.*

             O Thou, whose captain I account myself,
             Look on my forces with a gracious eye!
             Put in their hands Thy bruising irons of wrath,   110
             That they may crush down with a heavy fall
             Th' usurping helmets of our adversaries!
             Make us Thy ministers of chastisement,
             That we may praise Thee in the victory!
             To Thee I do commend my watchful soul   115
             Ere I let fall the windows of mine eyes.
             Sleeping and waking, O, defend me still! (*He lies
                  down and sleeps in his tent.*)

     Enter the GHOST *of young* PRINCE EDWARD, *son of Henry the
     Sixth.*

GHOST   (*To* RICHARD *as he sleeps*)
             Let me sit heavy on thy soul tomorrow!
             Think how thou stab'st me in my prime of youth
             At Tewkesbury! Despair therefore, and die!   120
             (*To* RICHMOND, *on the other side, as he sleeps*)
             Be cheerful, Richmond – for the wrongèd souls
             Of butchered princes fight in thy behalf!
             King Henry's issue, Richmond, comforts thee.

                                        GHOST *moves away.*

     Enter the GHOST *of* KING HENRY *the Sixth.*

GHOST   (*To* RICHARD)
             When I was mortal, my anointed body
             By thee was punchèd full of deadly holes.   125
             Think on the Tower and me. Despair, and die!
             Harry the Sixth bids thee despair and die!

The procession of ghosts
continues.

132   washed: drowned
   fulsome: sickening
133   guile: cunning
135   edgeless: blunted

138   battle: army

143   lance: long spear

---Think about ---------

• Should the actors playing
  Richard and Richmond stay
  motionless in their sleep or
  should they react in some
  way to the words of the
  ghosts? How would you
  direct it?

(*To* RICHMOND)
Virtuous and holy, be thou conqueror!
Harry, that prophesied thou shouldst be King,
Doth comfort thee in thy sleep. Live and flourish!   130

GHOST *moves away.*

Enter the GHOST *of* CLARENCE.

GHOST   (*To* RICHARD)
               Let me sit heavy in thy soul tomorrow!
               I that was washed to death with fulsome wine –
               Poor Clarence, by thy guile betrayed to death!
               Tomorrow in the battle think on me,
               And fall thy edgeless sword. Despair and die!   135
               (*To* RICHMOND)
               Thou offspring of the house of Lancaster,
               The wrongèd heirs of York do pray for thee.
               Good angels guard thy battle! Live and flourish!

GHOST *moves away.*

Enter the GHOSTS *of* RIVERS, GREY, *and* VAUGHAN.

GHOST (RIVERS) (*To* RICHARD)
               Let me sit heavy in thy soul tomorrow –
               Rivers that died at Pomfret! Despair and die!   140

GHOST (GREY) (*To* RICHARD)
               Think upon Grey, and let thy soul despair!

GHOST   (*To* RICHARD)
(VAUGHAN)   Think upon Vaughan, and with guilty fear
               Let fall thy lance! Despair and die!

GHOSTS   (*To* RICHMOND)
(All three)   Awake, and think our wrongs in Richard's bosom
               Will conquer him. Awake and win the day!   145

GHOSTS *move away.*

Enter the GHOST *of* HASTINGS.

GHOST   (*To* RICHARD)
               Bloody and guilty, guiltily awake,
               And in a bloody battle end thy days!
               Think on Lord Hastings! Despair and die!

The procession of ghosts continues. The ghost of Buckingham is the last.

151 **cousins**: nephews
153 **bosom**: heart

156 **the boar's annoy**: injury from Richard
157 **beget**: father
158 **flourish**: succeed

161 **perturbations**: disturbances

163 **edgeless**: blunted

166 **adversary**: enemy

168 **tyranny**: brutal rule

172 **yield**: give up

Think about

- When thinking about the ghosts from Richard's perspective, do they have to be the spirits of the dead, or could they be images from his troubled conscience? Do we have to decide between these two ideas, or might we think that both are possible?

(*To* RICHMOND)
Quiet untroubled soul, awake, awake!
Arm, fight, and conquer, for fair England's sake!   150

GHOST moves away.

Enter the GHOSTS *of the two young Princes (Edward and York,
sons of King Edward the Fourth and Elizabeth).*

GHOSTS   (*To* RICHARD)
Dream on thy cousins, smothered in the Tower!
Let us be lead within thy bosom, Richard,
And weigh thee down to ruin, shame, and death!
Thy nephews' souls bid thee despair and die!
(*To* RICHMOND)
Sleep, Richmond, sleep in peace, and wake in joy;   155
Good angels guard thee from the boar's annoy!
Live, and beget a happy race of kings!
Edward's unhappy sons do bid thee flourish.

GHOSTS move away.

Enter the GHOST *of Lady* ANNE *(Richard's wife).*

GHOST   (*To* RICHARD)
Richard, thy wife, that wretched Anne thy wife
That never slept a quiet hour with thee,   160
Now fills thy sleep with perturbations.
Tomorrow in the battle think on me,
And fall thy edgeless sword. Despair and die!
(*To* RICHMOND)
Thou quiet soul, sleep thou a quiet sleep.
Dream of success and happy victory.   165
Thy adversary's wife doth pray for thee.

GHOST moves away.

Enter the GHOST *of* BUCKINGHAM.

GHOST   (*To* RICHARD)
The first was I that helped thee to the crown.
The last was I that felt thy tyranny.
O, in the battle think on Buckingham,
And die in terror of thy guiltiness!   170
Dream on, dream on of bloody deeds and death:
Fainting despair – despairing, yield thy breath!

After the ghosts disappear, Richard wakes up and asks himself why he is afraid. He debates with his conscience. He fears that the souls of all those he has killed will take revenge in the coming battle.

173 **I died ... aid**: i.e. I died hoping to support you before I could do so

178 **Soft**: But wait
179 **afflict**: trouble
180 **lights burn blue**: a sign that ghosts are present
182 **none else by**: no one else here

185 **fly**: run away
186 **Lest I**: in case I take
187 **Wherefore**: Why

193 **several**: separate

196 **Perjury**: Lying
     degree: level of intensity or crime
197 **dir'st**: most terrible
198 **several**: different
     used: committed
199 **Throng ... bar**: crowd to the front of a courtroom (where sentence is given)

---Think about---

• Read Richard's soliloquy (lines 177 to 206) carefully. What emotional highs and lows, and changes in thought can you trace?

• How might you direct the scene to emphasise the contrasts between confidence and fear as Richard talks to himself during this long speech?

(*To* RICHMOND)
I died for hope ere I could lend thee aid –
But cheer thy heart and be thou not dismayed.
God and good angels fight on Richmond's side;   175
And Richard falls in height of all his pride!

GHOST *moves away.*

When all the GHOSTS *have gone,* RICHARD *starts out of his dream.*

KING RICHARD Give me another horse! Bind up my wounds!
Have mercy, Jesu! Soft! I did but dream.
O coward conscience, how dost thou afflict me!
The lights burn blue. It is now dead midnight.   180
Cold fearful drops stand on my trembling flesh.
What do I fear? Myself? There's none else by.
Richard loves Richard! – that is, I am I.
Is there a murderer here? No! – yes, I am.
Then fly! What, from myself? Great reason why –   185
Lest I revenge. What, myself upon myself!
Alack, I love myself. Wherefore? For any good
That I myself have done unto myself?
O, no! Alas, I rather hate myself
For hateful deeds committed by myself!   190
I am a villain! – yet I lie, I am not.
Fool, of thyself speak well! Fool, do not flatter.
My conscience hath a thousand several tongues,
And every tongue brings in a several tale,
And every tale condemns me for a villain.   195
Perjury, perjury, in the high'st degree;
Murder, stern murder, in the dir'st degree!
All several sins, all used in each degree,
Throng to the bar, crying all 'Guilty! guilty!'
I shall despair. There is no creature loves me;   200
And if I die no soul will pity me.
And wherefore should they, since that I myself
Find in myself no pity to myself?
Methought the souls of all that I had murdered
Came to my tent, and every one did threat   205
Tomorrow's vengeance on the head of Richard.

Enter RATCLIFFE.

Ratcliffe tells Richard not to fear bad dreams. Richard plans to eavesdrop on his troops to see if any plan to desert him. By contrast Richmond says that he has slept soundly, having had happy dreams that he will win.

208 **Zounds**: By God's wounds (a surprised oath)

209 **village-cock**: cockerel

210 **done salutation to**: greeted (by crowing)

213 **true**: loyal

215 **shadows**: illusions

216 **apostle**: Saint

218 **substance**: reality

219 **Armed in proof**: in strongest armour

222 **shrink from**: desert

Think about

• Do you think Ratcliffe is surprised to find Richard in a fearful state?

• What elements of set design and lighting might be used to draw out the contrast in mood between the two camps?

224 **Cry mercy**: I beg your pardon

225 **ta'en … sluggard**: found a lazy and late-riser

227 **fairest-boding**: best-promising

231 **cried on**: cheered for my

232 **jocund**: cheerful

RATCLIFFE	My lord!
KING RICHARD	Zounds! Who is there?
RATCLIFFE	Ratcliffe, my lord: 'tis I. The early village-cock
	Hath twice done salutation to the morn. 210
	Your friends are up and buckle on their armour.
KING RICHARD	O Ratcliffe, I have dreamed a fearful dream!
	What think'st thou – will our friends prove all true?
RATCLIFFE	No doubt, my lord.
KING RICHARD	O Ratcliffe, I fear, I fear!
RATCLIFFE	Nay, good my lord, be not afraid of shadows. 215
KING RICHARD	By the apostle Paul, shadows tonight
	Have struck more terror to the soul of Richard
	Than can the substance of ten thousand soldiers
	Armed in proof and led by shallow Richmond.
	'Tis not yet near day. Come, go with me. 220
	Under our tents I'll play the eavesdropper,
	To see if any mean to shrink from me.

Exit RICHARD, *with* RATCLIFFE.

RICHMOND, *on the other side, wakes and sits in his tent.*
Enter, to him, his Lords and Gentlemen (OXFORD, HERBERT,
BRANDON, *and others), with soldiers following.*

LORDS	Good morrow, Richmond!
RICHMOND	Cry mercy, lords and watchful gentlemen,
	That you have ta'en a tardy sluggard here. 225
OXFORD	How have you slept, my lord?
RICHMOND	The sweetest sleep and fairest-boding dreams
	That ever entered in a drowsy head
	Have I since your departure had, my lords.
	Methought their souls whose bodies Richard murdered 230
	Came to my tent and cried on victory.
	I promise you, my soul is very jocund
	In the remembrance of so fair a dream.
	How far into the morning is it, lords?
OXFORD	Upon the stroke of four. 235

Richmond tells his troops that God is on their side, and that Richard is God's enemy. He tells them that they will all be rewarded if they win the battle.

Think about

- Richmond claims God's support and speaks of Richard's evil. Which elements of his speech do you think would most fire up his soldiers?

- In what different ways could Richmond deliver this speech? Consider whether he might speak only to his men, or whether he might address the audience directly.

238 **leisure ... time**: lack and pressure of time

242 **high-reared bulwarks**: high defences
243 **Richard except**: Except for Richard

246 **homicide**: murderer

248 **made means**: plotted

250–1 **made precious ... chair**: made to appear precious only by the setting of England's throne

254 **ward**: protect and reward

258 **fat**: riches
your ... hire: you for your efforts

262 **quits ... age**: reward you in your old age
264 **standards**: flags
265–6 **ransom ... face**: i.e. price of failure will be my death
267 **thrive**: win
268 **The least ... thereof**: even the least important of you shall share in the profits of victory

RICHMOND   Why, then 'tis time to arm and give direction.

He comes forward from his tent. His speech to his army:

More than I have said, loving countrymen,
The leisure and enforcement of the time
Forbids to dwell upon. Yet remember this:
God and our good cause fight upon our side.   240
The prayers of holy saints and wrongèd souls,
Like high-reared bulwarks, stand before our faces.
Richard except, those whom we fight against
Had rather have us win than him they follow.
For what is he they follow? Truly, gentlemen,   245
A bloody tyrant and a homicide!
One raised in blood, and one in blood established;
One that made means to come by what he hath,
And slaughtered those that were the means to help him;
A base foul stone, made precious by the foil   250
Of England's chair, where he is falsely set;
One that hath ever been God's enemy!
Then, if you fight against God's enemy,
God will in justice ward you as his soldiers.
If you do sweat to put a tyrant down,   255
You sleep in peace, the tyrant being slain.
If you do fight against your country's foes,
Your country's fat shall pay your pains the hire.
If you do fight in safeguard of your wives,
Your wives shall welcome home the conquerors.   260
If you do free your children from the sword,
Your children's children quits it in your age.
Then, in the name of God and all these rights,
Advance your standards! Draw your willing swords!
For me, the ransom of my bold attempt   265
Shall be this cold corpse on the earth's cold face.
But if I thrive, the gain of my attempt
The least of you shall share his part thereof.
Sound drums and trumpets, boldly and cheerfully!
God and Saint George! Richmond and victory!   270

Trumpet sounds, and drums.
Exit RICHMOND, with his commanders and men.

Richard predicts that it will be a terrible day for someone, and is worried by the lack of sun. He sets out the details of his battle plan.

271   **as touching**: about
272   **up in arms**: to be a soldier

276   **Tell the clock**: Count the striking of the clock

278   **disdains**: proudly refuses
        by the book: according to the calendar
279   **braved**: shone in

283   **lour**: look angrily
284   **from**: away from

288   **vaunts**: struts and swaggers
289   **Caparison**: Put the harness on
290   **power**: troops

293   **foreward**: front-line troops
294   **horse and foot**: cavalry and foot-soldiers

Think about

- Richard drives away his fears with brave words and 'bustle'. Is anyone, including himself, convinced by these efforts to be cheerful?

Re-enter, on the other side, KING RICHARD *and* RATCLIFFE, *with*
CATESBY, *and soldiers.*

KING RICHARD What said Northumberland as touching Richmond?

RATCLIFFE   That he was never trainèd up in arms.

KING RICHARD He said the truth. And what said Surrey then?

RATCLIFFE   He smiled, and said 'The better for our purpose.'

KING RICHARD He was in the right; and so indeed it is.   275

A clock strikes.

                Tell the clock there! Give me a calendar.
                Who saw the sun today?

RATCLIFFE   Not I, my lord.

KING RICHARD Then he disdains to shine – for by the book
                He should have braved the east an hour ago.
                A black day will it be to somebody.   280
                Ratcliffe!

RATCLIFFE   My lord?

KING RICHARD   The sun will not be seen today.
                The sky doth frown and lour upon our army.
                I would these dewy tears were from the ground.
                Not shine today! Why, what is that to me   285
                More than to Richmond? For the selfsame heaven
                That frowns on me looks sadly upon him.

Enter NORFOLK.

NORFOLK   Arm, arm, my lord! The foe vaunts in the field!

KING RICHARD Come, bustle, bustle! Caparison my horse!
                Call up Lord Stanley! Bid him bring his power.   290
                I will lead forth my soldiers to the plain,
                And thus my battle shall be orderèd:
                My foreward shall be drawn out all in length,
                Consisting equally of horse and foot.
                Our archers shall be placèd in the midst.   295
                John Duke of Norfolk, Thomas Earl of Surrey,
                Shall have the leading of the foot and horse.

Richard dismisses a mocking rhyme aimed at Norfolk and himself. He talks to his army, insulting Richmond and his followers.

299 **battle**: division of soldiers
puissance: strength
300 **wingèd … horse**: protected on the sides by our main group of cavalry
301 **Saint … boot**: the help of St George too
302 **direction**: battle plan

304 **Jockey**: a nickname for John (the Duke of Norfolk's first name)
305 **Dickon**: i.e. Richard
bought and sold: betrayed

310 **in awe**: fearful and obedient

312 **Join**: Fight
pell-mell: fiercely, in hand-to-hand fighting

314 **inferred**: reported before
315 **cope withal**: fight against
316 **sort**: mixture
317 **lackey**: submissive
318 **o'er-cloyèd**: over-stuffed
319 **assured**: certain

322 **restrain**: steal
distain: rape
323 **paltry**: insignificant
324 **our mother's**: the mother country's, i.e. England's
325 **milk-sop**: mummy's boy
328 **over-weening**: boastful

330 **fond exploit**: foolish adventure
331 **want of means**: lack of money

Think about

- Compare Richard's speech to the troops with that made by Richmond in lines 237 to 270. Both men are trying to persuade their soldiers to fight hard for them. What are the similarities and differences between their methods?

- Look at lines 309 to 310. Where else in the play have there been speeches about conscience? Do they say the same things?

They thus directed, we will follow
In the main battle, whose puissance on either side
Shall be well wingèd with our chiefest horse.   **300**
This, and Saint George to boot! What think'st thou,
   Norfolk?

NORFOLK   A good direction, warlike sovereign.
This found I on my tent this morning.

He shows him a paper.

KING RICHARD (*Reads*) 'Jockey of Norfolk be not so bold,
For Dickon thy master is bought and sold.'   **305**
A thing devisèd by the enemy.
Go, gentlemen, every man unto his charge.
Let not our babbling dreams affright our souls.
Conscience is but a word that cowards use,
Devised at first to keep the strong in awe.   **310**
Our strong arms be our conscience, swords our law.
March on! Join bravely! Let us to it pell-mell –
If not to heaven, then hand in hand to hell!

His speech to his army:

What shall I say more than I have inferred?
Remember whom you are to cope withal –   **315**
A sort of vagabonds, rascals, and runaways,
A scum of Bretons, and base lackey peasants,
Whom their o'er-cloyèd country vomits forth
To desperate adventures and assured destruction.
You sleeping safe, they bring to you unrest;   **320**
You having lands, and blessed with beauteous wives,
They would restrain the one, distain the other.
And who doth lead them but a paltry fellow,
Long kept in Brittany at our mother's cost?
A milk-sop! One that never in his life   **325**
Felt so much cold as over shoes in snow!
Let's whip these stragglers o'er the seas again;
Lash hence these over-weening rags of France,
These famished beggars, weary of their lives!
Who, but for dreaming on this fond exploit,   **330**
For want of means, poor rats, had hanged themselves.
If we be conquered, let men conquer us,

The sounds of Richmond's army are heard. Derby has refused to join Richard, so Richard orders the death of his son George.

334   **bobbed**: battered
335   **record**: i.e. the historical record

337   **Ravish**: Rape

341   **welkin**: sky
        staves: spears

343   **deny**: refuse

348   **standards**: flags
        Set upon: attack
349   **word of courage**: battle-cry
350   **spleen**: anger
351   **helms**: helmets

Think about

• Despite Derby's desertion, Richard sounds confident. Is it still possible at this stage to believe that he might win the battle?

And not these bastard Bretons, whom our fathers
Have in their own land beaten, bobbed, and thumped,
And, in record, left them the heirs of shame.   335
Shall these enjoy our lands? – lie with our wives?
Ravish our daughters?

Drum beats in the distance.

                             Hark! I hear their drum.
Fight, gentlemen of England! Fight, bold yeomen!
Draw, archers, draw your arrows to the head!
Spur your proud horses hard, and ride in blood!   340
Amaze the welkin with your broken staves!

Enter a MESSENGER.

        What says Lord Stanley? Will he bring his power?

MESSENGER   My lord, he doth deny to come.

KING RICHARD Off with his son George's head!

NORFOLK   My lord, the enemy is past the marsh!   345
            After the battle let George Stanley die.

KING RICHARD A thousand hearts are great within my bosom.
            Advance our standards! Set upon our foes!
            Our ancient word of courage, fair Saint George,
            Inspire us with the spleen of fiery dragons!   350
            Upon them! Victory sits on our helms!

                                       Exeunt.

Shakespeare's Globe, 2003

RSC, 1992

RSC, 1988

RSC, 1995

In this scene ...

- The battle begins. Richard searches for Richmond.
- Richard refuses to run away and fights with great bravery.

3 **Daring an opposite**: challenging enemies

8 **Withdraw**: Fall back

9 **Slave**: Wretch
  cast: throw of the dice

10 **stand ... die**: accept the luck of the throw

12 **instead of**: in mistake for

---Think about---

- Richard remains brave and defiant to the end. Despite everything he has done, do we still have some admiration for him?

Bosworth Field.

Tents are removed, and soldiers march across.

Sounds of trumpet-calls, drums, and shouts (growing louder).

Enter CATESBY, meeting NORFOLK, with soldiers.

CATESBY	Rescue, my Lord of Norfolk! Rescue, rescue!
	The King enacts more wonders than a man,
	Daring an opposite to every danger.
	His horse is slain, and all on foot he fights,
	Seeking for Richmond in the throat of death!
	Rescue, fair lord, or else the day is lost!

Trumpet-calls. Enter KING RICHARD.

KING RICHARD A horse! A horse! My kingdom for a horse!

CATESBY Withdraw, my lord! I'll help you to a horse.

KING RICHARD Slave! I have set my life upon a cast
And I will stand the hazard of the die.
I think there be six Richmonds in the field.
Five have I slain today instead of him!
A horse! A horse! My kingdom for a horse!

Exeunt.

In this scene ...

- Richmond fights and kills Richard.
- Richmond takes the crown and declares that his marriage to Princess Elizabeth will unite the country and put an end to the civil wars.

Richmond kills Richard. Derby presents Richmond with the crown taken from Richard's body. Richmond learns that Derby's son is safe. He orders the burial of the dead and promises the end of civil wars.

2 **The bloody dog**: i.e. Richard

3 **acquit thee**: performed / acted

4 **long-usurpèd royalty**: crown that has long been in the wrong hands

6 **withal**: with

11 **Whither**: to which

12 **men of name**: i.e. important men with titles

15 **Inter**: Bury
becomes: is fitting for

17 **in submission ... to us**: i.e. who will accept Richmond's victory

18 **the sacrament**: a sacred oath

19 **white ... red**: the symbols of the houses of York and Lancaster

20 **conjunction**: union

---Think about---

- How might the simple direction 'They fight' be staged?

- In many productions this scene is an effective climax. How could it be made as exciting as possible?

The centre of the battlefield.

Trumpet-calls and shouting. Enter RICHMOND, *meeting* KING
RICHARD.

They fight. RICHARD *is killed.*

Trumpet sounds a retreat. Exit RICHMOND. *Noise of battle dies
away.*

Re-enter Richmond. Enter DERBY *(carrying the crown taken
from Richard's helmet), and other lords and soldiers (with
Richmond's banner).*

RICHMOND	God and your arms be praised, victorious friends! The day is ours. The bloody dog is dead.
DERBY	Courageous Richmond, well hast thou acquit thee! Lo, here, this long-usurpèd royalty From the dead temples of this bloody wretch 5 Have I plucked off, to grace thy brows withal. Wear it, enjoy it, and make much of it.

He presents the crown to RICHMOND.

RICHMOND	Great God of heaven, say amen to all! But tell me, is young George Stanley living?
DERBY	He is, my lord, and safe in Leicester town – 10 Whither, if it please you, we may now withdraw us.
RICHMOND	What men of name are slain on either side?
DERBY	John Duke of Norfolk, Walter Lord Ferrers, Sir Robert Brakenbury, and Sir William Brandon.
RICHMOND	Inter their bodies as becomes their births. 15 Proclaim a pardon to the soldiers fled That in submission will return to us. And then, as we have ta'en the sacrament, We will unite the white rose and the red. Smile heaven upon this fair conjunction, 20

Richmond prays that his reign and marriage will unite the country and calls for God's blessing on the new peace.

21 **enmity**: hatred

26 **compelled**: forced
    sire: father
28 **dire**: terrible
29 **Elizabeth**: Queen Elizabeth's daughter, Princess Elizabeth
31 **ordinance**: command

33 **smooth-faced**: i.e. peace is attractive, as opposed to the deformities of war
35 **Abate**: Blunt
36 **reduce**: return to

40 **civil ... stopped**: i.e. wounds caused by the civil war stopped from bleeding

---**Think about**---

• The play is over, and Richard is dead, but should we be entirely happy that he is gone? Do you think his evil completely overshadowed his wit, humour and sheer pleasure in shaking up the order of the world?

That long have frowned upon their enmity!
What traitor hears me, and says not amen?
England hath long been mad, and scarred herself:
The brother blindly shed the brother's blood,
The father rashly slaughtered his own son,   **25**
The son, compelled, been butcher to the sire.
All this divided York and Lancaster –
Divided in their dire division.
O, now let Richmond and Elizabeth,
The true succeeders of each royal house,   **30**
By God's fair ordinance conjoin together!
And let their heirs, God, if Thy will be so,
Enrich the time to come with smooth-faced peace,
With smiling plenty, and fair prosperous days!
Abate the edge of traitors, gracious Lord,   **35**
That would reduce these bloody days again,
And make poor England weep in streams of blood!
Let them not live to taste this land's increase
That would with treason wound this fair land's peace!
Now civil wounds are stopped, peace lives again –   **40**
That she may long live here, God say amen!

Exeunt.

RSC, 1984

RSC, 1988

Shakespeare's Globe, 2003

Richard III was written and first performed in the early 1590s, when plays about the history of England were very popular. The play is centred on Richard, Duke of Gloucester, who became King and reigned over England as Richard III between 1483 and 1485. Richard is presented as a cold-blooded villain: he claws his way to the crown through treachery and murder, killing everyone, including friends and family, who blocks his path to power. Perhaps surprisingly, this monster is also a highly entertaining figure who invites us to share in his laughter at the ignorance and foolishness of others.

A COUNTRY AT WAR

Richard III is set at the close of a period known as The Wars of the Roses. This was a violent civil war that divided England for more than thirty years until the defeat of Richard III by Henry Tudor, Earl of Richmond, in 1485. This play, and the three parts of *Henry VI* that Shakespeare wrote before it, shows the feud between two family groups that both claimed the right to rule England and Wales. On one side were the Lancastrians, known by their symbol of the red rose, and on the other were the Yorkists, represented by a white rose. It is important to know that this was not a local war between the counties of Lancashire and Yorkshire, but that 'Lancaster' and 'York' were the titles of different branches of the same family. At the start of *Richard III* the Yorkists, led by Richard's brother King Edward the Fourth, are in control. Henry, Earl of Richmond, who takes the crown from Richard at the end of the play, is linked to the House of Lancaster. By the time he becomes King Henry the Seventh, he has married Elizabeth of York, Edward the Fourth's daughter. The two feuding houses are at last joined together and the Tudor period begins. Queen Elizabeth the First, who was on the throne when Shakespeare wrote the play, was Henry the Seventh's granddaughter. This is probably one reason why Richmond is shown as a clean-cut hero whilst Richard is portrayed as such an evil villain.

HISTORY AS ENTERTAINMENT AND EDUCATION

History plays gave great opportunities to show colourful ceremonies, processions, and on-stage fighting, as well as displaying the private lives of the most important people in the country. In Shakespeare's time it was very difficult to write openly about politics; a writer could be severely punished just for daring to criticise the Queen. History plays were therefore exciting because they revealed the plotting and power struggles that went on behind the scenes.

Plays like *Richard III* were not written in order to give a fair and balanced account of history. Although playwrights based their stories on history books, known as 'chronicles', they believed that it was more important to entertain audiences and give a moral lesson than to give them a historically accurate account. *Richard III* shows that evil, no matter how attractive and devilishly clever, will be defeated in the end.

VILLAINS ON THE STAGE

Richard comes from a long tradition of stage villains. In Act 3 he says that he is 'like the formal Vice'. This is a reference to a special kind of religious drama, known as 'Morality Plays'. These plays were extremely popular until as late as 1560 and showed the battle between good and evil for control of a man's soul. On the side of virtue were characters representing qualities like 'Good Deeds'. On the other side the main temptation to evil was the 'Vice', a representative of the devil. The Vice was conquered in the end, but not before he, and the audience, had a lot of nasty fun at the expense of the other characters. Richard has many reasons to be bitter, but his spiteful pleasure in the sufferings of others shows that he is both a discontented Yorkist and a devilishly cackling villain who is firmly in the Vice tradition.

THEATRES AND STAGES

Richard III was written early in Shakespeare's theatrical career. It was probably first performed in 1592 or 1593, perhaps in the playhouse simply called The Theatre, in Shoreditch, on what was then the north-east edge of London. This earlier playhouse would have been of the same familiar type as the more famous Globe. The Theatre, in fact, was pulled down in 1598 and its timbers reused for building the Globe, so the size of the stage, with the yard and galleries round it, was probably much the same.

What we know about the early staging of *Richard III* comes mainly from the action of the play itself and the evidence of its stage directions. Most important is the continuous and varying use of the large main-stage platform (which may have measured as much as thirteen metres wide by nine metres deep). Only one scene, Act 3 Scene 7, has action on a level above the main stage: Richard appears *'aloft, between two Bishops'* (as the old direction says), pretending to be virtuously at prayer as part of his and Buckingham's play-acting to fool the Mayor and citizens of London. The only other special staging is in Act 5 Scene 3, before the battle scenes that end the play. Here, the tents of King Richard and his rival Richmond are set up on opposite sides of the broad stage.

ACTION, SETTINGS AND COSTUME

The action of the play in an Elizabethan theatre would have been fast and continuous, with no intervals between Acts or Scenes. New scenes are often marked simply by the entrance of new characters. Act 1 Scene 2, for instance, ends with Richard's triumphant soliloquy after his outrageous wooing of Lady Anne. As Queen Elizabeth enters discussing King Edward's illness with her family, a new scene begins in a new imaginary setting: indoors now, inside the royal palace. No scenery or stage-lighting, as we think of them, was used. The play's language and action were enough to suggest places and settings to the imagination of its audience.

'Royal' scenes, like King Edward's attempted peace-making (Act 2 Scene 1) or Richard's entry when newly crowned as King (Act 4 Scene 2), would have centred on the royal throne, brought out to a dominating back-centre position on the stage. The sound and colour of pageantry, trumpet fanfares and banners, would have contributed to a spectacular effect. By contrast, details of disturbed dress or appearance were important theatrical signals. When Richard and Buckingham enter wearing what the old direction calls *'rotten armour, marvellous ill-favoured'* (Act 3 Scene 5), this rusty gear marks their pretence that they have been caught out in a dangerous emergency. When Queen Elizabeth rushes in *'with her hair about her ears'* after the death of King Edward (the old direction in Act 2 Scene 2), this signals the wild extremity of her grief.

The outside of the Tower of London, which figures so threateningly in *Richard III*, would have been represented only by the rising wall of the dressing room area behind the stage, where the two main stage entrances would have suggested the gates. The same stage architecture could represent any building, like the fortress of Pontefract in Yorkshire, where Rivers, Vaughan and Grey are led to execution in Act 3 Scene 3. For the inside of the Tower of London, the difference between a prison cell and a council room would have been clear from the difference in characters appearing there, their language, costumes and some basic props. The lords at the council meeting that ends fatally for Hastings (Act 3 Scene 4) would have been richly clothed and seated at a table brought out for the scene. Clarence, a prisoner soon to be murdered (Act 1 Scene 4), is watched over by a keeper and has only a poor bed to sleep on. His clothing might also have signalled his distressed condition.

Costumes (armour for battle, indoor or outdoor dress, wealthy or 'poor') were important signals of character and setting for spectators. They were also the most valuable part of any theatre company's equipment, often costing far more than the sums paid to writers for providing plays. A play like *Richard III* would demand the display of rich costumes for members of the royal family and powerful lords. Servants would probably have worn the 'livery' (badge or 'uniform' colour) of their lords and masters. The King (Edward, then Richard) would of course have worn the royal crown, marking the summit of power. Richard is clearly still wearing a crown, over armour, when he is killed in battle: the crown and its power pass finally to Richmond.

'Aloft', tents, ghosts and terror

The imagined flat roof on which Richard appears *'aloft, between two Bishops'* (Act 3 Scene 7) would have been a railed gallery about three metres up on the back wall of the stage. Buckingham 'stage manages' the 'audience' (the Mayor and citizens) on the stage below for this pious performance. Richard, ironically, is nearer to 'heaven' (as the canopy over the main stage was sometimes called), and the real theatre audience finds itself watching a brief black-comic 'play' within the play.

Tents for King Richard and Richmond, in Act 5 Scene 3, would probably have been made of canvas and marked by their different banners. Needing to be set up or brought out quickly, these tents would also have been open enough for action partly inside them to be seen by the audience. This would seem to 'collapse' the space of the battlefield between the camps of the rival armies – rather as a modern film might use a 'split-screen' technique. This staging would also allow the sequence of ghosts to circle and visit each tent in turn with their echoing curses and blessings. The horror of the reappearances of Richard's victims would probably have been stressed by pale make-up, perhaps by blood-stained 'wounds', and by eerily ritualised movement and speech.

Richard's terror as he wakes, however, depends on Shakespeare's theatrical language for performance effects. His candle flames 'burn blue' (a sign of ghosts), Richard tells us, and he sweats with fear: 'Cold fearful drops stand on my trembling flesh' (Act 5 Scene 3, lines 180 to 181). But no audience in a large theatre could appreciate such effects except through the words that create them and the way they are performed. The lights would not have changed colour, as they might in a modern special effect, and the 'fearful drops' of sweat would not have been seen.

Doubles and a starring part

Richard III would certainly have been a challenging play for an Elizabethan acting company to put on. It has, for instance, a huge cast: there are more than fifty speaking parts. Yet an acting company, including the specialist boy-actors who took female parts (though old women like Queen Margaret may well have been played by men), would usually have had no more than about fifteen players. Parts had therefore to be 'doubled', which was usual practice in the Elizabethan theatre, and this would be assisted, in *Richard III*, by so many characters being killed off in the earlier Acts. The players of Clarence and Hastings, for example, might very well have reappeared, 'after death', as Derby and as Richmond. Some players would certainly have had three or four of the smaller parts. This would have been managed effectively by using changes of costume, and sometimes by also changing appearance with wigs and beards. Act 5 Scene 3, however, where many of the 'murdered' must briefly return as ghosts, would have stretched the acting company's resources to the limit.

The single role of Richard dominates the play. As a monstrous 'actor', gleefully sharing his evil designs with the audience for much of the play, Richard is intensely theatrical. The part has always been a vehicle for a star performer and was undoubtedly one of the roles that made a star of Richard Burbage, the leading player of Shakespeare's acting company for over twenty years.

Staging in Shakespeare's theatre may in some ways seem crude or simple by modern standards, but it was very flexible and powerful in playing to the imaginations of its audiences. And *Richard III*, as a supposedly 'true' history of nightmare violence and fascinating evil, had all the ingredients to make it a lasting theatrical success.

A play in performance at the reconstruction of Shakespeare's Globe

Richard III has always been one of Shakespeare's most popular plays and, since its earliest performances, great actors have leaped at the chance to play the scheming, murderous tyrant. There are many different ways of approaching the play in performance and directors ask themselves a number of key questions when they plan to stage it. These include:

- In what ways is Richard disabled, and how should his disability be shown to the audience?
- In what period should the story be staged?
- How should the ghosts scene be staged?
- Should we feel relieved at the end of the play or unsettled?

RICHARD'S DISABILITY

Throughout the play, Richard and others call attention to what he himself terms his 'deformity'. In Shakespeare's own time, many people believed that a person's ugliness was a reflection of a sinful or evil nature, or perhaps a punishment for past wrongs. But people no longer view disability in this way. So directors must decide how far Richard's evil should be reflected in his appearance – he acts like a monster, but should he look like one too?

In the 1995 RSC production **David Troughton**'s Richard had a noticeable hump on his back, but it was the ugliness inside him that was most important. He wore a jester's outfit for the opening of the play and afterwards dressed in short trousers so that he looked like an overgrown schoolboy. This Richard was a babyish clown lashing out at a world that he did not understand, and audiences both pitied him and were revolted by him.

When **Laurence Olivier** played Richard on film in 1955 his hunch-backed profile was a nightmarish shadow looming over all the action. In the 1996 film **Ian McKellen**'s Richard also has a hump, but his stylish uniforms mask this. Much more significant in this production is Richard's withered arm. Hanging loosely by his side, this arm makes usually simple activities like pulling on a glove much more difficult and time-consuming. But from the opening of the film, where we see him leading a commando assault on King Henry the Sixth's military headquarters, we realise that he has overcome his disabilities to become a successful soldier. This shows us that this Richard is a man of the greatest determination. It is through cunning and a gritty will power that McKellen's Richard defeats those blessed with better opportunities and good looks.

When **Antony Sher** played Richard in the 1984 RSC production he flew around the stage on giant crutches like a monstrous spider. Richard had the appearance of a vast and terrifying insect as the crutches and his long dangling costume combined to make him look eight-legged. His black, humped body and spindly legs matched the spider imagery of the play. Bent slightly, he always looked as though he were about to spring and devour his prey. After the coronation, Sher's Richard gave up his crutches for a throne in which attendants carried him from place to place. But this made him less mobile and matched his increasing loss of control as the play moved towards its end.

David Troughton in the 1995 RSC production

WHERE AND WHEN SHOULD THE PLAY BE SET?

At first the answer seems obvious: the events of the play take place in England in the late 1400s. However, directors must decide what kind of story they want to tell and how best to get it across.
Is the play to be a lesson from the history of five hundred years ago? Or should Richard's rise to power remind us of more recent historical events?

The set designed for the 1955 **Laurence Olivier** film was copied from medieval church architecture. Its pillars and corners suited eaves-droppers and spies. Richard hides in the shadows of great arches, his own shadow often falling across the scene as he observes others. This seemed almost like a fairytale world where the monster at the heart of the story haunts every dark corner.

The 1995 film starring **Ian McKellen** sets the action in the 1930s, a decade of tyranny and violence. This was the period when Germany, Italy, Spain, and the Soviet Union were fascist or communist states, and many feared that the United Kingdom would become a dictatorship too. McKellen's Richard has all the trappings of a 1930s dictator. He wears the smartly cut uniforms and medals of a senior military officer. His speech to the citizens of London becomes a Hitler-style propaganda rally. And his banners – red, white and black with a hog in the middle – look very like the Nazis' swastika flags. The film makes us recall the history of the 1930s, and Richard's rise to power seems sickeningly familiar.

Laurence Olivier in the 1955 film

STAGING THE GHOSTS

One particularly interesting question about performance concerns the ghosts who appear to Richard and Richmond before the Battle of Bosworth. How should this scene be staged? In the all-female 2003 Shakespeare's Globe production, in which **Kathryn Hunter** played Richard, the ghosts visited both Richard and Richmond, as in the original text. They wore bloodstained costumes and menaced Richard as they spoke to him. However, in the films starring Laurence Olivier and Ian McKellen the ghosts appear only to Richard.

The version of the scene in the **Laurence Olivier** film is very brief. Only some of the spirits appear and they speak only a few words. On awaking, it does not take much for Olivier's Richard to shake off the apparitions and to resume a warrior-like appearance. In the **Ian McKellen** film, the ghosts appear to Richard in a nightmare. We see him asleep but extremely restless, turning and flinching, his eyes flickering under closed eyelids. In his nightmare he sees the deaths of his victims, but from their viewpoints. Two particularly horrific moments are when Clarence is pushed under his bath water and a rush of blood billows away from the camera, and when Buckingham struggles in the back seat of a limousine as he is strangled. With such horrific images before him, it is no surprise that Richard wakes up with a scream of fear.

THE ENDING

At the close of *Richard III* the audience usually feels relief at the death of such an awful tyrant. At the end of the **Laurence Olivier** film, the Earl of Derby gives a happy smile as he picks up the crown and holds it aloft after Richard's death on the battlefield at Bosworth. The **Ian McKellen** film, however, ends very differently. Trapped at the top of a bombed-out building, Richard chooses to jump to certain death. But, as he topples backwards, Richmond pulls the trigger on his gun to shoot Richard and immediately looks directly into the camera with a grin of triumph. Richmond is now in charge but we do not know what kind of ruler he will make. As Ian McKellen himself said about the ending of *Richard III*, 'The future is a question mark.'

The activities in this section focus on different scenes in the play. The type of activities used can easily be adapted to focus on other sections of the play if necessary. Before beginning the activities you will need to have read the relevant scene.

ACT 1 SCENE 2: THE WOOING OF ANNE

Each activity in this section leads directly onto the next. However, it is possible to use any of them separately. The focus of the activities is on Richard's relationships with Anne, the world he creates around him and the audience.

The scene begins with Anne, the chief mourner for her father-in-law King Henry the Sixth, cursing Richard – the man who murdered both Henry and her husband, Prince Edward. Richard enters and has a powerful effect on the scene: within a few seconds the coffin-bearers are trembling and the body of King Henry is bleeding again.

1 **a** In groups of five take the roles of Richard, Anne, two coffin-bearers and King Henry's body. Create a freeze-frame of the moment when the King's body starts bleeding again.

   b Discuss what the audience might feel at this key moment.

   c Richard seems to have enormous power. Discuss whether the audience might believe that this power comes from the devil if he can make a body that was cold bleed again. We know that he has gone to woo Anne. Would the audience think that it is possible for him to succeed, do you think?

2 Richard's aims in this scene are very clear. He wants Anne to agree to marry him, and perhaps also wants her to be attracted to him. In pairs go through the scene and make a list of all the different tactics he uses to achieve these goals.

   Examples
   He flatters her beauty.
   He questions her Christian charity if she cannot forgive him.

3 a One of the ways in which Richard gradually wears Anne down is by remaining calm and not letting her comments and insults anger him. For example, when she spits at him he simply asks, 'Why dost thou spit at me?' (line 145). In pairs go through the scene and make a list of all the insults used by Anne and make a note of Richard's response to each one.

b How do you think the fact that Richard accepts Anne's attacks might affect the way that the audience sees Richard?

4 In this scene there are a few key turning points where what Richard does or says has an effect on Anne, helping to win her round.

a In pairs choose three moments in this scene that you think are turning points.

Example
Line 183: Anne realises that she cannot kill Richard and lets the sword fall.

b With your partner create a freeze-frame for each of the three moments you chose. For each one, write a line in which Anne speaks her thoughts. For example, for line 183, Anne could say, 'I've dreamt of this moment – of hurting him, killing him. Why can't I do it now?'

5 a The words in this scene are very important, as Richard wins Anne round with his intellect and wit. However the action of the scene is also very important. In pairs work out a version of the scene with just ten movements and no spoken words. Richard and Anne should have five actions each.

Example
1 Richard touches the body of King Henry.
2 Anne, seeing the body bleed, pushes Richard's arm away.
3 Richard kneels at Anne's feet.
4 She slaps his face …

b Show your scenes to the rest of the group.

c As a group discuss how the audience might interpret these actions. For example, what might the different effects on an audience be if Anne, at line 183, let the sword fall immediately, or held it for ten seconds to Richard's heart, willing herself to do it?

6 a In pairs one person should take the role of Richard and the other that of Anne.

b For about a minute think about the events of the scene in as much detail as possible, recalling everything from the point of view of your character. For example, if you are Anne you would be able to describe exactly what Richard was wearing, whether or not you liked the sound of his voice, and what the ring that he gave you is like. Think about exactly what emotions you felt during the scene.

c Talk to your partner about the experience using the first person (e.g. I felt …) and giving as much detail as possible.

Example
Anne: I could see Richard approaching, wearing black as usual …

d With your partner compare Anne's account with Richard's. Discuss the differences between how the two characters recall the action of the scene.

ACT 1 SCENE 3: FACTIONS AND CURSES

Each activity in this section leads directly onto the next. However, it is possible to use any of them separately. The focus of the activities is the effect of the unstable political situation on individual characters and on the atmosphere of the play.

This scene sets up the world of the play: a world of factions and curses. It establishes the tensions between the various individuals and groups, as well as the dramatic tension as the audience waits to see if the dreadful events called for by the curses will happen.

FACTIONS

By this point in the play Richard has managed to split the court in two. He has worked to persuade Buckingham, Derby and Hastings that most of the current evils, including the fall of Clarence, are due to the influence of the Queen and her supporters: her brother and sons.

1 a In groups of eight take the roles of the members of the two factions: Elizabeth, Rivers, Dorset and Grey are on one side, with Richard, Buckingham, Derby and Hastings on the other. Each faction should stand facing each other, if possible on opposite sides of the room.

   b With the other members of your faction discuss why your characters might be angry with one or more of the characters in the opposing faction. For example, Hastings might be angry that the Queen has more influence with the King than he does.

   c On a given signal both factions should advance towards the centre of the room where they will meet the opposite faction face-to-face. As you advance, each faction should shout insults, trying to be louder and more spiteful than the other side.

   d Discuss the hatred between the two factions and which of the grudges seems the stronger. Remember that the anger shown by Richard towards Elizabeth and her family is partly fake. His aim is to convince Buckingham and Derby that he believes passionately in the damage being done by the Queen and her people.

2 In lines 36 to 39 Buckingham reports that King Edward has called for the nobles because he wants them to make peace with one another. We do not see this meeting with the King in this scene.

   a Discuss whether you think a truce brought about by the King, rather than by the nobles themselves, is likely to hold strong after Edward dies. What would such a peace depend upon?

   b In groups of nine take the following roles: Elizabeth, Rivers, Dorset, Grey, Richard, Buckingham, Derby, Hastings and King Edward.

   c Improvise a scene in which King Edward brings each of his nobles forward in turn and makes them swear to be friends with each other. He could, for example, make them bow to each other, take hands or even embrace.

   d Discuss how each of the nine characters felt in this scene. For example, did Edward believe by the end of the scene that the peace would last?

CURSES

Margaret's function in the play is like that of a Chorus, telling the audience of past events, commenting on present actions and prophesying events to come. She is also a parallel to the character of Richard: powerful, articulate and a merciless child-killer. Before she launches into her stream of curses we learn that the Duke of York (Richard's father) cursed her when she had the young Rutland (Richard's brother) killed and that all of his curses on her have come true. This sets up the idea that if evil is called for against an evil done, it will be answered. God will punish people even if the hand of the law does not punish them.

1 At the end of the scene Buckingham says his hair is standing on end because of Margaret and her curses. Choose another character cursed by Margaret and write a short account of their response to what she has foretold. Consider:

   • whether the character believes in the power of curses and the supernatural
   • whether the curse affects their physical or emotional state
   • whether the character believes that the curse might come true.

ACT 1 SCENE 4: THE MURDER OF CLARENCE

Each activity in this section leads directly onto the next. However, it is possible to use any of them separately. The focus of the activities is on the role of conscience and the moral framework of the play.

CLARENCE'S DREAM

The scene begins with Clarence recounting to the Keeper the prophetic dream of his murder. This creates dramatic irony (when the audience knows something that one or more of the characters do not) and tension because the audience knows that the killers are on their way to Clarence. It also highlights the importance of the spiritual and supernatural in the play; like curses, prophetic dreams and premonitions do come true. Moreover, if Clarence is right about being murdered, it seems more likely that the second part of his dream, in which he is taken to hell and punished, will also come true.

1 a Imagine that you are directing a production and have decided to make a film of Clarence's dream to be projected onto a screen while Clarence is describing it to the Keeper. In pairs write a list of what camera shots you would use to create this dream sequence. One person should work on the first part of the dream, the murder (lines 9 to 33). The other person should work on the second part, the punishment in hell (lines 43 to 63).

   Example
   Shot of Clarence and Richard boarding a ship.
   Close up of Richard looking at Clarence.
   Shot of the rough sea around the boat ...

   b Discuss the effect that using a projection of your film in this part of the scene might have on an audience.

THE KILLERS AND CONSCIENCE

Conscience is often referred to in *Richard III*, perhaps most notably in Act 5 Scene 3, lines 309 to 310. Many characters, for example, die tormented by guilty consciences. Clarence's dream shows that he recognises his own guilt, and that he expects to be punished in the next life for crimes he has committed in this one. In this way many characters are punished more by themselves and their consciences than they are by justice or the legal system. The conversation between the First and Second Murderer before Clarence wakes is sometimes referred to as 'the conscience scene'.

1 a In pairs create a space to work in. Place a coat, or something to represent the sleeping Clarence, at one end of it and place a halo, or something to represent Conscience, at the other end. Take the roles of the First and Second Murderer and stand between the two objects.

   b In your roles read through the scene. Whenever conscience weighs heavily on your character you should take one or two steps towards the conscience symbol and whenever your character is determined to do the murder you should take a one or two steps towards the symbol of Clarence.

   c Discuss the way the murderers see conscience. Is it something that they wish to be rid of? Why?

THE KILLERS AND CLARENCE

1 a Read lines 149 to 256.

   b In groups of three take the roles of Clarence and the two murderers. Improvise a scene with Clarence trying to persuade the murderers not to kill him. The main arguments that he uses to try to save his life are listed below.

     • You do not have the hearts to kill me.
     • It is not lawful – I have not been found guilty of any crime.
     • If you are doing this for reward then my brother Richard will pay you more to keep me alive.
     • Imagine you were in my position and you were begging me for your life.

   c Discuss which arguments had the most effect on the murderers and why.

2 In the end the First Murderer kills Clarence alone. The Second Murderer gives up his share of the fee and wishes he had never been involved. How does this affect the way that the audience thinks about:

• the murder
• the character of Clarence
• the role and function of conscience?

ACT 3 SCENE 7: RICHARD ACCEPTS THE THRONE

Each activity in this section leads directly onto the next. Howe
is possible to use any of them separately. The focus of the activit
is on Richard's relationship with his supporters and with the peopl
of England.

ENGLAND'S CITIZENS

At the beginning of this scene Richard wants to hear from Buckingham
how much support he is likely to receive from the citizens of London if
he takes the throne.

1 a   In groups of four read lines 1 to 41.

   b   Use Buckingham's account to script a scene showing the meeting
       he describes. The scene should include Buckingham, the Lord
       Mayor and two citizens.

   c   Act out your scene.

   d   Discuss how you think the citizens feel about:

   • the prospect of Richard as King
   • the prospect of a child on the throne
   • the in-fighting amongst members of the royal family.

2 In this scene Buckingham, who is himself a descendant of one of the
  sons of King Edward the Third, establishes himself as a good speaker.
  It is also Buckingham who has the idea of Richard entering between
  two clergymen with a prayer book in his hand. In pairs discuss your
  views of the Duke of Buckingham. Consider:

   • What character qualities would be most important for an actor to
     bring to the role?
   • Why do you think he is such a strong supporter of Richard?

very little of Richard's reaction to the news of the citizens' of support in this scene. As a group discuss whether you think Richard expected a more positive response from the people of London.

Imagine that you are Richard. Write a short speech in which you voice your anger at or hatred of the citizens while you are preparing to meet the Mayor.

c   Do you think Richard's actions from this point in the play onwards would have been different if the citizens of England had given him their wholehearted support?

RICHARD'S RELIGIOUS MASK

Religion is very important in this play. As well as the prophesies, curses and warnings, many churchmen appear on stage, and there are numerous references to heaven, angels and saints and to Richard himself as a devil or fiend from hell. In many ways Richard's opponent in the play is God, rather than Richmond. In many scenes, perhaps most strongly in this one, Richard puts on the pretence of religious devotion.

1   a   In groups of three create a freeze-frame of the powerful image of Richard entering on a balcony, standing between two bishops and holding a prayer book. You could look at the photographs on pages 180 and 181 for examples of how this scene can be staged.

   b   In many productions this image has a strong effect on the audience. Each group should caption their freeze-frame with something that a member of the audience might think or say at this moment.

   c   Share your captions with the rest of the group, and discuss the different possible responses from the audience at this important point in the play.

RICHARD'S DISSEMBLING

In a brilliant display of dissembling, Richard pretends to refuse the throne and is then slowly persuaded to accept it. His speeches are simple and moving, far from the light, witty responses that have entertained the audience earlier in the play. His speeches seem to convince other characters that he is sincere in his religious devotion and in his reluctance to accept the throne.

1   In this scene the Lord Mayor moves from obvious wariness of Richard to enthusiastic support for him, strongly advocating that he should accept the throne.

    a   In groups of four take the roles of Richard, Buckingham, Catesby and the Mayor.

    b   Read lines 116 to 246. Any of the four characters can pause the scene by clapping. Each time someone claps, the Lord Mayor should speak his thoughts at that point.

    c   Discuss the reasons behind the Mayor's changes in attitude.

ACT 4 SCENES 2 AND 4: THE WHEEL OF FORTUNE TURNS

Each activity in this section leads directly onto the next. However, it is possible to use any of them separately. The focus of the activities is on the structure of the play and Richard's change of fortune once he is King.

In Act 4 Scene 2 Richard has achieved his ambition: he is King of England. However from this moment the wheel of fortune begins to turn, and very shortly we see not only the reversal of his luck but a deep psychological change in his character. Until now Richard has seemed dynamic, forward-thinking, witty and in control, but in this Act he becomes sluggish, forgetful and unable to control his emotions. He also leaves behind his mask and reveals his real intents, with disastrous consequences.

RICHARD'S FEARS

1   At the beginning of Act 4 Scene 2 Richard takes the throne for the first time, but instead of feeling triumphant in this moment of victory he is troubled and anxious about keeping the crown. When Margaret cursed Richard in Act 1 Scene 3 she demanded that the curse be set in motion when his crimes had taken their full effect: that time is now.

   a   In groups of three take the roles of Richard, Buckingham and Margaret.

   b   Richard and Buckingham should act out Act 4 Scene 2, lines 1 to 26. As they do so Margaret should whisper the lines below (Act 1 Scene 3, lines 218 to 220). She is speaking the fear that is in Richard's mind. Margaret could be circling Richard, for example, as she speaks the lines.

   MARGARET   O, let them keep it till thy sins be ripe,
   And then hurl down their indignation
   On thee, the troubler of the poor world's peace!

   c   How would you describe Richard's emotional state as he recalls Margaret's curses?

2   At the beginning of Act 4 Scene 2 Richard is more blunt and open
    than ever before. He tells Buckingham that he wants the Princes in the
    Tower dead. Buckingham does not know how to respond and we
    never know what his answer would have been because, when he tries
    to talk to Richard later in the scene, Richard changes the subject.
    However it is obviously an action that he would not want to
    undertake.

    a   In groups of three, two of you should take the roles of Richard and
        Buckingham and act out lines 1 to 26. The third person should
        speak Buckingham's thoughts before he speaks each of his lines.

    b   Discuss why it might be difficult for Buckingham to be honest with
        Richard. Has he been more open with him earlier in the play?

THE SECOND MOVEMENT OF THE PLAY

This play charts the rise and fall of Richard, and from the time that the
Princes are killed we see the tide of fortune turn against him. There are
several parallel scenes and events that highlight the play's two halves, for
example the dreams of Clarence and Richard, the murders of Clarence
and the Princes, and Richard's wooing of Anne and Elizabeth.

1   The scene between Queen Margaret, Queen Elizabeth and the
    Duchess of York (Act 4 Scene 4, lines 1 to 125) reminds the audience
    of Act 1 Scene 3, the scene in which Margaret cursed those around
    her. By this point most of her curses have come true. The Queens are
    sometimes referred to as the 'wailing women' of the play, grieving for
    the fall of the innocent and providing a link between the material and
    spiritual worlds.

    a   In groups of three put together a twenty-line version of Act 4
        Scene 4, lines 1 to 125. You can use lines from the text or make up
        your own lines. Remember that the women are still competing
        with each other over the amount of grief that each has felt, but in
        this scene they are also more accepting of each other's pain.

    b   Act out your scene.

    c   Discuss the relationship between the three women and the way
        this has changed since Act 1.

The wooing of Princess Elizabeth

Although Richard only sent for Anne to be his Queen in Act 4 Scene 1, having married her earlier in the play, in Act 4 Scene 2 he decides that he must get rid of her and instead marry Princess Elizabeth, the sister of the Princes in the Tower. In Act 4 Scene 4 Richard speaks to Elizabeth's mother, Queen Elizabeth, about the marriage. This scene is a direct parallel of Act 1 Scene 2 in which Richard, with enormous wit and charm, wooed Anne. This time, however, he has lost his skills: his arguments are weak and repetitive and his speech broken and blunt. It is as if he is trying to remember what he said to Anne, but cannot quite get it right.

1 a In pairs read Act 4 Scene 4, lines 200 to 430. Make a list of all the times when Richard appears to be struggling.

   b With your partner go back to Act 1 Scene 2 and pick out lines or arguments that Richard uses in both scenes.

   Example
   In both scenes Richard tries to blame his actions on the love of his intended partner.
   Act 1 Scene 2, lines 122 to 125:

   RICHARD   Your beauty was the cause of that effect –
   Your beauty that did haunt me in my sleep
   To undertake the death of all the world
   So I might live one hour in your sweet bosom.

   Act 4 Scene 4, line 287:

   KING RICHARD Say that I did all this for love of her.

   c Consider:

   • How has Richard changed between the earlier scene and this?
   • What do the two scenes tell us about Richard's attitude to women and to marriage?

ACT 5 SCENE 3: THE GHOSTS

Each activity in this section leads directly onto the next. However, it is possible to use any of them separately. The focus of the activities is on the contrast between the opposing armies, and the factors that lead, finally, to Richard's downfall.

In this scene the audience sees the two sides preparing for war. We are able to make direct comparison between the two. The scene is in three sections: preparations the evening before the battle, the night itself, and early morning pre-battle preparations. In each section Shakespeare shows us first one army and then the other, making the contrasts between the two very clear.

THE EVENING BEFORE

From lines 1 to 107 the action switches between the camps of Richard and Richmond. Both are pitching tents and preparing to meet for action.

1 a Read through this section of the scene. Make notes on the differences between the two camps. Consider:

- the states of mind of Richard and Richmond
- the level of support each leader has from his troops
- how organised they seem to be
- the values held by each army
- what each army wants to achieve through victory on the battle field.

b Make notes on the way that Richard's character has changed. For example, he now seems to be tired.

c Imagine that you are a TV news correspondent, reporting from the battle-field. From your notes made in parts **a** and **b** devise a report on the forthcoming battle and how ready the two armies are for it.

THE NIGHT

The last thing that Richmond does before going to sleep is to pray. This is in direct contrast to the religious devotion that Richard has pretended to have throughout the play, but has now abandoned. The ghosts of eleven men and women murdered by Richard appear to both leaders in their sleep. Their message to Richard is to 'despair and die'. Their message to Richmond is that they and God's angels will be fighting on his side.

1   Decide how you would stage the ghosts if you were the director. What effect would you want the scene to have on the audience? Consider:

   • Costume and appearance: for example, would you want the ghost of King Henry the Sixth to be covered in blood?
   • Lighting: would you use colours or special effects?
   • Sound: would you use music or sound effects?
   • Performance: how would you like the ghosts to speak and move?

2   In a few productions the director has chosen to have the ghosts gathering like a supernatural army behind Richmond, rather than exiting.

   a   Thirteen people should be chosen to take the parts of Richard, Richmond and the eleven ghosts. The rest of the group should act as directors.

   b   The thirteen actors should play through the scene. The rest of the group should experiment with the effect of having the ghosts staying on stage and forming part of Richmond's force. The group should consider how to:

      • give the impression that this force could never lose
      • show that the ghostly force is fighting on the side of 'good'.

   c   To highlight the chorus effect of this ghostly army, the group should choose a few lines for all the ghosts to speak together.

   Example
   God and good angels fight on Richmond's side. (line 175)

   d   As a group discuss the effects the presence of the ghosts on stage as part of Richmond's army might have on the audience.

THE MORNING

1 Richard awakes believing, in another prophetic moment, that he has
   lost his horse. As he remembers the dream he experiences growing
   terror, rather than relief. In his speech (lines 177 to 206) Richard is
   tormented by his conscience, even though earlier in the play, when
   Margaret cursed Richard in Act 1 Scene 3, saying 'The worm of
   conscience still be-gnaw your soul!' (line 221), it was hard to see how
   Richard might become guilt-ridden. This change is a huge challenge
   for the actor playing Richard to show.

   a In pairs one of you should be Richard and the other the director. As
      Richard reads the speech, the director should give advice about
      how to deliver it. Consider how you could show Richard's torment,
      distraction, loneliness and despair.

   b In your pairs discuss the reasons behind the director's choices and
      which method of delivery you felt most successful and appropriate.

2 To an audience the spiritual and supernatural seem very real in this
   play. For example, we know that the ghosts are not simply a product
   of Richard's dreams because they also visit Richmond.

   In pairs discuss how you would highlight the religious or supernatural
   elements, if you were the director. For example, you could have the
   sign of the cross built into the set.

3 a Divide into two groups: Richard's army and Richmond's army. Richard's army should choose one person to take the role of Richard, and Richmond's army should choose one person to take the role of Richmond.

b In your groups discuss how your army feels about your leader and the forthcoming battle. Remember that Richard's army outnumbers Richmond's army.

c Richmond should deliver his final pre-battle speech to his army (lines 237 to 270). His army should respond in the way it feels is appropriate, based on how the troops feel about him and the battle.

d Richard should deliver his final pre-battle speech to his army (lines 314 to 341). His army should respond in the way it feels is appropriate, based on how the troops feel about him and the battle.

e As a group discuss what the audience might feel at the end of this scene and what they might expect to happen in the next scene.